Come With Me, Grandma

And Other Stories

Best wishes!

M fi — ob

June 2001

Come With Me, Grandma

And Other Stories

by

Hertha Binder

1stBooks – rev. 1/11/01

For the five loves in my life:

Grandson Kurt, the inspiration for "Chuck;" sons "Kenny and Jeff" (Bernie and Ray) and Peter, the oldest; last but not least my husband, Rudi Binder, who has stuck it out with me for over 50 years. He didn't want me to use his real name either (so people wouldn't know who he is?), therefore I called him "Tom."

Without these guys my life wouldn't have been the same, and I couldn't have written the stories in this book.

Hertha Binder

Contents

Part I

Grandson Chuck

Hertha Binder

Part I   Grandson Chuck

"Come with me, Grandma!"

Our grandson, Chuck, four years old, is coming today to spend the last week of July with us, while our son, Jeff, and his wife go on a trip.

I am bustling with joy, having fixed the guest room just for him with teddy bears sitting on the bed. Grandpa had set up a swing set in the back yard. Everything is ready.

Really? Maybe I'm a bit apprehensive how Chuckie will like it. After all, he's been with me only for a few hours at a time. What is there to do for him the whole time? Will I be up to keeping a lively child happy and remain in control?

The horn beeps in the driveway, and there they are. After 20 minutes of laughter and a few glasses of lemonade, Chuck's parents are gone again.

The kid is ready to inspect the house. He notices every slight change we've made. "How come the green chair is in that corner, Grandma?"

"It has a wobbly leg, and over there it's not used as much."

"Why is the sofa now by the window? Does it have a wobbly leg, too?"

"No, but the light is better when Grandpa wants to read the paper."

Then he sees the new swing set in the back yard. "Oh, Grandma, look at those swings! Let's try them."

Let's?

He races out and wiggles onto the little seat. I follow and give him a push. "Higher, Grandma!"

Higher.

"Grandma, why don't you swing?"

"Oh, well, I haven't done it for such a long time."

"You sit on that big one over there, and I'll show ya' how to make it go."

5

With some hesitation I sit down on the swing, wonder whether the frame will hold us both, and gently rock back and forth.

"Push your feet like this," he orders.

Gingerly, I obey.

"Can't you do it higher, Grandma?

Now my pride gets pricked. I'll show that little twerp. I push myself off and suddenly enjoy the motion, the view of the clouds above. By golly, I'm going pretty high.

When I slow down, I see Chuck watching me. His swing has nearly stopped.

"Grandma, I need another push, but I waited till you were done."

After ten more minutes of the same, he attacks the slide. It's the old, tall one from the local school which Grandpa borrowed. The janitor there lives on our street.

Chuck eagerly climbs the twelve steps that lead to the top. "Watch me, Grandma!" And whe-e-e, down he goes.

"Grandma, come up and slide, too!"

"Grandmas don't go on slides."

"Why not?"

Why not? Actually, I don't know. It's not appropriate behavior for an elderly lady, but how would I explain that to Chuck. So, why not?

"Come on, Grandma!" he insists.

I climb the ladder and squeeze myself into the top of the slide. Gee, I haven't done this since I was a child. Well, come to think off, I did it a few times when *my* kids were little. That was such a long time ago. Holding on to the slide, I go down very slowly, half a foot at a time.

Chuck watches me and laughs. "No, Grandma, you have to go fast. I'll show ya'."

The second time around, I let go and just swoosh down. I nearly fall forward at the bottom and grin all over. He has an approving look on his face as we two try to lap each other.

6

I'm bushed but happy and need a rest. My low impact aerobics classes aren't half as much fun. "Want some chocolate milk, kiddo?"

"Is it cold? I don't want warm milk."

"It's in the fridge. Will that be good enough?"

After refreshments, he notices the lawn sprinkler in the neighbor's yard. "Oh, Grandma, can I run through that water?"

"That is not ours, it belongs to Mrs. Simon."

"Can't I go through her lawn sprinkler? Can't you ask her? Ple-e-e-ease. I'm so hot. See, Grandma, I'm sweating."

Wondering who controls whom, I pick up the phone."

"Mornin', Shirley. Say, could Chuckie run a few times through your lawn sprinkler? I can't get him off that idea."

"Well, of course. That's what lawn sprinklers are for, aren't they?"

We find his swimming trunks.

When I open the door for him, he looks at me with disapproval. "Grandma, you can't get wet with these clothes."

"I'll stay dry."

"But who will run with me through the water?" he complains. "Oh, Grandma, ple-e-e-ease, put on your swimming trunks."

I should have bought a new swim suit, but this faded one will have to do.

Chuck pulls me by the hand into the heaviest stream of water. My hair! The water from the sprinkler runs down my face. Chuck squeals with delight, and soon there are two more youngsters here -- Mrs. Simon's other neighbors. I could now withdraw since Chuck has company.

"Stay here, Grandma, you're not cold yet."

Do I like it? To be honest, I haven't had so much fun in a long time. I feel 25 years younger, like when Jeff was little. Chuckie looks just like Jeff anyway, particularly when his hair is wet. So I keep on running under that sprinkler, catching one of the kids after the other.

Someone has stopped in the Simons' driveway and is looking at the scene. Who cares? We are too busy.

When the children's lips are turning blue and their teeth are chattering, I call an end to it, give each a towel and invite them in.

A good snack calms them down, and our new friends leave.

Chuck looks out the window at the old maple tree with the crooked limb. "Grandma, is that the tree my dad was climbing when he was little?"

"Yes, it is. How do you know?"

"He told me. In our yard the trees are too thin for climbing. Can you come up with me?"

Climb the tree? That's too much. Or is it?

"We'll try it this afternoon" (Did I really say *we'll* try it?)

The tree must have grown since anyone climbed it last. One can't reach the lowest branch now. I get a sturdy chair, put it by the tree and help the kid up.

"Now you come, Grandma," he coaxes.

So I do, shaking my head in disbelief about myself.

Chuck likes the feel of freedom, to be off the ground. "This is great," he grins. "Did my dad like that?"

"Sure did. Watch out, that is a dead branch over there."

"And?"

"Dead branches can break off. See, its bark is loose. This branch here has smooth bark. That means it's healthy and can carry your weight."

"Can it carry your weight, too?"

We'll see.

Gradually we both work ourselves higher up. Fortunately, I am only 10 pounds overweight and not 25, or I wouldn't fit between these two branches.

When a gust of wind shakes the tree, Chuck says "Oooh!" For a moment he is scared, but then enjoys the swaying. "I like the wind."

So do I.

8

Grandpa is driving up. Today he came home early because the little one is here.

"Hi, Grandpa," hollers Chuck.

"Where are you?" Grandpa looks at the second floor windows.

"Up here, in the tree!"

He almost swallows his gum. "Well. I'll be... Take your time coming down, you two."

Back on the ground, Grandpa lifts Chuck high and gives him a whirl. Then he gives me a squeeze. "Hey, Dear, your cheeks are as rosy as when I proposed to you! Remember?"

"I don't remember what my cheeks were like when you proposed."

While Grandpa and Chuck are busy, I am thinking of our plans for the next few days. I can already hear Chuck's "Come with me, Grandma!"

He wanted to go to the big amusement park. By now I know I'll have to take all those rides with him, even the wet ones.

"Grandma, can you run from here to the fence?"

"What for? I'd rather walk."

"So we can race."

"Race?"

"Yes, see who is faster. Come with me, Grandma."

Hertha Binder

In an Amusement Park You Need a Kid

"When are we going to the 'musment park, Grandma?" Chuck asked the next day.

"Maybe we'll go to "Fantasy Park" when your folks are back. Then your dad can go with you on all those rides."

"Oh, Grandma, why can't we go today? Dad will be tired when he comes. Can't you drive there now?"

Hesitating, I said, "But I can't go on all those rides with you, Chuck."

"That's. O.K., Grandma. I'll show ya'." He put on his cowboy hat.

"All right, kiddo. Hop in the car."

Chuck squealed with delight and asked, "You got the money, Grandma?"

I double checked and showed him my wallet. Satisfied he buckled his seat belt.

****

"Aren't we there yet, Grandma?" he asked after five minutes. "Do you know how to get to Sam-taffy Park?"

"Fan-tasy. It's a long ride, Chuck; about another half hour."

The parking lot was huge.

"Grandma, how will we find the car? There are so many."

"See this red sign? What does it say?"

"Oh, I know. It's a C like in Chuck."

"And you know that number?"

"That yellow one is a 3. I know numbers," he said. "Is that how we'll find the car?"

"Right."

"I know a better way. You parked right beside that blue van. See, Grandma?"

"Yes." I wanted to say something else, but didn't.

11

Inside the park, he didn't know where to go first. "I want to ride this," he finally decided, pointing at some small electric cars that are supposed to bump into each other.

I sat down on a bench. "You go in. I'll just watch."

"He's too small to ride alone," said the man at the entrance. "Needs a grown-up with him."

"Come with me, Grandma!" Chuck grabbed my hand and pulled me in. With a condescending smile he watched how I lowered myself into the seat. He, of course, drove. Yanking the car left and right, he bumped others all the time.

"Watch out!" I yelled.

"Grandma, you're supposed to hit 'em. You hafta."

Chuck was totally absorbed in that game. Every time he knocked another car, he shouted, "Yeah... That's it...Gotcha...Hey, buster... wow... bull's eye!"

Then he got stuck in a corner and didn't know how to back out. He looked at me for help.

Turning the wheel, I said, "Put it in reverse, here at R. Then go slow."

He followed my advice. "I fixed it, Grandma; I got out of that corner. Did you see how I did it?"

For a moment I said nothing. "All by yourself?"

"Yeah. Didn't you see me?" He caught my eye. "Well, you told me how."

"Thank you, Grandma," *I* said.

Chuck looked at me. "Thanks, Grandma."

A bell rang and all the cars stopped. Chuck guided me to the next attraction.

****

There was a giant slide, light green and gleaming. One had to take a burlap bag at the bottom and walk the three flights up, sit on the bag and slide down. Simple.

"Grandma, I can do that all by myself!"

12

"Can't," said the attendant. She looked very stern. "You have to go with an adult."

"Grandma, are you an adult? Aren't you a grown-up?"

"It's the same, dear."

He ran ahead. "Come with me, Grandma. I want to slide. You want to slide, too?"

"Sure." I mumbled something under my breath.

When we were at the top, Chuck looked down. "Oh, Grandma, that's so-o-o far down." He clutched my leg.

"You scared?"

Clinging to me, he didn't answer.

While I sat down on the burlap, the guide told Chuck, "Let go of Grandma for a moment. I'll help you sit here in front of her."

Then he gave us a push and we zoomed down. Every time we hit a flat spot, I felt my stomach in my throat, and Chuck let out a squeal. At the end we spun around and landed backwards.

"Do we go again, Grandma?"

He seemed to hope I'd decline, but by now I had courage and said, "Sure, why not?"

Chuck hung back a bit climbing the stairs. On top he grabbed my leg again, but not as tightly as before. "You've gotta help me," he said to the guide.

The man picked him up and placed him in front of me. By now we were nearly experts and went smoothly with the bumps.

"Hey, we did it. We went straight this time!" Chuck was beaming.

I laughed.

The third time Chuck didn't need any more help. He deftly sat in front of me, and we went down like a pair of old pros. "Aren't you glad I showed you how to ride the slide, Grandma? Aren't you?" He looked at me eager for praise.

"We both learned it, didn't we?" I said. "Now let's have something to eat."

After a hot dog and a sticky snow cone, we were ready for new adventures.

"Grandma, see that merry-go-round? What's it called?"

Squinting my eyes, I read, " 'The Flyer.' You nearly fly when you're on it."

Lots of little kids were riding by themselves.

"Chuck, want to go on that without me?" I asked.

"Sure, Grandma. Will you watch me?"

"Of course, and I'll be standing right here."

He mounted a seat all by himself, and the guide locked the safety bar. The carousel started slowly, and Chuck waved at me every time he came by. Gradually the thing went faster and faster. Chuck slouched in his seat, not looking out.

When the "Flyer" finally slowed down and stopped, Chuck came off a bit wobbly and pale. "Grandma, I don't feel so good. Can you hold me?"

"Aren't you too big for that?"

He shook his head.

So I picked him up and carried him to the next bench. "Let's sit here in the shade a while, I'm sure you'll soon feel better." I stroked his back, his hair; I talked about the rides we had already taken (but not the last one) and about the ones we still might want to do.

"Look, Grandma, see how they splash in the water over there?" He pointed at a huge roller coaster. In the troughs it dipped into water dousing the riders. We heard screams at regular intervals.

"You want to ride it?" I asked.

"Yeah!" He jumped off my lap, his stomach and his spirits restored. "Come with me!"

This was a wild ride. The safety bar was so tight, I couldn't move. The car slowly climbed up the first grade and then rattled down clanking and creaking. Not knowing whether I should close my eyes or stare into the abyss, I held the bar with one hand and clutched Chuck with the other.

"Grandma, are you scared?"

Fortunately, he couldn't understand my answer.

The first time we got splashed, we were both too surprised to make a sound. Rising to the second peak, we were already braver. "Look, Grandma, how far...." and we swooshed down again. This time we screamed and yelled with the best of them. Making all that noise was half the fun.

There were five more crests, each one higher than the last. On every splashy bottom we screamed louder and longer. At the end we could hardly walk for laughing. We were soaked, dripping wet. Water was running from our shirts and shoes.

"Time to go home, kiddo."

"Oh, Grandma, let's do that ride one more time, ple-e-e-ease!"

Actually, I liked the idea. So we took that ride again, now feeling like experts. We were not frightened any more, rising and falling with the roller coaster. No longer fighting its movements, we didn't get sick either. When we stepped off, we were as wet as if we had fallen into a pool.

"Grandma, how do we get dry?"

"There is a blanket in the car. We can use it as a towel."

Chuck walked backwards. He watched the wet footprints. "Look, Grandma, your feet go this way and mine go the other way."

I spun him around so he had to go forwards and I backwards. In the parking lot, I said. "There's the C."

"And the 3 is over there." We found the car. Chuck looked around. "Grandma, that blue van isn't here."

"Probably went home," I said. "That's why you have to remember the signs."

We dried ourselves with the blanket. As soon as I started to drive, he fell asleep.

****

At dinner Chuck told about all the adventures. "Grandpa, you should 'a seen me on the water ride. We got all wet. And on the big green slide. I showed Grandma how to go down..."

"That's good," said Grandpa with a wink at me. "She needs you for all those rides."

"Why, Grandpa? Why does she need me?"

"If she'd go alone, people would think she's nuts. A kid like you is her excuse."

Angels and Letters in the Snow

Nobody can make you forget your sedate routine as quickly as a young child. When Chuck was four-and-a-half years old, he spent a few winter days with me. The first one went like this:

Looking out the window, he announced, "Grandma, I want to play in the snow."

"All right; let's get you dressed for it."

After sweater, snow pants, jacket, hat, scarf, mittens and boots were all on, he stomped out. "Come with me, Grandma, you have to help me."

"But, Chuck..."

"Come on, Grandma!"

"O.K. Wait a bit; I have to get dressed first."

When I stepped out, Chuck was lying on the snow, moving his arms like a swimmer.

"What are you doing, kiddo?" I shook my head.

"I'm making angels; can't you see?"

How could I not know? "Oh," I said. "Now I remember. Your dad used to make them."

Chuck got up without disturbing the imprints in the snow. "Make an angel, Grandma. We need a big one here beside mine."

"Chuckie, I can't..."

"Oh please, Grandma, you can do it. Just sit on the snow right here," he guided me, "and now lay down."

Stiffly I obeyed, moving my arms a little.

"Grandma, you have to get your arms all the way up to your head or the wings won't be big."

I tried harder.

"That's good, Grandma! Now you made huge wings."

Then I attempted to sit up.

"Watch it, Grandma; don't put your hand on that fluffy snow, or the angel won't be nice."

17

Finally I sat up without the support of my hands.

"Oh, Grandma," Chuck was all excited. "Your angel has no head!"

"He doesn't?"

"You have to put your head in the snow real deep."

So I leaned back again -- as if that were a big deal -- and put my head firmly into the snow. A big gob got into my collar against the neck.

"Is that good now?" I asked.

Chuck tried to look without stepping on the smooth snow. "I can't see, Grandma. Sit up!"

Ooh boy.

"Yeah, it's good. Look, the angel has a head now. See it, Grandma?"

"Chuck, I can't unscrew my head. Give me time."

He gave me a hand up.

I turned around and laughed. "Chuck, that angel looks so plump, it won't be able to fly."

"What's plump?"

I showed him with my hands.

"Oh, you mean fat, Grandma. That's O.K. He doesn't have to fly. He can stay here."

"Now what?" I asked.

"Now I'll make another angel, then you and then me. Lots of angels."

So Chuck made five more to my three, all the way to the driveway. Then he stumbled and fell across one of the big ones. "I'm sorry, Grandma; I didn't mean to." He was afraid I'd be angry.

"That's all right, Chuck." I picked him up and whirled him around twice. "See, my angel is giving your angel a hug."

"Grandma, can we make a snowman now?"

"Guess so; let's go to the other side of the house and bunch up some snow."

We pushed and patted it, shoved and squeezed it.

18

"Now he needs a head," Chuck said.

Over by the big tree was a deep drift. "If we pack the snow well, it might make a big, round head," I said. The head was heavy to lift, and I nearly knocked over the snowman's body. Finally the head was on.

"He needs eyes, Grandma. Let's get some stones."

Beautiful grey eyes. The right one was a little larger than the left; I wondered if the snowman was sick.

"He needs a nose, Grandma. Do you have a carrot?"

"No, we don't."

"Lets try a stick."

We got many little twigs. One made a pretty good mouth, but they all were too thin for a nose.

"Well, Chuck, what else can we use?"

"I have it, Grandma! Let's take a pickle."

"A green nose?"

"Yeah. It'll be just right." He was hopping up and down.

"All right. A green nose is better than none."

We went into the house, tracking snow into the kitchen. While I got the pickle, Chuck tried to make the puddles bigger. Then he looked whether I had noticed.

"Come on, kiddo, let's give the snowman his nose."

"Grandma, he'll also need a hat, won't he?"

"Good thinking. He'd get cold without a hat." I grabbed an old hat of Grandpa's and a scarf.

"Grandma, I want to stick the nose in, please."

After several tries the wet pickle froze into the snowman's face.

"Can I put on the hat, Grandma? You'll hafta lift me up."

While he gave the snowman his hat, the big eye fell out. We found a better one.

"Grandma, you put on the scarf. I can't reach."

We stepped back and looked at our work of art.

Chuck smiled. "He looks like Grandpa."

"Let's hope it won't get warm," I said.

19

"Why?"

"So the snow won't melt."

"I hope it stays real cold," said Chuck. "For a whole year."

"It might do just that."

Then he looked at the other side of our yard. "Grandma, can you write in the snow?"

"With a stick?" I asked.

Chuck laughed. "No, Grandma, in the snow you write with your feet. I can write a C." He carefully put one foot in front of the other and tracked a recognizable C. "Can you make C-h-u-c-k out of it, Grandma?"

I stomped the H and the U into the snow. "Now comes another C," I said. "Put it here."

This one was reversed, but -- maybe -- to the earthworms it looked all right. I finished the last letter, K.

Just then Grandpa came home.

"Grandpa's here, Grandpa's here." Chuck got all excited and ran to the car.

Grandpa picked him up and gave him a bear hug.

"Look, Grandpa, what I made in the snow." Chuck gave him a guided tour to angels, letters and the snowman. "Grandma did this one. I showed her how."

"It's great that you teach Grandma this snow art," said Grandpa and winked at me.

"I know." Chuck smiled. "Grandma is a good learner."

I blushed. Best compliment I ever got.

Let's Ride the Sled, Grandma

One wintry morning Chuck brought along a red sled, big enough for two.

"Maybe you can take him to Grandview," said his mother. "They have a little hill right by the first tee."

At Grandview, Chuck cut a face. "That's a baby hill, Grandma. And look at those kids, they are babies! I'm bigger."

He rode the sled fast, lying on his stomach, nearly knocking over one of the little tykes.

"Why don't you take him to the state park," suggested one of the worried mothers. "They have a much bigger sled hill."

****

At Punderson one cannot see the slope from the parking lot.

"Where's the hill, Grandma? I don't see it," he whined.

"Just over there by those brown posts."

We walked through the snow. Then Chuck looked over the edge -- a drop of about 150 feet. Some older teenagers were riding a toboggan. They looked at us with surprise.

"Oh-oh, Grandma, that's a big mountain." Chuck's voice was small as he held on to my coat. "You've gotta ride with me on this one. Those big boys can run me over."

"Chuckie, I've not ridden a sled for ..." He wouldn't understand how long.

"Let's see." I was thinking out loud. "If I stick my right foot into the snow, that darn thing should turn right; poke in the left foot, turn left; dig in both, slow down. It shouldn't be too hard! Now all we need is the guts to do it."

"Come on, Grandma!"

"Let me sit down first, and then you come here in front of me."

21

We pushed off and began sliding with controlled speed. Half-way down the hill, I felt safe and let loose.

Chuck got a lot of snow into his face. "Grandma, I can't breathe."

"Want to ride in back the next time?"

He nodded.

Now came the long walk up. "Grandma, can you pull me?"

"O.K., sit down." After a short stretch I was winded. "Chuck, if you want to keep sledding, you'll have to walk or I'll get too tired."

The second time down, we went much faster and Chuck shrieked behind me. As we came to a stop, he said, "You know, I helped you steer."

Was that why it always veered to the left?

"I could do it only with one foot, Grandma; I can't reach with both."

"Aha."

The teen-age kids stared at us. "Having fun?" one said trying to be friendly -- but he meant, "What's that old broad doing here?"

I smiled at them. "It's great."

After several more runs of "reckless" sledding, Chuck wanted to try it by himself. The lower half of the hill seemed safe enough. He aimed straight into the shrubs and thought that was the way to do it. "Grandma, did you see me?" He giggled.

Pulling the sled up the hill by himself, he nearly reached me. Then the rope slipped out of his mittens, and the sled got away. Chuck ran after it, nearly catching it twice, but didn't quite make it.

I had to laugh.

"Grandma, come help me!" He was close to tears.

"Want to quit?" I picked up the sled.

He shook his head.

The big boys had watched him and one asked, "Want to ride the toboggan with us?"

Chuck's face lit up. "Can I, Grandma?"

I nodded.

They took him for three rides. I heard Chuck squeal with delight when they went down and chatter importantly while they walked up.

Then his new friends had to go home. "See ya', buddy."

"They are brothers," he explained. "Brothers can ride a toboggan."

"Can't friends?" I asked.

"Not so good."

****

When his mother came for him, Chuck hopped up and down with excitement. "Mom, I was riding on a toboggan!"

I explained to her the day's events.

"Next year, Mommie, can I have a toboggan?"

"Maybe," she said.

"And a brother, Mommie? I need a brother for the toboggan."

Chuck Was Right!

Two weeks ago, after we had been sled riding, Chuck asked, "Next time, Grandma, can we go to a bigger hill?"

"I don't know a bigger sled hill around here, but would you like to go skiing?"

His face lit up. "Yeah, let's go skiing.

"But I'm not as strong as your dad is," I said. "I can't carry you to the lift as he did -- you'd have to do it by yourself and stand on your own feet."

"I will. I'm bigger now. Let's go, Grandma."

"Well, O.K." I hesitated. "If there's no blizzard and if the snow lasts, then we can go skiing to 'Harvest Mills' next week."

"Is that Mills a big place? Like the one my mom and dad were at?"

"Big enough for you."

****

Tuesday morning it was raining. When I picked him up, I asked, "What do you want to do today?"

"Go skiing," he said with a small voice.

"Oh, Chuck, it's raining. We'd get all wet."

"M-hm."

"Would you like to go sled riding?" I asked. "That's not as far, and we could go for just a little while."

"No." He shook his head.

"Would you like to go to the mall?" (He always did.)

"No, Grandma." His voice was still peepsy.

"What do you want to do?"

"Go skiing."

"You'll get wet and be sick," said his mother.

"No, I won't," he whispered.

"All right," I said. "Take along your ski clothes. We first have to go back to my house and pick up my stuff. We'll drive to Harvest Mills. Maybe it'll clear up in a while."

His mother nodded in agreement, glad she could leave the argument to me.

Chuck grabbed his ski pants and mittens, put on his hat and skipped to the car.

At our house, my husband was just leaving for work. When Chuck saw him, he hollered, "Guess where we're going, Grandpa. We're going skiing!"

"Really? In the rain?"

"I don't mind."

Grandpa gave me a skeptical look.

"We'll drive there and see how the snow is." I shrugged.

On the way to Harvest Mills Chuck asked, "Grandma, how do you know it's raining there?"

"I just guess. It's not that far, so it'll be the same as here."

He did not answer.

When we got to the Harvest Mills Ski Area, all lifts were running, but not a soul was out.

"It's raining," I said.

He smiled. "It's nice here."

I gave in -- bought tickets and rented the equipment for Chuck. "Do the boots fit? Don't they hurt?"

"They're fine, Grandma." (I remembered how he had complained about the stiff boots the year before.)

When we walked out to the slope, it had stopped raining. Chuck gave me a triumphant look. With a little help from the lift guy, he got on the chair lift. "Hey, this is neat. How will I get off at the top, Grandma?"

"I'll tell you where to stand up, and then you'll just slide away. My arm is right here behind you."

The maneuver went off without a hitch. The snow was nice and soft. I let Chuck hold on to my ski pole and together we made a few turns down the hill. Towards the end I told him, "Let go of the pole and ski the rest by yourself."

"I did it, Grandma, I skied all by myself. Do we go again?"

"Sure, champ. Back to the lift!"

Second time down, Chuck wanted to go faster and fell a few times. He did, however, not complain, struggled up and went on. I let him go by himself from higher up than before. A radiant smile was my reward.

Third time down, Chuck saw a rope tow on the other side of the slope. A two inch thick rope slowly moved up the hill, propelled by a motor. Skiers could hang on to it and be pulled up. He had never been on one, and I was afraid he'd get his legs and skis all tangled up.

"You've got to keep your skis straight," I said when I put him on the track. The lift attendant had his finger on the OFF switch should Chuck fall, but he didn't.

We went up and down that slope a few more times. Then other people came, and I wanted to make sure Chuck wouldn't run into them. "When you want to go this way, you have to lean to the right," I said.

He gave me a blank stare

"Oh, I forgot. You don't know right and left." I bent down and tapped his right knee. "This is the peanut-butter leg, and this," touching his left knee, "is the jelly leg."

The kid beamed.

"Now when I say 'Peanut butter,' you lean on this leg..."

"... and when you say 'Jelly leg,' I do that."

People looked at us in surprise when they heard me yell "Peanut-butter" and then "Jelly," and I never found out whether they understood our code, but Chuck got down the whole hill without running into anyone.

"I did it, Grandma," he shouted. "I made turns."

"Want to go in and eat now?" I asked.

"I'm not hungry."

But I saw that he was getting tired. "O.K., one more time. Then *I* want to go in and get something to drink. We better take a rest."

The not-hungry Chuck ate a big cheeseburger, an apple pie, and had a large Coke. Then he started yawning.

"Let's return your stuff and go home."

He did not object. However, he insisted on a side exit from the rental department, and there was the souvenir shop with exciting ski hats. A wolf's head on top of a cap. It looked fearsome. "Grandma, ple-e-ease, can I have that?"

Usually I let Chuck have one toy, so this was today's choice.

In the car, I said, "You are a real good skier by now, and we sure were lucky it stopped raining."

He buckled his seat belt. "It's raining again." Giving me a big smile, he settled into his seat and fell asleep within a minute.

****

"You have rosy cheeks, kiddo," said Grandpa at dinner. "What did you do today?"

"We went skiing. I told you we'd go."

"Yes, but it rained all day. You skied in the rain?"

"Grandma didn't want to, but when we got there, it didn't. And it was nice till we left."

"So how did you ski?"

"You tell him, Grandma."

"He skis much better than last year, and we had a great time," I said.

"Well, Chuck, without you Grandma wouldn't know what's good for her."

"Right," said the kid and bit into a drum stick.

Bad Words

One summer day I was driving on a deserted street with five-year-old Chuck in the back seat. Apparently I went too fast because an officer stopped me, lectured me and gave me a ticket. In the rear view mirror I saw Chuck watching intently.

When I pulled back onto the street, he said with urgent concern, "Grandma, don't you have to say bad words now?"

Our Personal Ravine

This story spans several years, and therefore the child's age is out of sequence in some sections

When Chuck was two and a half years old and could walk fairly well on level ground, I took him to a nearby park. The trails were too rough for the stroller, so we left it in the car.

"Chuck walk," he said and he did for about 50 feet. Then he raised his arms. "Hold me!"

I obliged. Soon he wanted to get down again. When there were roots in the way, I either lifted him over the obstacle or guided him by the hand. When we rested, Chuck took a few sips of juice from his bottle. He carefully inspected caterpillars and mud puddles.

After a stretch the trail passed along the rim of a steep valley, about 150 feet deep. I picked him up so he could see over the underbrush. In the depth of the ravine a large creek was glistening in the sun.

"See the water down there?" I didn't think he could recognize it, about half a mile away and partly hidden by the trees.

"Pool," Chuck said triumphantly. Oh yes, every outdoor water was "pool" to him, from a puddle to the Great Lakes. "Pool, pool," he said again, pointing and straining towards it.

"You want to go down there?"

He nodded emphatically and said "pool, pool" another 20 times.

"That won't be easy." I had been in this ravine many times when my own kids were little.

"The path is steep and rough. You'll have to let me help you."

31

The trail was in part slippery with dry sand and on other spots it had high steps, outlined by exposed roots. Man-made stairs had broken down but still provided a firm hold for the foot. Chuck let me pick him up and put him back on the ground many times without complaint. He held on to my hand when told to do so.

It was a tedious trip, and after a while I asked, "Have enough? Want to go back up?"

"Pool!"

"O.K." Actually, I was quite proud of the little adventurer and happy that he gave me an excuse to test my skills on difficult terrain. This was a challenge.

Finally we were down and had to cross a little water run. I stood on a rock in the middle and swung Chuck from one side to the other.

He beamed. "Fall in?"

"No, we made it, and besides, the water is not deep, see?" I reached to the bottom and showed him that the water didn't even come up to my wrist. "It's warm, too. Feel it." I helped him bend down and put his hand into the water.

Chuckie just smiled. Then he realized that this little trickle was not what we had come down for. "Big pool?" He turned to look for it.

Yes, where was it? "Just over there," I said, "behind those trees."

We walked another 20 feet and there was the big creek. A sand bank was on our side, a cliff on the other.

"Go there?" He pointed at the bluff.

"No. The water is too deep, We'll have to stay here. Look at all those rocks." I picked up a few and threw them into the water.

Thwoop. Six rocks fell into the deep part. Tlap. Three pebbles hit the shallow part.

"Chuck, too. Chuck, too," he whined.

"Look, there are so many rocks. Pick them up."

He did and with a big swing of his arm threw the stones. The first ones barely missed my head, but then I could position him so that his projectiles fell into the water.

Why do kids enjoy throwing rocks? I thought. But I liked it, too.

"Let's go back, kiddo," I said after a while.

He made no fuss. Before the steep incline, Chuck saw a garden snail with its beautiful little house. It was moving up a tree just at the kid's eye level, leaving a silvery trail. I showed him the snail's dark eyes on long stalks and how it quickly pulled them in when touched.

"That's a snail," I said.

"Nail?"

"Close enough."

Now came the trip up. First I carried Chuck piggyback. I had to support him with both hands because he didn't hang on close enough. Then I tried to hold him on one arm, but he was quite bulky, diaper and all. So I put him on the ground ahead of me. "Stand still now," I said.

That was trickier than I had thought. He wanted to hold his body at a right angle to the slope and that, of course, would not do. I had to support him on his back or on his bottom while I stepped up to his level. Then this procedure was repeated. It took a while, but we finally made it to the top.

When we were again on the rim of the gorge, Chuck looked down and waved. "Bye, pool!"

A group of people approached, and one of them asked, "Is that trail to the creek steep?"

"We made it," I said. "It's fun."

****

A year and a half had gone by. There had been a dry spell and frost for a week in December. Chuck and I went to the park and again wound up by the rim of the gorge.

33

"Oh, Grandma, throw rocks?"

"You mean into the pool?"

He looked surprised. "Grandma, that's not a pool, it's a river. Don't you know?"

"You are right. But today you'll have to walk all by yourself. You are too heavy to be carried."

The descent was easy this time. I held Chuck's hand, pointed out slippery spots to avoid, and showed him good, solid rocks to step on. We were down in a jiffy.

He stopped in front of a tall tree. "Snail?"

"A snail?" I asked. "No, not in winter. But you are right, this *is* the tree where the snail was.

"I know." He smiled.

The little water run was covered with thin ice. We carefully broke off large pieces of it, and then Chuck threw them on a rock and watched them splinter. What a burst of glitter as the sun hit the little chips. Some even showed rainbow colors. When all the "useful" ice was broken, we went to the big creek.

A large rim of ice outlined the shore. First, we picked up little rocks and threw them as far as we could, judging again the depth of the water by the thwoop and tlap sounds when the stones fell in. Then one of the rocks didn't reach the water but skidded over the ice. Chuck liked that.

Now we let the stones slide along the ice. Sometimes the rocks didn't fall right into the water but bounced off it. This was easier than skipping stones in summer. The flat ice set them on the right course.

Among the many pebbles that Chuck picked up, he found two very pretty ones. A smooth white quartz and a bright round red one. That was actually a piece of brick, smoothened by time and water, but the kid was all enthusiastic about the "red rock."

We put them on a safe place by a tree. "We'll take them along when we leave," I said.

A few yards upstream, a large tree lay across the river, its bark long gone. "Can we go on that tree to the other side?" Chuck asked.

"No. The wood is slippery and we might fall in. It's much too cold now to go with wet clothes."

He looked longingly at the tree. "What's on the other side?"

"Don't know. Tell you what. We can come back here next summer and go across. Then it wouldn't matter if we get wet. But now we better leave."The hike up the hill was a cinch. Most of the time Chuck was ahead and only waited for me to steady him on a few spots. Near the top he was running, and when he arrived at the crest, he had a triumphant smile "Beat ya'!"

"You sure did," I admitted. "Now it'll be easy to walk."

"Oh, Grandma," he cried. "You forgot the rocks!"

"Hmh. *We* forgot them. You didn't think of them either, right?"

"Grandma, can we go get them?"

"Go back down?"

"Ple-e-ease!"

I realized it wasn't only the rocks he wanted, he liked to climb some more. So down we went again, Chuck now with more ease because he remembered the bad spots, I a little slower because I was getting tired.

"They are here," he shouted. "Can you carry them?"

I put them into my pocket.

Up once more, and agin Chuck ran towards the top. "Bet ya' again! I'm faster than you, Grandma."

"You sure are." I stroked his head.

A little way on the easy trail, he stopped raising his hands. "Grandma, can you hold me?"

"Carry you, after you beat me up the steep trail? Aren't you much too big for that?"

He shook his head.

"All right." I picked him up. "I suppose that means 'I love you,' doesn't it?"

35

He pressed his head against my shoulder in response.

Not much later he wiggled off. "I can walk now, Grandma."

****

The following summer Chuck and I had been to the zoo, to a deer park and to the beach. We had rented a row boat and visited an amusement park. Soon Chuck would start Kindergarten

"Where do we go today, Grandma?" he asked one morning.

"Don't know. What do you want to do?"

"Can we go throw rocks?"

"Throw rocks?"

"M-hm. And walk across the tree?"

"Oh, all right," I said. "Do you have good walking shoes?"

He showed me his lace-up tennis shoes.

"These might do, and they can get wet."

At the park Chuck led the way to the ravine and walked ahead of me. At a slippery spot he held out his hand. "Hold on to me, Grandma, so you don't fall."

"Thanks, Chuck." Gladly, I accepted his help. "Wouldn't make it without you."

He gave me a proud, beaming smile.

The big old tree was still lying across the creek, but it had shifted somewhat and now didn't reach all the way to the other side.

Looking at it, Chuck suggested, "We can hop from the tree to the shore."

I wasn't so sure and threw a rock into the water where we would have to jump. It made a deep "thwoop."

"Oh, it's deep." Disappointment was on the kid's face.

"Yeah, and I don't want us to fall in there. We might twist an ankle. Let's look at the river farther up."

We walked a bit upstream, first scampering on a strip of sandy beach, then struggling under vines. Later we came to a shallow stretch with several larger rocks sticking out. They made crossing easy.

Near the other shore I saw that the water was not more than a few inches deep, so I just waded to the other side. Chuck still balanced on a rock.

"Grandma, can I walk in the water, too?"

"Sure, it will be below your knees. Just watch your step."

He did. "Look, Grandma." He had a big grin. "I got my shoes all wet, just like yours."

On the other shore we walked downstream a little way.

"Grandma, can we go up?" He pointed to the rim of the steep embankment. "We don't know what's there."

After we climbed up, we could see over the top. Wildflowers everywhere, bumblebees humming and a meadow lark trilling its song. We sat down.

"Look, the lark is way up there." I pointed.

"I see it," said Chuck. "Hear it sing?"

A dragonfly landed on my hand.

"Oh, Grandma, it's pretty. See its wings? They are green."

Slowly it took off again, playfully drifting in the breeze.

"Want to go back?" I asked.

"Do we have to find the same place to go across?"

"Oh, let's see whether we find a spot shallow enough to wade across here."

"Wade again?" His eyes sparkled. "Yippie!"

By now we felt like experts at fording this little stream. Back on the home shore, we found a large puddle, full of wiggly black tadpoles.

"Oh, Grandma, look. What are they?"

"They are little frogs, polliwogs."

"That's a funny name," said Chuck.

"These poor little things will all die, though."

"How come? Why will they die?"

"See, they got here when the water was higher. They probably liked it by the shore where it doesn't flow so fast. Then the water level sank..."

"What will happen?"

"This puddle will probably dry out and the polliwogs will die."

"Can't we save them?"

"We have nothing to scoop them up with." I shrugged.

Chuck tried to get a few tadpoles into his cupped hands. "What do I do with them now, Grandma?"

"Throw them into the river."

He did. Now both of us got busy evacuating tadpoles into the stream. With each scoop we got about 20 of them. We watched as they happily wiggled away in the creek.

"Will they all grow up to be big frogs? Ribbet, ribbet?"

"Some will," I said. "Most of them will be eaten by fish."

"Are the fish bad?" asked Chuck.

"No, they are not. They just have to eat."

"Let's go now, Grandma," he said with a small voice. "I wanted to save those little frogs."

A few steps further his good cheer returned. On the way up the slope, Chuck again steadied me. He was visibly proud of that role reversal. "Remember when I was a baby, Grandma?"

"You mean when I lifted you up here step by step?"

"M-hm." He chuckled. Then he ran towards the crest. "Beat ya' again," he beamed.

I put my hand on his shoulder. "You are such a big guy now."

****

Later that day Chuck told his mother about the trip into the ravine.

"You know," she said to me, "we wanted to go there last week, but Chuckie refused. He said that's for him and Grandma only. It must be a special place for the two of you."

"We've been there," I said. "Every time we go, we remember what adventures we had before. Right, Chuck?"

He gave me a bear hug.

Seagull Encounter

The phone rang and a little voice said, "Hi. Tomorrow is Grandma-Day, right?"

"Oh, hi, Chuck. Yes, tomorrow afternoon you'll be with me."

"Grandma, can we feed the seagulls on the beach? Like last year?"

"Sure, if you like to go to the beach."

"Yeah. Bring lots of bread, O.K., Grandma?"

"All right -- and you bring your nice new beach towel."

I heard him talk to his mother.

"I wanna go in the water, too, Grandma."

"We can do that if it's not too cold."

****

A beach at Lake Erie is just a short drive from our home. When Chuck and I arrived there, we saw only a few gulls, but as we started to feed them, more and more came.

"Grandma, throw the bread in the air. See if they can catch it."

I tried. First the bread pieces just fell back on the sand. A few gulls squawked over them till one could grab a chunk and take off. After a while, though, I found a new trick: if I tossed the bread slices like a Frisbee, they sailed pretty high, and then the more adventurous seagulls caught them in the air. This attracted a whole flock of them. As Chuck and I got better at throwing bread, the birds seemed to get more skillful at catching it.

"Grandma, will they eat out of my hand?"

"I don't know. Give it a try."

He held out some bread. The birds eagerly looked at it but didn't take it.

41

"Why don't they get it, Grandma?"

"I think they are scared. They don't come any closer than three feet."

So we threw some more "Frisbee-bread." A few people stopped to watch, and a woman laughed out loud when she looked at Chuck. I turned.

There he stood, stuffing a whole slice of bread into his own mouth.

"Well, Chuckie, didn't you have lunch?"

"Oh, yes, but I wanted to find out why the seagulls like it so much. It's go-o-o-od!" He enjoyed the attention of the gulls and of the people. "Grandma, the seagulls learned a new trick from us. I bet they've never done that before."

****

As we walked down the beach, we placed our blanket near the water.

Chuck ran into the lake. "Come on, Grandma! Come with me! I need you here."

So I went in too, first thinking it too chilly, but soon getting used to it. The kid needed me for company. He did handstands, swam between my feet and let me pull him as a "dead man." We even used a real Frisbee in the water.

When we came out, he played with another boy, Jim, in the sand while I chatted for a while with Jim's mother.

"Grandma, do you like our sand castle?"

"Sure do. Only to me it looks like a volcano."

Pride was in Jim's voice. "We've got the only volcano on the beach!"

****

Before we left, we each had a Coke and a hot dog. A few seagulls came curiously close.

42

"Bye, birds," waved Chuck. "See ya' next time!" To me he said, "Those birds were the funniest thing today -- don't you think so, Grandma?"

I stroked his hair.

In the parking lot we met Jim and his mother again. "How can you, as a grandmother, be so active?" she asked. "I saw you with those birds and then in the water."

"Why shouldn't I?" I laughed. "I can still move and think and swim. I've no trouble being alive. It's fun."

Why Shouldn't a Kid Pick His Own Presents?

Most people like shopping -- I don't. Buying groceries is a chore. Clothes, I order from a catalogue. Even getting toys for Chuck, our grandson, is a nuisance to me. But with the right help, shopping can be fun.

****

It was close to Chuck's birthday, and I had no idea what to get him. Yes, his mother had suggested some clothes and had told me Chuck's size for anything from hats to boots. I think, though, grandparents should provide some presents just for fun.

"Chuck, want to come with me to shop for your birthday?" I asked.

"You mean now?" His eyebrows went up.

"Sure."

"What presents will you get?" He was beaming.

"I don't know. That's why *you* should choose them."

"You mean, I can pick what I want?"

"Sure. I wouldn't know what you like best. Just don't go over $50."

He snuggled into the car seat, and a mixture of concentration and bliss played on his face. "Fifty dollars is a lot of money."

"True, but your birthday is only once a year."

After a while he asked, "Which store do we go to, Grandma?"

"Which one do you want? You decide."

He immediately named one of the better known chain stores. Once there, he took a cart and briskly walked into a far corner.

Passing by an array of colored boxes, I asked, "What are these?"

"Those are Nintendo games, Grandma. They cost way too much."

45

I got a glimpse of a price tag. Was he ever right!

He didn't let that delay him, though, and marched right to the end of an aisle. "Grandma, can you reach that yellow truck up there?"

I could. It was a large carrier with many little cars.

"You can load it with this lever," he showed me, "and here you unload it. But we need batteries."

"How do you know that so well?"

"Jerod has one like it, and sometimes I play at his house."

"Really?"

He put the truck into the shopping cart. "Come with me, Grandma." Swiftly moving to another aisle, he looked around. "Here they had blue and green scoops with a ball. Now I can't see 'em."

"There is a sales lady. Ask her where the scoops are."

"You are right," she said. "They were here, but the boss moved them to aisle C."

We found them. "Grandma, how much money is left?"

"About 25 dollars."

We backtracked into the previous aisle and he picked an oven for *Creepy Crawlers*. Expertly, he showed me all the written and pictured instructions on the box.

"Is that too much?" he asked.

"No. You have another four dollars left for batteries."

He nodded approval. "Grandma, I want to look at the bicycles." He raised his hand as if to ward off my objection. "I know, they are too expensive. I just want to look."

Not only did he look, he also gave me detailed explanations about the special features of each bike.

I had expected that he'd want to wheedle an extra toy after the $50 were gone, but no attempt came. He didn't whine, beg or bug me for more. His parents obviously had taught him well.

But I thought that I had to get him something practical, so we went to a clothes store. He still talked about the Creepy Crawlers.

When I asked him to pick a matching shirt and trousers, he chose light gray pants and a top in green and yellow.

"How about these green pants?" I asked, "or the gray top?"

He shook his head, so we bought his "matching" set.

"Chuck, these toys will stay with me till your birthday."

He nodded.

On the way to his house, he said, "You know, Grandma, the best thing is that I could pick my own presents."

"Chuck, we did the same thing for Christmas."

"Well, no." He grinned. "At Christmas you wanted to trick me."

"I did?"

"You said you had to buy toys for another little boy and I should help you pick them. But when I saw you smile, I knew you were just teasing."

The Quiet Sides of Nature

On a sunny spring day last year, Chuck and I went to LaDue Reservoir. By the shore was a family of Canadian geese, the parents and five goslings. The gander stuck out his neck and hissed at us as a warning to keep our distance. The little ones found a frog and chased it. Because all of them wanted to catch the same prey, they tumbled over each other, and the frog escaped. Mama goose, however, made two quick steps and picked up the wiggly snack. She divided it into manageable bites and stuffed them into eagerly gaping beaks. Then papa led his troops into the water while the little ones followed single file and mama brought up the rear.

Chuck had been watching without moving. "Neat," he said, "but I wouldn't want to eat a frog."

When the geese were out of sight, we rented a boat, received life jackets, oars and instructions.

"I'll carry the paddles," announced Chuck and went into the boat.

After I had put the life jacket on him, I explained, "These are not paddles, they are oars."

"I know, Grandma." He slid the oar pins into their locks.

"Let me steer into the open water, Chuck. Then you'll row."

When he took over, he imitated what he had seen others do. That always looks easy, but at first our boat spun wildly out of control, then went on a zigzag course and finally crunched onto the shore. There were again our Canadian geese. This time they did not hiss, they just ran.

Gradually, I taught Chuck the mastery of the oars so that our craft would advance in the same general direction with every stroke.

He improved. "Grandma, can you row now by yourself? I have helped enough. Right?"

"Sure." I did my best not to show relief. ."See the many little waves glittering in the sun?"

He studied the water. "M-hm. Over there they look like happy faces, don't they?"

With some imagination one could say that.

From the north side we went under the causeway bridge. With the water level being very high, we had to duck so we wouldn't hit our heads on the beams. Cars and trucks rolling just a few feet above us made a deafening roar.

Chuck was scared. "Will they fall through?"

"They haven't yet."

On the south side of the causeway, the lake was as smooth as glass. No waves, no fishing boats. Willow trees on the shore seemed to have an hour-glass shape, one crown above, the other mirrored in the water. The stillness impressed me. Suddenly we seemed to be living in another dimension, relaxed and away from noise and haste.

While I relished the calm, Chuck was face down and watched schools of little fish in the clear water. "Why do they all swim in the same direction, Grandma?"

"They're playing follow the leader. It's safest for them."

"Look at the neat whirls you're making with the oars. They are cool." He slid on my seat. "Can I try?"

A few of his strokes turned out all right.

****

This year we went again to the reservoir. Chuck's navigational skills have miraculously improved over winter, and he could handle the boat by himself now. But I liked the exercise and wanted to feel needed, so I was rowing, too.

Around a bend in the shoreline, we came again upon a family of Canadian geese.

"Are they the same from last year, Grandma?"

"The parents could be the same; they might even have stayed here over winter."

He counted. "There are seven little ones. Do they have more kids every year?"

"I doubt it. Seven babies is quite a crowd to feed."

A little farther out, thousands of little waves glistened in unending motion. "Look, Grandma, how it sparkles. They look again like happy faces. Remember them?"

I nodded and soaked in the calm that nature provided for us.

"Here are the little fish, too," said Chuck, staring into the water. "Are they the same we saw last year?"

"Probably not. After a year they would be bigger."

A lazy heron stalked in the shallows looking for food.

What comfort, that in our ever changing world a few things remain the same, year after year: baby birds guarded by their parents, the lake scintillating in the sun, the calm and solitude in wind protected parts, the rhythmic squeaking of the oars in their locks, hundreds of tiny fish swimming in unison and a rambunctious little boy taking in, for a while, the quiet sides of nature.

Observing a Single Ant

Sure, we all have seen ants, hundreds of times. Many of them, running in every direction.

On a recent outing with Chuck, I was able to observe *one* particular ant. We spent time by a little creek. He was busy skipping stones and trying to catch tiny fish with his bare hands, so he didn't need my attention right then. I sat on a large rock by the water's edge. In front of me were three tufts of grass, each with three or four blades sticking our horizontally.

One ant was climbing up on a stem. When it came to the first blade, it turned and ran along the slim leaf, visibly with less effort than on the vertical shaft. When the ant came close to the end, its weight suddenly bent the blade down. Frantically the little guy hung onto the tip, upside down, kicking with the back four legs while it clung with the front two to the blade. Finally it got a better hold, struggled for about an inch on the underside and then moved to the top of the narrow leaf.

It seemed to breathe a big sigh of relief, hesitated as if to collect itself and then calmly ran back to the stalk. There, this tireless insect climbed up to the next blade. Again an easy stroll until the weight let the tip of the blade drop. Once more a desperate struggle to hang on, at one time with only one leg, then a little rest and the return to the shaft.

On up to the next blade. Oops, that one came from another stalk. No good, not this time. A little higher up was a leaf that belonged to the first stem -- same sequence of events.

On top, my little friend turned, seemed to look around and then climbed down.

"Grandma, come here!" called Chuck.

"I can't."

"Why not?"

"I have to watch an ant."

"An ant? What's he doing?"

"Come and look. It's climbing up on the second stalk."

"He's just running on that grass. Oh, now he's falling off." Chuck got interested. "Look how he's holding on, Grandma. Oh, no. With just one leg! Made it. Now he's running upside down, Grandma. See?"

"Now on top again," I said.

At the next blade, the ant made a few steps, stopped and then turned back.

"Why is he not going to the end on this one, Grandma? Is he scared of falling?"

"The ant goes on each blade only once -- it's already been on that leaf."

"How does he know where he's been?"

"I believe the ant can smell its own scent on the leaf."

"Why is he running all over, Grandma?"

"I don't think that ant is a *he* and -- maybe it's looking for food or just wants to have fun, but I really don't know."

"We are too dumb to understand an ant?" Chuck's primate superiority was offended.

"In a way. There are many things we don't have to understand, but we sure can admire how hard he works and how he sticks to his job."

"Now *you* said 'he.' " Chuck laughed. "He's still running up and down like crazy."

I nodded. "Let's go back."

On the way home Chuck held on to a branch and kicked his feet.

"What are you doing?"

"Trying to get on top like the ant did, but I can't."

"That's all right," I said. "The ant can't do many things you can do."

"Like what?"

"Smile, like you do."

"Without my two teeth?" He grinned. Then he lifted his arms to me.

"Yes, and he can't give a hug like you." I picked him up and gave him a whirl.

"Oh, Grandma," Chuck squealed. "I'm hanging on with only my hands. Just like the ant."

Promoted to Fisherman's Helper

Going fishing with our grandson, Chuck, has always been my husband's job and privilege. There seems to be some male bonding between the two guys, and Tom, my husband, thinks he knows everything about fishing. I'm not aware that he ever fished, but then, he doesn't build car engines either and knows all about them.

This year there was trouble with scheduling. When Grandpa had time, it was either raining or Chuck couldn't come over.

"Well, when do we go fishing?" Chuck became impatient.

After two weeks, I said to Tom, "We have to keep our promises. If you can't take Chuck fishing, I'll go with him."

"You can't do that," spoke my lord and master. "You don't know how to fish."

"So tell me," I said. "Well need the fishing rods..."

"We have only one -- for Chuck. You just watch."

"Good. One worry less. Where are the hooks?"

He showed me safely packed hooks, floats and sinkers. "You also need a bucket in case you do catch something."

"I know; that tan one."

Tom also gave me a box with "Off," a knife, more fishing line and -- what joy -- a jar with worms.

"Of course you have to call the Hendersons," he said as he gave me a doubtful look before he left.

Bill and Sue Henderson, friends of ours, have a small pond right by the house and a large one in back of their land, half an hour's walk through weeds and mosquitoes. Chuck had been there last year.

"Anytime you want to come," Sue had said.

After school, when Chuck saw the fishing gear in my car, he got all excited. "Is Grandpa going fishing with me?"

"He has to work today, but I'll go with you."

He gave me a long look. "You? Do you know how to fish?"

"No," I admitted, "but you can teach me. Grandpa made sure we have everything we need."

"You have the worms, too?"

"Sure do. Gramps told me how to put the hook through them."

"Good." Chuck heaved a sigh of relief. "Because I don't know how."

"You don't know or you don't want to do it?" I like to keep 'em honest.

"Well," he hesitated. "A little of both."

When we arrived at the Hendersons', Chuck decided to try the small pond first.

"That's fine with me," I said. "We can go to the big pond if they don't bite here."

Carefully, we put a hook on the line. And then the worm.

"If *you* take the worm out of the jar, I'll put the hook through him," I said.

He did, and I did. Then Chuck cast and within seconds he had a fish. Not big, maybe five inches, but a fish. I ran to fill our bucket with water. "Grandma, you take out the hook."

Next time, it took probably two minutes before another one took the bait. Then someone ate most of the worm, but didn't get caught.

Grandpa Henderson came out. "What have you got? -- Oh, bluegills. See their color?" He duly admired them, and Chuck beamed. To me Mr. Henderson said, "You've got too much worm on the hook."

"They are all so big. How do I get less worm?"

With a condescending smile, he pinched a worm in half. With his bare fingers! "There you go."

I was quite grateful for his help.

Chuck and I stayed for about two hours, and he caught 21 bluegills, anywhere from three to ten inches long.

By now I had become quite proficient in handling the worms.

58

"You are real good at that," Chuck said with a happy smile.

Finally -- to me delight -- we ran out of worms. Before we left, I took pictures of Chuck and all his fish. Then Bill Henderson collected the dead fish for the cat, and Chuck let the live ones make a high dive back into the pond.

At home, Tom was waiting for us. "How did it go?"

"Grandpa, I caught 21 bluegills!"

"You didn't! Where are they?"

"We threw them back into the pond," said Chuck.

Grandpa had a smirk on his face indicating that he didn't believe us.

"I took pictures with all of them lined up in front of Chuck," I said. "You'll be able to count them."

"You know," Chuck said to Grandpa, "Me and Grandma, we are a real swell fishing team."

An Olympic medal or a Purple Heart couldn't be as good as that.

Hertha Binder

No Senior Discount on the Waterslide!

The first warm days are here and our thoughts drift ahead to summer. Basking on the beach and sunburns; cookouts and mosquito bites; hikes in the woods and poison ivy; bicycle rides and band-aids; little league and frustration ... it'll be so wonderful, just as in all the years before. And yet, even in dreaming about summer, there is a little boredom.

Wouldn't it be nice to do something different for a change? Put a little pizzazz into the lazy hazy days of summer. Seven-year-old Chuck and I found just the right cure for laziness.

One day we wound up in an amusement park in Geneva, on the shore of Lake Erie. There is a huge double slide of gleaming white plastic supported by a sturdy wooden structure. It's 70 steps to the top (that's about five floors high).

"Grandma, look at that slide! Can we go on it?"

"Guess so." I was a bit worried for him, but I asked for a ticket.

"Grandma, we need two tickets!"

"Why?"

"I need one and you need one."

"Oh, I won't go," I said. I don't like fast rides where I can't control my speed and the track.

"Oh, Grandma, ple-e-e-ease!"

By now several people were waiting behind us, mumbling and shuffling impatiently. So I bought two tickets. "You give a senior discount?" I asked the cashier.

She shook her head and gave me a wan smile. "We never had a request for that."

We put on our swim suits, picked up one glorified innertube each and marched up. I wasn't sure whether my heart beat so fast because of the climb and the 90 degree heat or because I was scared.

"Come with me, Grandma, hurry up!"

61

The guard at the top looked me over as if to judge whether I might sue them for a heart attack.

"Bet you don't have many grandmas here," I said with forced cheer.

He just shook his head.

Chuck pushed off with a mixture of fright and enthusiasm, managed a few curves, then spun around and landed backwards in the pool. He looked back up. "Come on, Grandma!"

So I went. As soon as I was in the winding trough (it's called a flume), I remembered the luge races at the Olympics. People lying on their backs slide down a curving course on a bob sled. It occurred to me that, maybe, I'd have some control over the descent by shifting my weight. Whatever I did, it must have worked because even before I splashed in, I heard Chuck shout, "Grandma, you came down straight!" Was that a compliment?

"Let's go again!" He ran ahead. Then he looked at me. "Grandma, why do you walk so slow?"

"I can't go any faster."

"I can run. Why can't you?"

"Ah, because I'm old."

He accepted that explanation.

Second time up, the guard didn't consider me a liability any more.

Now Chuck wanted to race, so we went side by side. To everyone's surprise, I won.

"Grandma, how come you got here first?" .

"Because I'm heavier." That statement didn't hurt his little ego.

After two more trips up and down, I busied myself with taking pictures of the slide, the trees, the lake and Chuck. That gave me a chance to catch my breath without being quizzed about my "infirmities."

We became more familiar with the flumes and went down with more speed, more skill and more laughter.

In the end, I had walked up those stairs 12 times and Chuck 15. I didn't need to exercise on the Stairmaster that day.

We finished off the afternoon with some putt-putt golf and a few games in the arcade.

On the way home, Chuck said, "Next time when it's Grandma-day, can we go on the slide again?"

"Sure." Why not forget about "acting your age" and whoop up with the kids?

Hertha Binder

Water Wonderland

"Where are we going today?" asked Chuck when I picked him up for his weekly visit.

"Oh, not far. How would you like Pioneer Lake?"

"You mean Pioneer Waterland?"

"Yah."

"Why do you call it Pioneer Lake. Grandma? Don't you know its name?"

"Long ago it was just a swimming lake -- neat and clean. When your dad and Uncle Kenny were little, they used the diving boards for hours. We went there many summers."

"It was just a lake? They have much more now."

"Have you been there?"

"Yeah. Last year with my mom and her friend. They have a humongous slide, but I couldn't go on it. I was too little. Now I'm big enough."

When we got there, I was amazed. "My goodness, what they all have!" I could not believe my eyes. A regular amusement park.

"Grandma, let's do the dry stuff first."

"Good idea. When we get hot, we can go in the water."

Chuck sampled kiddie locomotives and go-carts. Then he tried the baseball batting cages, several different arcade basket balls and knock-'em-down machines. What he lacked on finesse, he made up in energy, and the balls bounced all the way back onto the grass.

I just sat in the shade and watched.

Now came the bumper cars. You need at least two cars going, or there is nothing to bump against. Just when Chuck wanted to ride, no other youngster did. So, a guard drove one of the cars (not the worst part of his job) and showed Chuck how to make it spin and jump.

65

"Did you see me, Grandma? That guy showed me all those neat tricks."

By now we were hot. The first water attraction was a "river" with people floating on fancy innertubes. Didn't look too exciting, but Chuck wanted to go. "Are you coming, Grandma?"

"Sure."

He hopped on an innertube and floated off.

I tried to get on another, but when I sat on its edge, the other side whacked me on the head. "Try it at the steps," someone suggested.

In the shallow water by the steps, I got on the raft with ease; however, I was unbalanced and the whole thing flipped, dumping me head over heels. I sputtered and finally got on. By that time Chuck had disappeared.

"So you made it after all," said a friendly man.

"You did stay on -- good for you," said a woman.

I didn't really want all that attention while I made a fool of myself. Fortunately, Chuck was waiting at the exit, and we went once more together, this time without mishaps.

Now he looked at the huge water slide. "Grandma ..."

"You want to go on it?"

"Yes, but..."

"Want me to come along?"

"Yes!" he blurted out. "It's more fun."

On the top he hung on to me, peeked down and said, "Ask her how high that is."

"Six stories high," said the guide who had heard Chuck's question.

There were two slides. One straight and steep, the other winding.

"Let's go on the curved one," decided Chuck.

I had gone with him on similar slides before, so I was not afraid.

Chuck went first. The curves were tight like hair pins, and I got a bit dizzy. I felt klutzy when I splashed into the pool and couldn't walk straight.

"That happens to most people," said the guide with an encouraging smile.

On the next trip we felt like pros. Chuck wasn't scared any more, and I didn't get dizzy. After three more trips on the slide, Chuck asked, "Now what are we gonna do?"

"Want to go swimming?"

"Yeah, in the pool. Is this the lake where my dad was jumping? Was he bigger than me when he jumped?

"Oh, yes. At least 12 years old."

And then we swam. The water was warm and clean, and Chuck decided for the first time to swim where he couldn't stand. He did like me close by, so I served as a floating dock, something to hold on to. Of course, there was a life guard who didn't let us go "beyond those posts," and "You can't swim in the deep water with a doggie paddle or float on your back." I had been swimming on my back so I could see Chuck better, but -- you can't win them all.

When we were tired, Chuck had nachos and I took a hot dog. Then we did more floating on the river (we even raced) and went two more times on the big slide.

Chuck was not interested in the pedal boats nor the put-put golf. "Let's do that next time," he said. Instead he played more games in the arcade.

Quiet Times in Autumn

In fall I had a few hours on a sunny day with Chuck, now seven years old. We went to Swine Creek Reservation, a park we had not yet explored. Road signs pointed to a "Kildeer Lake." There we found a large playground and a well groomed picnic area. No lake, just high weeds beyond the mowed lawn.

"Where's the lake, Grandma?"

"Don't know." I was puzzled.

He climbed on the jungle gym. "Oh look, Grandma, there's water behind that tall grass."

On a few spots the grass had been bent down, probably from animals walking through. Low and behold, a sizeable pond was hidden behind the tall rushes.

We walked along the shore and came upon a sturdy wooden dock with two benches -- apparently intended for fishermen. From here one could see the entire lake, not much larger than a basketball court.

A pair of ducks leisurely swam away from us, pulling an ever widening V-shaped wake behind them.

"Look at those fish, Grandma! See them?"

"No, I can't. There is glare from the sun."

"Come down here, where I am." He was lying prone on the dock, looking into the water.

What the heck! I lay down beside him. So close to the water's surface, there was no glare. On the contrary, through the green water one could see every detail on the bottom and two schools of little fish as if they were in an aquarium. The members of one group were three to four inches long and black; the others were only one inch long, tan, gleaming in the sun.

A fly fell into the water, and the larger fish tried to catch it, but apparently were not yet skillful enough. They just pushed the fly farther and farther towards the shore with every attempt to grab it.

Two little pairs of orange feet were paddling on top of the "fish tank." I had to look above the water surface to make out what they were: attracted by the commotion, the ducks were returning hurriedly. The drake was repeatedly nudging the fly towards the female. Was he so caring?

"He doesn't like flies." Chuck had the prosaic explanation.

While we were still on our stomachs, we heard a strange noise behind us, something breaking through the brush. A woman's voice was calling out. Before we had a chance to get up, two huge Labradors came running and stopped just a few feet from us, tongues hanging out.

Apparently they didn't know what to make of horizontal humans, so they lost interest and waded with much splashing into the pond. Wouldn't they have liked to catch a duck! The birds, however, casually took off.

By now the dogs' master had arrived and called them back. Because neither Chuck nor I had enough sense to get up before the dogs returned, we got a solid shower when they shook off the water. This was not the time of the year to get wet.

Fortunately, we each had a dry jacket in the car, put it on and looked for a place to hike. Chuck gets bored walking on smooth trails; he likes rough ground. A dry river bed was just the right path for us.

There were unwieldy rocks, patches of wet sand, huge uprooted trees and thorny shrubs barring the way. I was barely able to get through this wilderness, occasionally steadying myself on a branch.

Chuck relished the place. He jumped from rock to rock, balanced on slanting tree trunks, jumped over puddles -- sometimes not all the way -- and chose the steepest part of the bank to get up. He did, though, want my never-ending attention and admiration, which I gladly gave if I wasn't about to tumble.

Chuck boasted. "I got up here without hands. Can you do that?"

"Guess not, I had to hold on to that branch."

He gave me a tolerant smile.

When it started to get dark, we agreed to end our adventurous trip. Walking past the pond, we again saw the ducks, now huddled in a dip for the night. The Labradors barked in the distance.

Challenges and Discoveries at a Rock-Park

Just a few miles from our home are the "Nelson Ledges." The land drops off sharply towards the east, and huge rocks protrude on that break in the Earth's crust. I had been there a few times when our kids were little, and now I took Chuck.

"Oh, Grandma, Look! These stones are monsters. They are huge!"

"You like them?"

"Sure. Can we go on that trail?" He didn't quite wait for an answer and ran ahead.

Following at a more sedate speed, I hollered, "Not there, Chuck. The trail goes here!"

"How do you know, Grandma?"

"See these red marks? This is called the Red Trail. Over there is the blue one. When you stay on a trail, you don't get lost."

He looked. "I see the next red sign, Grandma!" He pointed ahead. A little later he said, "Wow, these rocks sure are big."

I nodded and looked. Good chance to catch my breath.

We came into a very narrow passage.

"Watch! It's tight here. I can walk straight, but you have to bend down, Grandma, don't you?"

"Yes, if I'd stand up straight, I'd get my head stuck."

"Or you'd bump it." He hopped along.

Splash, splash, squish. "Grandma, watch out here. It's wet, but you can walk through it. I've checked it out for you."

"Well, aren't you nice. Now step out of that water or your shoes will be all soaked."

"That's O.K., Grandma. They are already wet."

Ahead was a steep descent with high steps. Several times I sat down on one of them and reached with my feet to the next level. Chuck watched me doubtfully but was satisfied with my progress. He had to sit down too, while going down.

"Grandma, look at the stones. Was this an ocean?"

"I guess so. But that was a long time ago, many million years."

"Oh, yeah." He nodded. "That's what I mean."

In second grade, he knew that? I wondered who told him, but he was too far ahead to hear me ask.

"Look, Grandma, I'll jump down here."

"Watch out, Chuck. Those rocks are slippery."

He jumped anyway with an amused smirk on his face.

Then came an uphill climb with roots for steps. He was of course ahead. "I got up here without holding on." A challenge was in his voice.

"You little twerp," I mumbled. "I'll show you."

He didn't hear me, but he watched.

"Ha, I made it just like you," I bragged. I didn't remember, though, that those rocks were so exhausting 30 years ago. Could they have become steeper, I wondered, and the steps higher?

"Grandma, I'm climbing up there."

"O.K., but jump down on the trail here, not over to that other rock." I had seen his measuring glance.

He jumped -- to the other rock. And grinned again.

"You are not very good at listening," I said. "Whatever I tell you, you do the opposite."

"Oh, Grandma, you always worry that I'll get hurt. But I never do."

Maybe I'm a worry-wart. He sure has proven me wrong time and time again.

The fall leaves on the trees were red and golden, and when a little breeze came up, they playfully sailed to the ground. Chuck wanted to catch some, but you can't run over boulders and look up at the sky at the same time.

"I can't reach them, Grandma." His feeling of superiority was a little dampened.

"You'll have to try chasing leaves where the ground is flat. There you don't have to look as you run."

74

****

As his grandfather and I took him home later that evening, he boasted, "We were at those big rocks, Grandpa. It's so tight there. And Grandma didn't get stuck, but she had to go sideways."

"What would you have done if she did get stuck?" Grandpa laughed.

"Oh, I'd have pushed her back out."

Chuck slid over to my seat, and I lifted him onto my lap.

"Grandma, I'm big -- I don't hafta sit on your lap," but he held still while I fastened the seat belt around both of us and he let me stroke his arm.

Hertha Binder

A Different Point of View

Have any plans with Chuck this week?" asked my friend Sue.

"I don't really know yet."

"Look at this ad." She showed me a page in a newspaper. "I thought of you when I saw it."

A local fruit grower was inviting families to come and harvest their own apples. Tractor rides to the orchard were offered. Business hours and modest prices were listed.

"That sounds like a great idea," I said. "I bet Chuck will like it."

****

When school let out, I was waiting for Chuck.

"Where are we going today?" he asked.

"Apple picking."

He gave me a long look. "Where?"

I told him.

"Do you have any ketchup?" he asked while looking over the snack I had brought. Then he explained how the toy from the "Happy Meal" worked and how many others he had already collected.

He'll like to pick the apples once we get there, I thought.

His eyes widened when we pulled into the driveway. "Look at those pumpkins!"

In the large farm store pumpkins of all sizes, Indian corn, gourds, cider and tons of apples were on display.

The woman at the counter was busy with her register. -- Seems the tape was stuck.

"Hello," I said after a while.

She looked up.

I put a hand on Chuck's shoulder. "We came to pick apples."

"Oh, that's only on weekends," she said.

"You have a big ad in the paper." I tried to keep my voice down. "It says nothing about weekends only."

"I know." She shrugged her shoulder. "What can you do if they forget to print a line?" She pointed to the back of the building. "Try our 'Farm Festival.' The tractor will take you."

Chuck was pulling my hand. "Let's go to that festival, Grandma."

While we walked out, I bit my lip.

"What's wrong, Grandma?"

I grumbled something.

A tractor pulled a large wagon to the festival area.

Chuck was beaming. "This is great. Don't you like the ride, Grandma?"

"You're the only ones here," said the driver. "I'll come back for you when you're ready. Have fun!"

In a large pavilion, hay bales were arranged to form a maze. Chuck hopped over them and only glanced at the three foot slide. "That's for babies." Now disdain was in his voice.

"Look," I said. "A pumpkin carving contest." But there were no pumpkins and no contestants.

Chuck saw a sign. "Grandma, it says here 'Hiking Trail'." He was proud of his reading skills.

"O.K.," I said. "Let's try it."

We bounced over a wobbly rope bridge, Chuck with abandon, I with hesitation. Then came a winding trail, marked by sap buckets. I laughed out loud.

"What's so funny, Grandma?"

"These sap buckets are fastened to any kind of tree," I said. "This pail is on an oak, the other on a tulip tree, and the next one hangs on a beech."

Chuck looked at the leaves. "But this here *is* a maple." He was right.

Now he was hitting each pail with a rock. "Grandma, I'm testing them." What a din!

I should have stopped him, but that joyful racket resolved my tension. Inspecting two buckets after he had hit them, I found no damage. "Take just little pebbles or small twigs."

He was a good marksman, and each tin pail announced our presence to the woods. Birds were flushed out and squirrels rushed for cover.

A little brook had a three foot high bank. Chuck went down to watch the whirligigs. "Come down here, Grandma. Jump!"

"Yeah, yeah."

He gave me a sideways glance while I struggled down.

Back on the trail, Chuck pointed. "Look, there's a lid on the ground."

"Maybe the wind blew it off. Put it back on!"

He picked up the lid, I lifted him high, and he restored the sap bucket to its full glory.

Once more, we crossed the swinging rope bridge.

"You've got to run, Grandma. Then it bounces more better. See?"

I ran. It bounced. Chuck approved.

When we returned from the hike, the man with the tractor was waiting. Since we were alone on the huge wagon, Chuck was moving about freely. He stood on the running board. "Look, Grandma, no hands!" He had complained before that I worried too much, so I said nothing. Then he jumped off, ran beside the wagon, and hopped on again, several times. The driver didn't notice.

At the end of the ride, we went once more into the store.

The cashier lady had fixed her tape and smiled at us. "Did you have fun?"

"The tractor is cool," Chuck said to her, and to me, "You should buy apples for Grandpa; he loves them."

I chose two bags of Golden Delicious, and Chuck hugged a pumpkin.

"Grandma, can I have this one?"

"If you can carry it."

He pressed it over his head like a weight lifter.

"Isn't that great, Grandma? Now I have my pumpkin, and you got the apples, and we didn't even have to pick 'em."

Chuck Goes Voting
or
Government 001

Chuck spends one day a week with me. When I picked him up from school, the second grader asked, "Where are we going today, Grandma?"

"Voting."

He looked surprised.

"Know anything about it?" I asked.

He stuffed a chicken nugget into his mouth and shook his head. "M-mh."

How should I explain our political system in two minutes? "There are two parties."

"Like birthday parties?"

"No." I hesitated. "More like two groups of friends; large groups, though, all over the country." I steadied his Coke before it spilled. "One of these parties wants doctors to get less and less for our work, for treating patients. If this keeps on, soon we won't have enough money to go to Seaworld..."

"...or skiing!!" He understood that. "And the others?"

"They leave doctors pretty much alone."

"So you vote for the ones that leave you alone."

"You bet."

At the polls I was greeted by neighbors. "Oh hi, Mrs. Binder," said someone. "Hello, Hertha." -- "Good afternoon, Dr. Binder."

"They all know you?"

"Many do. They all live in this township."

After I signed the registration book, I had to state my name two more times. Then we had to wait a little and sat down on the bench.

"Why did you have to write your name into that book, if they all know you?"

"They have to make sure I have the right to vote, have lived here long enough and am an American citizen. When Great-grandma was visiting here, she would not have been allowed to vote."

"She could only vote in Austria?"

"Right. You also have to be 18 years old..."

"I know, I can't vote yet."

"Then they make sure that no one votes twice."

"That would be cheating!"

Now it was our turn to go into the booth.

"Hi, Aunt Carolyn," I said to the woman who handed me the ballot and a special pencil.

"This must be Chuck," she said. "My, how you have grown!"

"Is she your aunt?" asked Chuck.

"She was a babysitter for your dad and Uncle Kenny. They called her Aunt Carolyn.

Once in the booth, I let Chuck close the curtain. "Why do we have to close it, Grandma?"

"So nobody can see how we vote."

I had prepared a list with the names of the candidates of my choice. "Do you want to fill in these circles?"

"Oh, yes." He could barely see on top of the little counter, so I lifted one knee and let him sit on my leg. "Don't wiggle," he said, "or I can't write."

I pointed out the names on the ballot, and he marked the circles. "You don't have to show me, Grandma. Just read the names, and I'll find them."

When we came to the county commissioner, Chuck slipped off my leg. We rearranged him on the other side. When we were finished, Chuck was beaming. "I filled them all out, Grandma, I did it."

Outside the booth, Aunt Carolyn handed us a flat box, like a stiff envelope.

"What do we do with that?" I asked.

"Chuck can put the ballot in here. Then I'll tear off the small stub, and you dump the ballot into this big box."

Chuck dumped, but the ballot floated to the ground. "Oops." He giggled.

"Good," said Carolyn. "It fell on the buttered side."

"Why is that good?" asked Chuck.

"So I can't see how you voted."

On the second try the ballot found its correct way, and Carolyn put an "I voted" sticker on Chuck's coat.

In the car, he asked. "Why can't she see how we voted?"

"Imagine," I said, "there are two third grade teachers, a tall lady and a short one. You kids can vote who your teacher will be next year."

"Neat."

"You pick the short one, but the tall lady gets more votes and will be your teacher. Would you want her to know that you had voted against her?"

"Oh, no! She wouldn't like me."

****

"Guess what I did today, Grandpa," Chuck said at supper. "I voted!"

"Really?"

"Yeah, I filled out all the circles. Well, Grandma told me which ones. And we kept it a secret from your Aunt Carolyn. Didn't we, Grandma?"

I smiled. "Chuck was a big help."

Hertha Binder

Amazing Progress -- Phase One

"Grandma, wait up! You have to hold me."

"How come? Last year you could already ski by yourself."

"Yeah, but here it's steep."

Chuck and I were standing near the top of Alpine Valley's main lift. In the evening sun, the little village, Fowlers Mill, looked as if Grandma Moses had painted it.

"All right, then. Come on." I straightened his skis and let him hold on to my pole for stability. "I hope my back won't give out." Slowly and carefully we wound our way down, turn after turn.

The lift attendant wisely slowed down the approaching chair to let us get on safely.

Riding a chairlift was still very exciting for Chuck. "Look, Grandma, I can lean on this, see?"

"It's the safety bar -- keeps you from falling down."

"And, Grandma, look at the shadows!" This was the first time Chuck skied after dark, and the artificial lights cast distinct silhouettes. "Is that us?"

"Sure. Just watch." I waved an arm and wiggled a ski, and the shadow returned the greeting.

Chuck squealed with delight and waved with so much enthusiasm that he nearly lost a mitten. "Oops! What would we do if it fell down?"

"You'd have to freeze till we got there and could pick it up."

Now a dark object by the woods caught his attention. "Grandma, do you see this?" He pointed. "Is that an animal?"

"I'm not sure; we'll see when we come closer."

"Looks like a groundhog, doesn't it? Oh, it's just a piece of wood. Is it here for decoration?"

"I doubt it."

"But it looks nice. Doesn't it, Grandma?"

"Sure does. Watch when you get off the lift."

Preparing for the next run down, he reached again for my trusty pole. "Grandma, can we go faster?"

"Do you want to go alone?"

"No. With you, but fast."

I obliged, and we curved down the hill with "dizzying" speed. Chuck leaned heavily on me. And then it happened. We wiped out, but good. I fell on top of him, and our skis were all tangled up. Snow was in my goggles and in my collar, the ski pole had stopped 10 feet up the hill. Chuck didn't know whether he should laugh or cry, so he did a little of each.

Just then the ski-patrol came by. "You O.K.?"

"Yeah; guess so. Thank you."

He handed me my pole. "You shouldn't go so fast with the little one."

"Yessir." Then I untangled Chuck's skis, pointed them in the right direction and lifted him up. "Soon, you should do that by yourself," I said.

We finished the run and two more without any further mishaps. Close to the lift, two little kids -- obviously younger than Chuck -- passed us. They skied quite well. One had a red hat, the other a pink snow suit. "Look," said the pink one pointing at us. "Me and my mom did that when I was little."

Chuck watched them for a long time and was unusually quiet on the ride up. "Grandma, I want to go by myself," he said as we started the next run.

"Good! I'll be right behind you. If it gets too fast, sit down."

He skied all right. When he fell, I helped him up. "Want to hold on again?" I asked when I saw he was getting tired.

"No."

"Want to go in and eat?"

"I'm not hungry."

"But *I* need some hot chocolate."

Reluctantly, he came along.

At a table sat a boy all by himself; he was a little older than Chuck. When we joined him, he was glad to find an audience and told abut the snow, about the food, his dog and his teacher. Chuck was spellbound. It is not often that a 10-year-old pours out his heart to a second grader.

When the nachos were finished, when the hot chocolate cup had been emptied for the second time, I asked quietly, "Chuck, want to go out again?"

He got up. "Well, see ya'," he said to the boy.

Outside, while I helped him into his skis, I said, "We can do two more runs. Then we have to leave."

"Why?"

"Your mom wants you home by 8:30. Tomorrow is school."

When we were ready to quit, the little pink skier had fallen. Chuck skied very close, "accidentally" covering her with a spray of snow.

"Hey!" she cried.

Chuck pretended not to notice.

In the car he asked, "Didn't I ski good today, Grandma? You didn't have to hold me." He took a sip from his can of pop. "Well, yeah, at first; but in the end I skied all by myself."

"You were great." I patted his hand.

He buckled his seat belt and took a cold French fry. "That pink girl -- she was a pest."

I just smiled

Hertha Binder

88

Phase Two

"Aren't you glad it snowed again, Grandma?"

"Yeah. After two weeks of rain, we deserved it." Chuck and I were again at Alpine Valley, riding the lift. When we got off, I had to adjust a buckle on my boot. "Wait a bit, Chuck."

"Grandma, look at those houses." He pointed at Fowlers Mill. "Don't they look like a Christmas card?"

"Sure, like one of those cute ones."

He didn't dream of holding on to me any more. I skied a few feet ahead, and he followed my turns. When he fell, he called out, "I've got it, Grandma. I'm O.K." He had mastered the skill of getting up.

Soon the careful turns bored him, and he made them steeper and faster. "Follow me, Grandma!"

Obediently, I did.

Later, he said, "I don't have to make turns any more, I can do this." For the first time, he had his skis in a perfect snowplow, or wedge, the essential stance to slow down or stop. So, with the ability to control his speed, he went down straight, and I was right behind him.

"I like to go fast. Don't you, Grandma?"

"Sure do."

At the next run, I again followed closely. Towards the flatter end, though, I just let my skis run and passed him.

"Grandma, how could you do that?"

I shrugged.

"I mean, how come your skis go faster than mine?"

"Oh, probably because I'm heavier than you, and my skis are longer."

On the next ride up, he looked at the second chairlift, the one leading to the top. "Grandma, when I'm 10 years old, can we go on that lift?"

"Oh, sure."

89

****

A week later, we were again at Alpine, Chuck skiing fast and hollering, "Follow me, Grandma!"

In the middle of the slope, skiers were neatly lined up for a lesson, their instructor standing in front. Chuck scared them all when he whizzed between them.

Laughing, I told him, "Listen, you have to ski around a class with an instructor, not between them."

"Oh." He ducked. "I didn't know."

On the next ride up, I asked, "Do you want to go on the upper lift?"

"You mean now? And I'm only seven-and-a-half?"

"Sure. Let's give it a try. Up there it's a bit steeper, so you'll have to be careful."

He was impressed with the difference between the two lifts. On this one, we had to load from the side. "How is it at the top, Grandma? How do we get off?"

"Stand up and slide away. Just like on the other one."

"Grandma, what does that say?" He pointed at a sign "Ex...?"

"Experts only. That means..."

"I know what it means. Let's go there!"

He took off, and all I could do was try to keep up with him and worry. This trail had a narrow section with a sharp S-curve. Would Chuck hit a tree? But he zoomed through and just gave me a quick glance.

Then he saw other kids jump over three bumps. His eyes widened. "Grandma, can I jump?"

I hesitated. "You could hurt yourself, and I'm responsible for you."

"Grandma, ple-e-e-ease!"

"Well, all right, but be very careful. You..."

He was off, jumped and fell. "I'm O.K., I'm O.K. I've got it, Grandma."

He struggled up and tried the next jump. Fell again.

"Look, I think you have to get the back end of your skis on the ground first." I showed him with my hands.

The third time was a success. "I jumped! Grandma, I did it! Did you see me?"

I duly admired him.

"Let's hurry, Grandma. I want to jump again."

After we had done the trail with the bumps three times, Chuck jumping and I skiing around them, he asked, "Grandma, can you jump?"

"Yeah, but I don't like to."

"Why not? Because you are so old?"

"No." I took a deep breath. "I didn't like to jump even when I was much younger."

"You mean when my dad was little, you didn't jump either?" He shook his head in disbelief. "Can't you at least try it once?"

"All right, to keep you happy."

Next time down, he stopped to watch me. I did jump, got all the way into the air, whacked the skis with the obligatory clap on the snow and, lucky me, didn't even fall.

He gave me an approving nod. "See, you can do it."

****

When Chuck had left, I told Grandpa about our adventures.

"Chuck jumps?" he asked. "I thought he's holding on to your leg."

"Oh, that was a month ago."

"Really? Amazing progress."

Hertha Binder

A New Park for Grandma

"So where did Susan say we have to go today?" asked eight-year-old Chuck when he got into the car.

"What?"

"Your boss at the newspaper. Where does she want us to go?"

I had to laugh. "She didn't send us anywhere."

"But she wants you to write about another place, doesn't she?"

"It would be nice. I anyway wanted to explore a new park with you."

He stuffed a chicken nugget into his mouth. "A new one?"

"Well, I haven't seen it and I think you haven't either. So it's new for us. Now snow and mud are gone, and the bugs aren't out yet. Just the right time."

"What's there?"

"Don't know yet. It's not far from our house, right beside those huge gravel piles."

"Where the little airport is?"

"Right."

He seemed to think about that.

When we approached the Best Company (the gravel outfit), I slowed down to find the entrance to the park.

"It's the next driveway, Grandma. See that sign with the bird on it?"

"Oh, -- yeah. It's so good to have someone along like you who can read. Do you know this place?"

He didn't answer, too busy finding the last French fries in the bag.

The small, paved parking lot was neat and clean -- no debris from winter's broken branches or dead leaves.

We took a trail leading west, separated from the gravel hills by a fence. After a while, another path split off.

93

"Let's go there, Grandma." Chuck pointed. "Maybe we'll find something neat." Skipping over a few puddles, ducking under low-bent shrubs, he was ahead of me.

"Oh, look," I said. "There's something like a gazebo -- and here's a lake! See the geese?"

He hopped on the grass. "Grandma, those are ducks." He sounded like a teacher trying to correct a hopeless student.

"Oh, I didn't quite see them through those bushes."

We watched as a family of ducks -- mother, father and four little ones -- sawm towards the shore. They checked us out and turned as if in disgust when we didn't have any food for them.

"Look at those tiny fish, Grandma!"

A school of about 20 sand-colored fingerlings, less than an inch long, swam synchronized as if under one control. Chuck threw a pebble into the water, making the fish scoot in all directions. "Ha, I showed 'em."

After a while we turned back and now walked along the shore. This lake is about as big as two football fields and has the shape of half a doughnut.

"Grandma, see the people fishing from those docks?" He pointed across the lake. "They have the feet in the water. Can I do that too?"

I took a step back to look past a branch for a better view.

"Sque-e-e-eak!" A bicycle had skidded, barely missing me. We both came away with the scare.

"Hey, neat," said Chuck. "I wish I had my bike here." Seems the feet in the water were forgotten.

From a narrow bridge that leads across the tail end of the lake, we looked into the water. "Yikes, see that fish?" called Chuck. "Isn't he big?"

"He's so different." I tried to avoid the water's glare. "So slim and restless. Must be over a foot long."

"That's a pike," shouted Chuck. "In our science book, there's a picture of a pike and it looks just like him."

94

"You see that scoundrel?" asked one of several fishermen sitting at the shore. "That's why we can't catch 'em here. He chases all the others away."

"They don't want the pike to eat them," Chuck explained to the man who cut a face.

A little farther, Chuck went on one of the small fishing docks and with his eyes asked me whether he could take off his shoes.

I shrugged.

"Oh!" He was dangling his feet from the edge of the dock. "I can't reach the water. It's too far down." Slowly he got up again.

Near the western end of the lake, the trail is blocked by a split-rail fence.

"We can't go in there, it's for the animals only," said Chuck. "See the sign, it says 'Closed–wild–life–preserver.' "

"Wild Life *Preserve*," I read aloud. "Interesting."

"It's so that people don't bother the birds and the fish and all the others."

"O.K. Let's go back." I put my hand on his shoulder.

Last year's growth of tall rushes and cattails with their furry spikes stood along the shore line in all shades of reddish brown. When the evening sun came out, they shimmered as burnished golden stripes against the millions of light green dapples that were the new leaves. I wished I could paint.

While strolling back, we came to a long, winding wooden bridge over a ravine.

"Let's see what's there," I said.

"Oh, that only goes to another parking lot."

"I don't think so."

We skipped along the bridge, making it bounce.

Chuck giggled. "Are we supposed to do that?"

"Guess not. But its' sturdy, we didn't break it." From then on we walked very softly to make up for our earlier rudeness to the structure.

95

And there was a parking lot!

"How did you know that?" I asked.

Chuck turned away, but I saw his big grin and the mischievous twinkle in his eyes.

"You know that place! When were you here?"

"Last year with my mom."

"And why didn't you tell me?"

"You wanted a new park, Grandma, so..."

I gave him a big hug.

Our Family's (Harmless) Encounters with Guns

This story does not mean that I am officially either for or against the principles of the American Rifle Association, nor that I take a political stand on guns. It just tells about our personal experiences.

In Austria, where I grew up, civilians were not permitted to carry fire arms except for professional hunters. I don't remember knowing anyone who owned a pistol or a rifle.

When we came to Geauga County and lived on an old farm with 65 acres of unspoiled land, my husband, Tom, was impressed that here we could own guns and even shoot them on our land. While Pete was little, and when Jeff came along, the three guys sometimes went target shooting in our cow lane or aimed at clay pigeons. On the landing above our stairs was a gun rack, holding five weapons. One was a rifle, I was told, another a shot gun, and I don't know what the others were.

The kids were interested in shooting as one might be in sled riding. Occasionally it's fun, and at other times one doesn't care. They left the gun rack alone.

This situation changed when we adopted Kenny, then not quite five years old. His foster family's main past time was hunting, and even the little one had experience with guns. The ones on our rack fascinated him, so one day Dad took the boys shooting behind the house. It turned out that Kenny hit more targets than his big brother and Dad together.

"Bull's eye!" Kenny shouted when he came in. "I got a bull's eye every time!"

I didn't quite believe it, but Tom said, "He's great. Never heard of a kid shooting that well."

Jeff's disgusted look confirmed the little one's marksmanship.

Kenny must have been born with a talent for shooting, with various guns -- even B-Bs -- or a bow and arrow. A few years later, when aiming for clay pigeons, he rigged the thrower so that it ejected three discs at the same time. Kenny went "boom-boom-boon" and hit all three, just like that. Later, while in the Army, he received special recommendation for his excellence as a sharp shooter. When at home, he often went hunting with his mentor, Bill Henderson, who owns a large piece of land.

Last summer, Kenny came one Sunday with his friend Ron, for a short visit. "Hi, Mom," he said. "Is Jeff here yet with Chuck? We'll go target shooting to the Hendersons."

Jeff, Kenny's older brother, drove up, and Chuck jumped out of the car. "Uncle Kenny!"

Ken picked him up and gave him a whirl. "Nephew Chuck, so good to see you."

"Let's get going," said Jeff. "Mom, are you coming too?"

I hadn't planned on that, but then, it was a nice day. "Tom," I hollered, "I've got to go along and take pictures."

Bill Henderson had set up a target, provided different guns and ammo and placed a tarpaulin on the lawn to catch the shells. The men took turns firing their weapons, walked to the target, doubted the others' success and put fresh paper on. My camera caught each of the macho guys in action.

"Don't you want to try?" Bill Henderson asked me. "This 22 doesn't kick much at all."

"No, thanks."

"Chuck, come here," said Kenny while squatting on the grass. "Sit right in front of me."

Chuck did, and Ken placed a rifle in his hands, guiding the kid. Jeff watched carefully.

Quickly I got ready to take a picture of this historic event. Did I see right through the view finder? I checked outside the camera. Yes. Chuck had his eyes tightly shut as he pulled the trigger. Kenny, being behind him, could not notice that.

The two of them prepared for the next shot, "Chuck," I said, "I'm pretty sure you're supposed to keep at least one eye open when you aim."

Kenny looked at him. "Are you scared? You have to line up that grain here, see, between these two pins, and then the whole thing with the target."

Chuck nodded in understanding and closed his eyes again.

"Hey, kiddo," said Kenny. "It doesn't bite ya'."

Chuck did open his one eye and shot, still with Kenny's guidance. Then he and his dad went to the target, admired the results and took the paper along as trophy.

"Why don't you shoot, Mrs. Binder?" asked Ron, Kenny's friend.

"Oh, I don't like to."

Bill Henderson, who had listened, shook his head and mumbled, "Women, don't know what life's all about."

Back at our home, every marksman reported his success to Tom.

"But Grandma didn't shoot," said Chuck.

"Grandma?" Tom laughed. "She'd have to cry."

"Why'd she cry?" wondered Chuck.

"Mom in tears? I can't believe it." Kenny looked at me.

I smiled. "You tell 'em," I said to Tom.

"When we first moved out here from the city, we set up a shooting range in the cow lane. Many of our friends came and practiced, and even four-year-old Pete was quite good. Mom just watched."

"Is that true, Grandma?"

"M-hm." I nodded.

"One day I thought she, too, ought to know how to handle a gun. Took me a while to talk her into it." Tom's voice reflected his old frustration. "We had a new rifle, very easy on the trigger. And for her, we had an old trash can of tin, a big one, as a target."

"Why a trash can, Grandpa?"

Ron had experience with that. "You can hear it when the bullet hits the metal. It makes a nice 'Ping'."

Tom continued. "So Grandma hit it three times in a row. 'Come and look how well you've aimed,' I urged her. But she didn't move, just kept sitting on the grass. Then I saw how tears were just streaming down her cheeks, and she even started sobbing."

"You did?" Kenny got up.

"Sure did."

"I patted her head," said Tom. " 'If you're so upset, dear, you won't have to shoot any more.' Then she smiled."

"I can't believe it, Grandma." Chuck was emphatic.

"You were not much different, kiddo, when you squeezed your eyes tight today instead of aiming."

"Say, Dad, do you have a gun in the house now?" asked Jeff.

"Oh sure, right in my night stand."

"You better keep Chuck away from it, then."

"He can't get hurt," said Tom. "The ammunition is locked in the safe." Tom is a very safety-conscious person.

"You mean," Ron burst out, "when a burglar comes, you have first to go to the safe? Your family sure has strange habits with guns."

A Cloudy Day at Lake Pymatuning

During the night, it had been raining. Now it was overcast, humid and damp; thunder rumbled in the distance.

"Guess you'll have to stay home today," said Chuck's mother when she dropped him off. "It's supposed to stay bad all day. What a summer."

I nodded in resigned agreement.

"Be a good boy for Grandma." She gave him a kiss and left.

Chuck looked at me. "So, where are we going?"

"Want to feed the ducks where they walk on the fish?"

"M-hm. Can I get another toy there? One of those spears they have?"

"What happened to the one from last year?"

"It broke when I shot it at the house. I need a new one."

"Well, if you *need* one, we just have to go there."

Chuck smiled, old enough to understand the joke. "What's the lake called? Pun..."

"Pymatuning."

"And it's in another state, right?"

"The one side is still in Ohio, but the other side, across the causeway, is in Pennsylvania."

"I know." He played with three of his little Hot Wheels cars.

Most people from northeast Ohio and adjoining parts of Pennsylvania have seen the spillway at Pymatuning Lake. Fishing is prohibited above it to protect the fingerlings, but feeding is allowed. Cheap loaves of stale bread are available and visitors throw it to the carp. The fish crowd in the "No Fishing" zone in such numbers that they sometimes seem to get stuck on each other. No space is left between them. Therefore, if a duck ventures into that section, it has no room to swim and is literally walking on top of the carp. It's quite a sight and sounds odd when hundreds of big fish smack their lips. Of course some rodents and seagulls scavenge for the bits of bread that don't reach the water.

A flock of the birds came out of the fog.

"Grandma, now throw the bread into the air for the seagulls."

I tried it – Frisbee style.

"Yes, yes! He got it!" Chuck was jumping with excitement. "Oh, that one was too dumb. Grandma, you hafta throw it right in front of them. They can't change direction quickly."

"Yessir. Why don't you try?"

He made little balls of bread, pitched them at the birds and even hit one. Before we left, we bought an ice cream cone for each of us and in the souvenir store an "Indian" spear for Chuck. The tip was rubber.

"Where do we go now?" he asked.

"Don't know. I saw a sign to a beach."

We found the drive to "Tuttle Beach."

"Is it closed?" asked Chuck when we could see it.

I wasn't sure. As we walked towards the lake, we found a lifeguard sitting in his high chair, reading a book.

"Are you open?" I asked.

Startled, he looked up. "Oh, yes." He gave us a hesitant smile while he shrugged his shoulders at the grey sky. "Lots of space for you today. It just stopped raining."

"Let's change," I said to Chuck.

"But Grandma, we have no swimming trunks!"

"Oh yeah, I have some in the car."

"Mine, too?"

"Of course, wouldn't leave home without them."

Ready for the water, I said to him, "Maybe we find a dry place for the towels; on the grass they'd get sopping wet."

The lifeguard pointed under his seat. "You can leave 'em here."

Then Chuck ran ahead. "Oh, the water is warm!"

"Always feels that way when the air is cool."

A large area was roped off for safety, where the water got deeper very gradually. In the past, Chuck had always been swimming quite close to me, using me as a floating dock. Today he kept his distance, maybe 15 feet from me. I smiled at him.

A good way's out, he asked, "Grandma, can you still stand?"

I tried. "On my tippee toes."

"Then it's over my head." A mixture of pride and fear was in his face. "Let me rest, Grandma." He held on to me, piggy-back. After a few minutes, he said, "I can swim again. Let go of me, Grandma."

"Chuck, I'm not holding you." I showed him my free hands. "It's you who has to let go."

He laughed and pushed off, dunking me under and splashing into my face. Then he dog-paddled back to the shore.

The lifeguard had watched us. "You're taking good care of him."

Chuck ran after a Canadian goose just for the fun of it and then came back. "Let's go out again."

"Yeah, but don't dunk me."

Mischief played on his face.

After three more trips into the deep part and lots of splashing, Chuck was tired.

At the concession stand, the lifeguard was having a sandwich. He waved at us. "Good swimming with nobody else around."

On the way home, I had to turn the windshield wipers on high while Chuck gave me a happy smile and fell asleep.

****

"Guess, Mom, what we did today. I swimmed all by myself in the deep water!"

"You swam in the bathtub?"

"No, no. In a real lake where it was over my head. And I hit two seagulls."

103

I explained.

She shook her head. "With your grandma, you never know."

Chuck grinned and waved his spear at me. "See ya' next week!"

A Wild Trip on the Niagara River

Rafting thrills of white water combined with the comfort of sitting back, relaxing and letting others do all the work – sounds unlikely? Well, try a jet boat ride from Niagara-on-the-Lake, Ontario and you'll agree. The big river with its huge rapids interested me, so I took Chuck, then age nine, and my son Kenny, his uncle, to Niagara.

We had been white water rafting before, on smaller rivers where one has to paddle. Here was a new adventure.

Kenny is very young at heart, which means he and Chuck tease each other all the time, like brothers. Each one comes back for more; more poking, wrestling, arm-twisting or tricking the other by telling fibs.

However, Kenny can also be very protective. At the falls, he carried Chuck on his shoulders to lift him over the elbows and heads of the crowds. Chuck could get a better view than anyone else.

Although Kenny had been enthusiastic about this trip, he seemed to have second thoughts now. "Say, Mom, isn't that boat ride dangerous?"

"Not by the folks who told me about it. They had a ball; nothing unsafe."

Kenny shook his head. "Chuck is so little."

"No, I'm not, Uncle Kenny. I'm strong."

As answer, Kenny squeezed him hard. "Oh yeah?"

"Kenny, they take six-year-olds. Can't be too bad. For regular rafting, kids have to be at least 12."

At dinner, Kenny talked non-stop, about high school friends, college, his buddies in the Gulf War and his job. Chuck and I couldn't get a word in edgewise. The little one looked at me and, with a grin, shrugged his shoulders.

The next morning was different. When we signed in for the ride, we were advised to leave jewelry, dentures, toupees and anything else that isn't grown on, in the car because it might get lost. Most people laughed, but Kenny was mum, not a word. No banter, no jokes. He walked away.

"Grandma, is Uncle Kenny scared?"

"Looks like it. Are you afraid, Chuck?"

"Oh, no! Are you?"

"A little. I'm excited, but that's part of the fun."

The trip starts where the Niagara River empties into Lake Ontario and goes as far up as the "Whirlpool" which most people have seen before, from above.

When Kenny saw the boat, he heaved a sigh of relief. "Oh, that's big!" Suddenly he smiled and helped Chuck get on. I followed.

The jet boat seats about 20 and looks rather tame while sitting at the dock. It is, however, maneuverable like a speed boat and our skipper, a young guy named Oogy, wanted to show off and did "doughnuts" by driving in circles with only a 10 foot hole. The boat banked sharply and the passengers squealed with excitement when hit by the massive spray. Kenny had one arm firmly around Chuck and clutched the safety bar with his other hand. Both grinned at me.

Once in the gorge, we hit the rapids. Going upstream with all that jet power made them look and feel rather harmless, but coming down ... wow, wowee! I really took a hard grip on the bar in front of my seat now. The giant waves drenched everyone in spite of the windshield and our raincoats. Water ran down our necks, our front and even into our mouth because we laughed so much. And contrary to rafting with a paddle, this boat turned around, went back up and did the same rapid over and over again.

In the "Whirlpool" we had just time enough to wave at the cable car above, before we were in the next rapid. The water was quite warm. Only when Oogy cranked up the jets to about 40 miles per hour (pardon me, 60 km per hour – it's metric in

Canada), did we feel chilly. But that was on the way back, and a cup of hot chocolate awaited us at the dock.

"Hey, Mom, you did great." Kenny gave me a pat on the shoulder. "Nothing to it."

Chuck looked at me, a mixture of a smile and a grin on his face.

We each had a set of dry clothes ready in the car.

"Will we see the falls once more, Grandma?"

"We can, on the way home. You have enough time, Kenny?"

"Please, Uncle Kenny!"

Ken looked at his watch, lifted Chuck high and gave him a whirl. "Yes, Nephew Chuck, we can enjoy that world wonder one more time."

Among the many visitors, a man said to no one in particular, "This falls, it ees the most greatest in the world. No?"

Chuck whispered, "He should 'a been in the rapids, then he'd know what's great."

The ride home was peaceful. My two heroes soon fell asleep while I drove.

****

"Grandpa, you should have seen those awesome waves." Chuck beamed.

"Were you scared?"

"I wasn't, but Unc ... "

"Oh, Mom isn't afraid of anything," said Kenny. "The whole thing was her idea. But on that huge Niagara River you really get a wild ride."

White Water Rafting With a Child

Well, the water wasn't very white, but it was fun anyway.

Our family has enjoyed rafting for many years. (The kids and I, that is. Tom is much too sedate for such foolishness.) We often talked about it, and nine-year-old Chuck wanted to raft, too. On most rivers, people have to be 12 years or even 16 years old for safety reasons. Ohiopyle State Park in Pennsylvania, however, has a very mild river section, the so-called Middle Yough, where little ones are allowed.

My son Jeff and I had taken kayak lessons there a few years ago. We thought it wouldn't be very exciting to raft it, but went there anyhow as a birthday present for Chuck.

Chuck's spirits were high, and he talked non-stop on the bus ride to the river. He carried the paddles while we dragged the raft to the water. The two men sat in front, and I behind Chuck. They paddled with varying effect while I tried to counterbalance Chuck's enthusiastic strokes.

Soon after the intake, the river shows quite a few ripples, called a Class One rapid. The water flows a little faster and some rocks cause the foam. We got stuck on a rock, but Jeff swung the raft around, and we glided a little stretch backwards.

Chuck was thrilled with the spins. "Did you see, Grandma? We turned the boat all the way!"

"I was sitting in it, Chuck. How could I not notice?"

On a smooth section, Chuck said, "Dad, Grandma doesn't have to do anything. We can row all by ourselves."

I didn't quite hear Jeff's answer, but he gave me a funny look. When Chuck lost his paddle and I retrieved it, he didn't consider me useless ballast any longer.

On this "soft" river, we had a chance to observe the little things. "Chuck, be quiet for a moment and listen," I said. "Hear the water? When it runs over rocks, it makes a sound – light and gentle."

"M-hm," he said. "It's just a little noise."

"Look at the dragon fly on your paddle," said Jeff. "See the green wings?"

"Catch it, Dad! Get it!"

"What would I do with it? Just let it rest a while."

The dragon fly was smart and sat down on the raft beside me – out of Chuck's reach.

At a slightly bigger rapid, Chuck worried. "Grandma, the water sounds different here, deeper. Is there more water?"

"It flows faster," said Jeff.

Later on, when we were again drifting in a smooth section, Jeff said, "I love these hills. There must be 200 different shades of green." The slightly yellowish locusts provided the highlights; quaking aspen leaves glittered in the sun; darker oaks and maples grew in large numbers; sumacs polka dotted the shore with their red fruit clusters; the grey-green willows dipped their branches in the river and a few bluish evergreens stood sentinel at the scattered homesteads.

Jeff felt hot and just rolled overboard to cool off.

Chuck was stunned. "Dad, did you want to do that? Did you fall in?"

"The water is great," said Jeff. After a few minutes, he heaved himself back into the raft.

"Dad, can I go in, too?"

"Sure. Jump in."

Chuck did and was surprised by the coldness of the water and by his own courage. Then he tried to come back in as Jeff had done, but the raft was too high for him.

"Give me your hand," said Jeff. "On three!"

Chuck counted and his dad lifted him in like a soaked puppy.

"Grandma, are you hot too?"

"Yes, but I want to go in the water by the shore where it's shallow so I can get back into the raft on my own."

After lunch we saw a doe, right by the river. She looked at us but did not move.

"Don't make any noise," whispered Jeff. Quietly we paddled towards the shore. The doe was 10 feet from us. She must have known that people can't jump quickly out of a boat because she leisurely shook off flies and nibbled on leaves. Gradually, we drifted away.

"Neat," said Jeff. "This one didn't even bash in my car."

At the take-out, Chuck gave us again directions how to handle the raft. Changed into dry clothes, we went to the car.

"Grandma," asked the kid, "can we raft again for my next birthday?"

"Sure." I smiled.

"I was afraid," said Jeff, "such easy rafting might be boring, but it wasn't at all. It was so quiet; I had time to look and think and relax. If it hadn't been for Chuck, we would have missed that."

Have You Ever Seen a Mountain Slide?

I don't mean a mud slide in California or a rock avalanche. What I'm talking about is a slide built on a mountain slope for fun. Often this can be found in a ski area that calls itself a "Four Season Resort." There is a hill, and they already have the ski lift to take people up.

After our white water rafting in Pennsylvania, there were several daylight hours left, and Jeff wanted to go to Seven Springs where we had skied the previous winter. "I'd like to see the place in summer," he said. Chuck fell asleep during the half-hour ride.

At the resort, Jeff woke him gently, and Chuck staggered and stumbled as any sleepy kid would. However, he did notice the slide. Suddenly, his eyes were wide open. "Let's go, Grandma! Come on, Dad!" He pulled me towards the slide.

"Well, hold it, Chuck. First, we need tickets."

"Are you going, too, Mom?" Jeff asked.

"Sure." Did it show that I was scared?

There were extensive explanations by the lift operator: "Stand on the red line, look at the chair, sit down, close the safety bar, don't bounce..."

Chuck got impatient. "I know that. It's just like in winter."

I took the chair behind them. My two guys turned and yahooed at me. From the lift, I could see the entire slide. It was like a bobsled run. Two ribbons of concrete wind from the very top of the mountain all the way down, each about four feet wide. They bank a bit in the curves. A sign says that the difference between the height from top to bottom is 700 feet – not just a little hill.

People came down at various speeds, teenagers seemingly as fast as it would go, parents with measured haste while holding their little kids. The whole thing didn't look as scary as I had imagined.

113

On top, Chuck was hopping up and down with eagerness and anticipation. "Dad, you go first, and I'll come right after you, O.K.? You gotta go fast or I'll bump into you."

His father just nodded agreement.

"Grandma, you can come right after me. I'll keep the track open for you."

What would we have done without him?

I lifted a little cart on the track. One sits on it like on a sled, but of course it has wheels.

After more instructions from an attendant, we were off.

This is really neat, I thought. Not quite as good as skiing, but exciting enough. The slide has pleasantly sharp curves and two steep drop-offs where my stomach seemed to rise into my throat. Great fun! By using a lever, a timid rider can slow down or even stop completely.

When I arrived at the bottom, Jeff and Chuck were just getting off.

"Oh, look," said Jeff. "Grandma is already here."

"Wasn't that fun, Grandma?" Chuck asked.

"Terrific." I grinned as broadly as he.

"Let's go again," urged Chuck.

"Tell you what," I said. "You two go by yourselves, and I'll wait and take pictures."

When they were down the second time, Jeff said in a beseeching voice, "Mom, would you wait while we go *one* more time?"

"No," I said.

He was surprised by my seeming rudeness.

"I want to slide, too," I said.

"Oh, good." He bounced to get more tickets.

This time, Chuck said, "Dad, you go on this side, and I'll go here. We can race; O.K., Dad?"

"Yeah," said Jeff, "but I might beat ya."

"No, you won't." Then Chuck turned once more. "They should have three tracks so Grandma could race with us."

"You'd win anyway," I said as they took off.

This time I even looked into the distance, at the beautiful hills of Pennsylvania, crest after crest. Such tranquility beyond the exciting, noisy slide.

At the bottom, Chuck got up just an instant before I could bump into his sled. He looked at me with a "You didn't get me" grin.

When we walked to the car, Chuck's main concern was, "Grandma, when we go rafting next year, can we come to the slide, too?"

Jeff put his hand on Chuck's shoulder and answered for me, "We'll plan on that."

****

If you have a chance to go on a mountain slide, do it. It's not dangerous – it's not scary – it's just fun.

A Day at Peek 'n Peak
(A Ski Area In Western New York)

It started like a regular skiing day. For my birthday, I wanted all of us to go to Peek 'n Peak, just over the state line in New York. My two sons, Jeff and Kenny, hadn't skied together for many years with four years in the Army for Kenny and an injured ankle, business demands and conflicting schedules. Chuck, Jeff's son, was by then a pretty good skier, fast and fearless.

Kenny had spent the night at our house, and early in the morning we picked up Jeff and Chuck.

"Say, Mom, can you drive? I need more sleep," said Jeff.

"Me too." Kenny reclined the car seat, and Chuck snuggled up to his dad.

One and a half hours later, in Pennsylvania, I heard them stir.

"Breakfast coming up," I said. "Chuck, what do you like? At this exit we can get French toast sticks. Egg Mc Muffins are at the next."

"French toast sticks! Yummie."

So I pulled off the road. By now all my guys were wide awake. Jeff blew the cover of his straw right onto Kenny's plate.

"Oh no, you don't!" Kenny laughed. He snipped the paper back to Jeff, and a few crumbs of scrambled eggs flew along

"Dad!" Chuck gasped. "You're not supposed to do that in a restaurant!"

"Kenny started it," grinned Jeff, but they settled down for the time being.

"You know, Grandma," said Chuck while trying to wipe the syrup off his fingers, "you and me, we've skied with my dad or with Uncle Kenny..."

"...or just the two of us," I said.

"Yeah, but never all together. I can't wait."

117

At Peek 'n Peak, Jeff helped his kid tie the lift ticket to his coat. Kenny was already on his skis and pretended to slip, bumping Jeff who barely could catch his balance. Jeff quickly fastened his bindings and hurried after his brother to the lift. On this one, three people could sit side by side on each chair.

"Hey, Dad, wait up for us!"

"Where's Grandma?" Kenny looked for me.

"Go ahead," I said. "I'll be on the next chair."

The two men took Chuck in the middle, and I saw them talking, laughing and gesturing. Chuck turned his head from one to the other, like watching a tennis match.

When I arrived at the top of the lift, Jeff glanced at me to make sure I was all right, and then he and Kenny took off, racing each other.

Chuck followed them, taking a few little jumps. "Did you see me, Grandma?"

"Great jumps."

When we caught up with Jeff and Kenny, they were just throwing snowballs at each other.

"Dad, did you see me jump?"

"Not really. I had to race this guy. But if you caught air over that big root up there, you're really great."

After a few more similar runs, we switched to a lift that seats only two people, a so-called "double chair." Jeff and the little one were one chair ahead of Kenny and me. I saw Jeff put his arm around Chuck's shoulder but then he turned. "Hey, Kenny, let's take that run with the bumps over there."

"Since when do you like bumps?"

"I like moguls, Uncle Kenny. Don't you?" hollered Chuck.

These little hills ("mogul" is the Austrian word for "bump") are created by skiers, all making turns on the same spot. Skiing over them is harder than on a smooth trail. They also slow you down with all the turns you have to make. Jeff and Kenny took off again, while Chuck and I trailed a bit. He, with his much shorter skis, went straight over the moguls; I tried to find a path on the side of the slope where they were not as high.

We saw that Jeff reached for Kenny's binding. One ski fell off, and Kenny hit the ground. Jeff laughed so hard, he sat down on the snow beside Kenny.

"What are you doing?" asked Chuck.

I wondered that, too.

"Now," Jeff was still laughing. "Now I've achieved everything I ever wanted in skiing."

"What's that?" asked Chuck.

"I made Kenny fall. Sweet revenge for 'Single Jack.' "

"Oh, but I got you at Single Jack much better than that." Kenny was grinning.

"Grandma, what's a single Jack?"

"It's the name of a ski run out in Utah. I remember that Jeff fell there and lost one of his new skis. He had to hobble down half the mountain on one ski."

"Did he find the one that got away?"

"On the bottom of the run, someone had nicely stuck it into the snow. You couldn't miss it."

"And why is Dad mad at Uncle Kenny?"

"I really don't know," I said.

"Kenny unsnapped my binding. That's why I fell and the ski came off."

"Really? I didn't know that," I said.

Jeff and Kenny looked at each other. "Maybe now, 15 years later, it's time to tell Mom about it," admitted Kenny.

Then they both took off for the lodge.

Chuck frowned. "I thought only little kids do that." Then he yelled, "Wait up for me, Dad!" But Jeff didn't hear.

At the end of the run, we decided to go in and have a snack. I saw Jeff stooping down to Chuck and helping him with something.

"Any problems?" I asked.

Jeff shook his head. "No, he's just jealous," he said quietly.

119

"Hey, Chuck," said Kenny in the cafeteria, "it's great how you ski. You're not a little kid any more who needs to be watched all the time. You're really one of us guys in a fast group."

Chuck carefully dipped a nacho into the melted cheese, slowly licked it off and crunched the chip. He tried the hot chocolate. Then he took a deep breath and sat up straight. A faint smile started around his eyes, and he shoved the nachos between Kenny and Jeff. "Want some, guys?"

They accepted the offer.

"Is Grandma a guy, too?" asked Chuck.

"For skiing, she's always been one of the guys," explained Kenny.

Chuck seemed satisfied. Then he said. "Today was not a regular skiing day, today was special."

"It's Grandma's birthday," said Jeff as he got up. "She's a year older, but so are we all."

"Me too?"

"Sure. You've grown a lot today." Jeff lifted Chuck high and let him ride on his shoulders to the car. "But I can still carry you."

Chuck answered with a happy little squeal.

A Homebound Day – Not Bad

We ran through the rain to my car.

"Chuckie," I asked, once we had a roof over our heads, "do you have a lot of homework today?"

"No, I did it all in school," he said with a proud smile. "Why?"

"I know nothing special to do. In that rain, we can't go into a park or ..."

"But we still can go to your house, right?"

"Sure."

"I know lots of things to do there." He checked the snack I had brought along and settled comfortably into the seat.

At home he went instantly into his toy corner and brought out a sturdy plastic sheet. "Can I use this?" he asked.

"The sled? For what?"

"To slide down the stairs."

"Will that work? Won't you get hurt?"

He was already upstairs. Thump...thump..thump, thump, thump he came bouncing down the steps. "That's great, like the moguls in skiing. This kind of looks like a snowboard anyway, doesn't it, Grandma?"

It needed more imagination than I had, to see a snowboard in that four-dollar piece of plastic.

Next time down, he went faster. "Yikes. Awesome!"

I had to answer the phone and could not watch him for a few minutes.

"Grandma, I can ride that thing standing up!"

"You'll fall!"

Too late. He landed with a somersault and bumped his head. "Ouch." Gingerly, he rubbed a sore spot.

"You better stop that now or you'll bust your head."

Reluctantly, he agreed. Then, "Grandma, can I put the couch cushions on the floor?"

121

"What for?"

"So I can do flips."

We have sectional furniture, so all the upholstery can be taken off and be put on the floor.

Chuck is a gymnast (although not yet Olympic class) and can do all kinds of jumps, twists and flips. He covered most of the living room floor with the six inch thick cushions, started running from the kitchen and did flips. Forwards, backwards, with or without a twist, landing on his knees, his feet, his side or his butt.

He took off his sweatshirt. "I'm hot."

"Say, Chuck, are you doing such jumping every day at home?"

"Oh no! My mom doesn't let me."

I didn't probe any further.

"We have nothing soft to put on the floor, and once I slipped and flew against our picture window."

"You did?"

"I wasn't hurt real bad, and the glass didn't break either. It just made a funny noise, like 'cre-e-ek,' and my mom, she got all scared. She's always fussy."

Hmm. I could understand her concern.

"But here I jump away from the window, so you don't have to worry." He tried a double flip.

Grandpa came home. "My goodness, has a hurricane struck?"

"Yeah, Hurricane Chuck."

"Let me change my clothes and then we can feed the fish," said Grandpa.

Chuck helped for a little while to pick up the mess, and then the two guys disappeared into the basement to entertain the goldfish.

After a few minutes, the kid came running up. "Grandma, my shirt is like soaked. Can you put it in the dryer?"

"Did you fall into the fish tank?"

He laughed. "Not all the way."

"Put on your sweatshirt," said Grandpa. "You won't be hot anymore. We'll play 'Wheel of Fortune.' "

"Like on TV? How will we do that?"

They took a paper plate and drew many small pie sections on it with a number in each – five, three, eight. With a nail stuck through the center, the plate could be twirled. Grandpa drew little boxes for letters on a piece of paper. On a note pad he wrote down the puzzle words and hid them from Chuck. The little one spun the plate and if he guessed a correct letter, he received credit for the amount.

I left the two of them alone for a while. When Chuck's mother came for him an hour later, we watched.

"Look, Mom, now we have to add up all the pennies that I won."

Grandpa kept track, but Chuck had to do the adding.

"Four dollars and 36 cents. I'll get all that!"

My husband had a hand full of change. "Here, Chuck, now you find the right amount."

Chuck carefully made four little stacks of quarters, then he found three dimes, a nickel and a penny. "Is this right, Grandpa?"

"You did it, you are real good at it."

"You had to know spelling," said Chuck's mom. "You had to add and then find the coins. That's more than you learned in school today, isn't it?"

"Yeah, and look how much I won. Awesome! Can we play again next Tuesday, Grandpa?"

"If it's again raining, and if I still have some money left, we'll play." He patted Chuck's head.

"You know," Chuck said to his mother, "Grandma was worried because when it like rained, we had to stay home. But that's how we could play all these games. Awesome."

Hertha Binder

Oops – 't Was the Wrong Hobby

We older folks, grandparents and such, always try to entertain and educate the kids with activities that we like. I've loved skiing all my life, so I'm teaching it to Chuck and am proud of his and my achievements. When we go to a playground, I use the swings and slides with him. The same goes for wave running, swimming and hiking.

Now Grandpa has set up in our basement six fish tanks "for Chuck." The kid is here half a day per week, and Grandpa lovingly takes care of the critters the rest of the time.

He and Chuck even built a divided cage of plywood, about 4 x 2 x 2 feet with a front panel of glass. Grandpa taught Chuck how to drive in nails and he let him hold a drill. Of course, Grandpa steadied it. Then he bought a pair of hamsters and two iguanas to live in the beautiful new cage.

A day later, while Grandpa was away, Chuck came over. He was all excited and decided to name the larger hamster Gus and the female Rachel. Then he wanted to let them out.

That, however, was a different story: those animals are *not* my hobby, an I don't like to handle them.

"Grandma, can't you take Rachel out so I can pet her?"

"No. Tell you what: *you* take her out while I take off this glass door."

"I can't reach."

"Stand on the other side and grab her with your left hand."

"Grandma, when you open that door, how do we keep Gus and the iguanas from getting out?"

"Don't know. I'll just try to shoo them back in."

Chuck touched Rachel very gently – or gingerly – and the lively ball of fur slid away several times. Meanwhile I tried with my two hands to keep the other three animals from coming out.

Chuck did coax Rachel into a shoe box and covered it. I put the transparent front panel back on.

125

"Watch it, Grandma. You're pinching the tail of the iguana. It can break off."

I really didn't care what happened to its tail, but I lifted the glass out once more. The tail was slowly withdrawn, and at the same time Gus got a foot caught.

"When will Grandpa come home?" Chuck knew the right solution to our dilemma.

"In an hour, but you wanted the hamster now." Finally, I could shut the cage without dismembering anyone.

Now Chuck put the box with Rachel in the middle of the living room and stroked her lovingly. "Grandma, why don't you hold her? Pet her. Feel how soft the fur is."

I'm a bit squeamish about such a little animal that tries to get away and scratches with all four feet at 200 RPM, but the fur was indeed soft and pleasant to the touch. Chuck slowly let go, and I held and cuddled her. He seemed proud that he had taught me to enjoy his furry friend.

Just when Chuck was ready to take her back, Bob, our handyman, stopped by. "What have you got? A brown mouse?"

Chuck felt insulted. "Don't you know a hamster?" He looked at Bob.

That one second was enough for the animal to get loose. She dashed under the couch. Chuck and I were lying on the floor, trying to locate the fugitive. The sofa was too heavy for us to lift, and even if we could do it, Rachel would run away again.

"Grandma, we could push her out with a broomstick." Chuck, ever so lightly, nudged the hamster out.

"Where is she now?"

"In that corner," said Chuck. "There we can get her." But Chuckie's arms were not long enough. "Grandma, can you reach her, please?"

So I lay on the back of the couch and stretched down behind it. Ouch, my shoulder hurt. To my luck, the hamster seemed so scared, she let me grab and pull her from the nearly inaccessible

126

spot. Chuck took over once more, carefully guarding his little friend.

After a while, he said, "Grandma, can I feed the fish now? I know what food they get in each tank."

"All right, let's go in the basement. Do we put the hamster back?"

"M-hm. She can have a rest."

I needed a rest as well.

This time I was already more skillful with the glass panel. No one escaped, no one was pinched.

Chuck generously dumped large amounts of fish food into the tanks.

"Isn't that too much? Grandpa had said what they don't eat spoils and fouls up the tanks."

"Sorry," said Chuck. "I didn't mean to."

So I scooped some of it back out, getting my sleeve all wet.

Just then Grandpa came home. After giving Chuck a hug and a whirl, he looked at me. "How come you look so bushed? You are the one who wants to play with your grandson."

"Yeah, but ..." I didn't really want an argument, so I said no more and happily left the two of them in the basement.

While I fixed myself a cup of tea in the kitchen, I heard Chuck tell how the iguana nearly lost his tail, and how Rachel got away. "Grandma didn't hold her right."

When I looked out the window, it was snowing a little. Great! Maybe next week we can go skiing.

Hertha Binder

The Second Generation Tree House

All winter long, Chuck and Grandpa had been discussing how to build a tree house in our big spruce. They had drawn plans and studied the sketches. Finally it was spring, and on a bright Sunday, Chuck with his father, Jeff, and Grandpa were ready. Two sawhorses were lined up, and Chuck was sitting on a board to weigh it down while Jeff was sawing. Then the kid was allowed to use the power drill.

"Don't press down," said Grandpa. "Let the drill work itself in."

"Hold it straight." Jeff watched it intently. "Move the top a bit towards me."

Being curious what was going on, I busied myself with some yard work close by. When I looked up again, a 12 foot tall 4 x 4 had been erected, anchored to the tree with a board.

"Don't come close, Mom." Jeff laughed. "I'm pretty sure it'll fall down."

"But, Dad, it can't fall. It's hooked on the branch. See?" Chuck had no doubts.

While I struggled by the hedge with some deadwood that the last storm had broken off, I heard a commotion, mostly Chuck calling, "Uncle Kenny's here! Uncle Kenny!"

Unannounced, Kenny had shown up. He lifted Chuck high while the little one squealed with delight, then gave Tom a hearty pat on the back and put his arm around my shoulders.

"Hey, little brother," Jeff called from above. "Quit all that hugging and give me a hand here."

"I know you can't do it without me." Kenny raised the second 4 x 4 while Chuck climbed back up and was driving in nails.

"Let's measure and make sure that those posts are the same distance apart on top and bottom," said Grandpa, the architect.

Jeff checked it. "Fifty-four inches," he said tossing the tape measure to Kenny who caught it casually with his left hand.

"What's the distance down here?" Grandpa was serious.

"I can't believe it. Fifty-four inches!"

"Oh, that's an accident." Jeff chuckled. "We never build things parallel."

"Isn't it good, Dad, if those beams are straight?"

"Sure is, but *our* tree house wasn't straight. It had a jaunty angle."

"It was crooked like this." Kenny showed Chuck with his hands.

"*You* had a tree house here too, Dad? How come?"

"Chuck, I lived here and grew up in this back yard; I've spent more years of my life on this place than anywhere else. So did Ken. We didn't just have a tree house – it was in *this* tree. It even had a name."

What was it called?"

"Camp Kennychev. Sounded Russian, but really it was our two names put together." Kenny was now handing Jeff a saw.

A little later I brought fried chicken from the store and used a clean board as the table.

While we were all munching, Kenny pointed into the tree. "Say, is that the branch where I got stuck?"

"I'm pretty sure it is." Jeff stood up. "That's where the tree house was."

I looked at them with raised eye brows.

"Oh, that's one of the things we didn't tell our mommy right away," said Kenny, and they both grinned.

"So what happened? Can you tell me now, 20 years later?"

"Kenny climbed out the window. I don't know what for."

"Your tree house had a window, Dad? Will mine also get one?"

"Sure, maybe two. One on each side."

"So what happened when he was out the window?" I asked.

"Kenny slipped off."

"Jeff was supposed to hold me."

"Yeah, but you let go of my hand." Jeff buttered an ear of corn for Chuck. "Kenny would have done all right if he had just fallen off..."

"...but my shoes got stuck on the branch, so I was hanging upside down."

"I jumped off the tree," said Jeff, "and wanted to catch him, but before I could run over, he slid out of the shoe and fell on his head."

"You didn't tell me?"

"Didn't need to, Mom. He was all right. Only at night, he threw up ..."

"... and Mom thought she had let me eat too many strawberries."

Chuck was looking from one to the other in speechless amazement. Like most youngsters, he never considered that his elders had once been kids. Was this the first time his dad and uncle had admitted some imperfections? Surprise and delight played on his face.

While we grownups were still resting in the sun, Chuck climbed back up the tree, a drum stick in his hand. He sat down on the small planks with a serene and far-away look. This rudimentary structure, a few boards fastened to the branches, was his. No girls allowed. Seems all boys like to be there. Why? Away from supervision? Solitude? That could be found as well on other places. Is there any connection with our very distant ancestors who lived in trees for safety? Some scientists might think so.

Our good old pine had such a long history: kids climbing up, storms nearly upending it, the first tree house, 12 German shepherd pups chewing on the exposed roots, the drought of '88 killing the top third and now a second tree house. That spruce really seems part of our family and it is the ideal place for our grandson's new retreat.

"Grandpa, when do we build the roof?" he called down.

131

"Next time you come. It shouldn't take us too long."

When Will We Waterski, Grandma?

"So, Grandma, when will you take me waterskiing?" asked Chuck last March. "I'm big enough now."

"Waterskiing? I don't know."

"Can't we go in summer?"

"It's not as easy as that. For snow skiing, we can just go by ourselves. For waterskiing, we need a boat..."

"You have to buy one?"

"No, we could rent it, but we'd need three grown-ups because you are too young to be a driver or an observer."

"What's he do?"

"When the boat pulls a skier, one person has to face backwards in the boat and watch the skier all the time – observe him. If the skier signals that he wants to go faster or slower, the observer tells the driver. If the skier falls, the boat has to turn fast, check whether he is O.K., pick him up or at least bring the rope back to him."

"You and my dad and Uncle Kenny are three grown-ups. We can go."

"Yeah, and we all need a vacation at the same time."

"M-hm," he said with so much confidence that he got me on the track to think and plan.

****

In July we were at a beautiful lake in western Maryland, a reservoir created years ago by damming the Deep Creek. It has many small coves where the tributaries ran into the main river, an excellent location for skiing, because there are no big waves.

"Mom, you go first?" asked Jeff.

"Sure." I was a bit shaky, but I jumped in. "Let me have a ski."

133

Chuck plopped it in, and it stopped pretty far from me. I had to swim for it. When I was ready for the second ski, I saw that Jeff explained the art of scooting a ski exactly to the person in the water. Chuck watched with surprise how his father set it on the water and how I barely had to stretch my arm to grab it.

Kenny, the driver, picked up the slack of the rope.

"Hit it," I yelled bravely.

Oh, it was great to glide again over the water. We hadn't done it for a few years. I waved happily at my crew not watching some cross waves and wiped out. Oh well, the skis didn't even come off, and I was ready for more.

"Grandma, why did you fall?"

"Guess I was klutzy."

"Do you want to go again, Grandma?"

"Of course," said Jeff. "Don't you, Mom?"

"What else?" I grabbed the rope and just had to nod at Kenny who was watching me. This time I went the better part of the lake's length, grinning from ear to ear.

When I quit, Chuck was impatient to try it, but his father said, "You'll do better if you watch a bit longer. I'll ski now, then Kenny, and then I'll help you."

My two sons, both in their early thirties, skied with skill and abandon.

"Will I ever ski as good as Uncle Kenny, Grandma?"

"I'm sure you will, but it'll take you a year or two."

Jeff went with Chuck into the water and showed him how to put on the skis, how to handle the rope and get into position for take off.

"If the kid should get up today," Kenny said to me, "we won't be able to stand his bragging."

Chuck did get up after a few tries, but fell instantly either forwards, backwards, left or right. He huffed and puffed when he came back into the boat "Boy, I'm tired now."

"I saw you getting up," Kenny complimented him. "Don't think I could do that the first day."

Chuck had a wan smile. It seemed he wasn't sure whether he should be proud of his moderate success or disappointed that he wasn't equal to the water skiers at Sea World yet.

We went back to the marina and rented a glorified inner tube, mostly for Chuck. On that he was quite comfortable and – we assumed – could have been bouncing on it for hours.

The next day it rained, but two days later it was just perfect; the water smooth as glass because it was windstill and no other boats were out early in the morning. We had a ball. Chuck overcame his wobbliness and could stay up for about 70 yards.

"Will we water ski again next year?" he asked.

"Sure," said Kenny. He pointed at another boat with two skiers in tow. "Look at those guys, see how they cross over and switch sides? Grandma used to do that with us when we were kids. Next year *you* can ski like that with her."

"Really?" Chuck had a wide-eyed smile.

Jeff put his hand on the kid's shoulder. "Yes. By next year you'll ski well enough for that. It'll be the perfect summer fun for an 11-year-old and his grandma." He looked at me. "Right?"

My smile was just as happy as Chuck's.

At the Hale Farm, Cows Have Udders, You Know

Do you enjoy being outdoors, take a leisurely stroll and discover something interesting? Consider a visit to the Hale Farm and Village, located near Bath, Ohio. The farm, close to the crossing of interstates 271 and 77, lies within the Cuyahoga River Valley Recreational Area.

It takes you 150 years back to the daily life of settlers in the Western Reserve with people wearing the period clothing: for women long gingham dresses, aprons and white bonnets with a ruffle; for men button down shirts, dungarees and leather suspenders.

Chuck and I were at the Hale Farm earlier this summer. From the parking lot, we saw cattle grazing in a pasture. Scattered over several acres, we found a sawmill and shops for woodworking and pottery. We watched a blacksmith in his forge. At the broom maker's we received a sample of corn straw, the material for brooms.

Chuck liked the hands-on exhibits best: at the basket weaver's, a lady explained how baskets differ depending on their intended use. Thin strips of hardwood were soaked in water to make them soft and pliable. "Now they can be woven," she said. "Over and under, over and under."

Chuck tried it.

"Watch out here, you skipped one and went under two."

Chuck pulled the strip back a little and proceeded carefully around the basket's circumference.

"Great, beautiful," she said.

Chuck beamed. "I didn't know I could do that."

We admired the glassblower, although visitors can't do any work there for safety reasons. The glowing glass is 2,500 degrees hot. From a shapeless gob, the man made a delicate little bowl.

"Neat," said Chuck. "He didn't even break it when he knocked it off that long pipe."

At the Spinners and Weavers' Chuck was allowed to card the wool with two wire brushes to make it clean and fluffy. "That's like brushing the dog." He tried also a large loom, switching the rows of thread with foot pedals and scooting the shuttle through. He produced about 1/8 inch of a three foot wide runner.

At our next stop, a lady explained cheese making. "We get the fresh milk every day from our cows. In this pot we heat it and let it turn to curds and whey."

"And that's what Miss Muffet ate?" asked Chuck. "Yukk, I wouldn't want that."

A thunderstorm passed over the area, and the cheese woman invited us to sit on the large milk cans until the rain let up.

"What made you work here?" I asked.

"I loved the area and often came here to hike," said the round faced, middle aged lady, her bonnet a bit askew. "The job I had before was a high pressure position with deadlines and demanding customers." She put some kindling wood into the stove. "When they had an opening here, I was happy to take it."

"Are you always here with the cheese?"

"Most of the time, but we have to learn about all the other trades too so we can fill in elsewhere."

Meanwhile, her fire had gone out. Chuck offered his corn straw from the broom shop. With a safety match she lit it, and the fire flared up. "Thanks," she said to Chuck. "Better than using flint."

The rain had let up and we left. As we passed a barn, Chuck said, "Can we go in and look?"

Two heads of cattle and a young woman were inside.

"Are these the cows that give the milk for the cheese shop?" I asked.

"These are our two oxen, Beech and Birch," she said brightly with a smile reserved for city slickers. "The cows are out in the pasture."

I got a red face.

"Grandma, a cow has an udder," instructed Chuck, shaking his head in disbelief. "Grown-ups are supposed to know that stuff."

In spite of my embarrassment, I had to laugh. "I couldn't see their bellies and from the horns I couldn't tell."

Chuck gave me a sideways look and mumbled, "What an excuse."

We entered a historic home to escape the renewed rain. Not much was on exhibit there, but two guides, young women both, had a bag full of old fashioned toys. That was really the nicest thing for Chuck. One had a heavy piece, a large button or such, in the middle of a three foot long string. When one first twists the string and then pulls on it, the button whirls and makes a humming noise. Therefore, it's called a "buzz saw." Another toy was made of a stick with notches on one side and a little wing, like a pin-wheel, fastened to its end. When one rubs the notches with something hard, the pinwheel turns.

"I wish I could have one of these," said Chuck, aware that the toys he played with were not for sale.

"They might still have some in the souvenir shop," said one of the young women.

So we went to the gift shop which looks quite modern, bought Chuck's toy and a "present day" lunch.

On our way to the car, a "mooh" came from the near pasture.

"See, Grandma, that's a cow. It has..."

I put my hand over his mouth. "Oh, you hush."

Editorial Help

Every writer benefits from the suggestions of another person. A husband, friend or grown son is a handy critic for any literary attempt. They find confusing sentences, misplaced commas or vague words that can be improved before the article is submitted to the editor.

Having learned English only as a second language, I still have troubles with sentence structures. Occasional, a "throw the cow over the fence some hay" slips in. When Chuck was about nine years old, he knew that his father checked my articles.

"Grandma, what does my dad really do when he reads your stories? Does he correct your spelling?"

I was taken by surprise. In the past, when I had read to him a tale of our common adventures, he had listened with barely concealed boredom. And now that sudden interest?

"Not so much the spelling. If I don't know it, I can always look it up in the dictionary."

"Then what does he check?"

"He makes sure I write the way people really talk. Coming from another country, another language, I don't always get it right."

"I know that." His smile was slightly condescending. "Dad's often busy. I can check your papers. I know English; I'll tell you what you should change."

Wow. 'That little twerp,' I thought. 'What's *he* gonna tell me?' But then, he was the first person who *volunteered* such help, so I asked, "What do you think I should do differently?"

His answer came promptly. "Don't use long words. If a kid wants to read it, he can't understand it."

"I always try to use simple words..."

"But you wrote 'commotion' when the ducks came back."

"What would be better?"

"I would say 'fuss.' Everyone knows what that means."

141

"But, Chuck, the books you bring from your school library have long words."

"That's different. Those are scientific books."

"And you know, I don't really write for kids, I write for grown-ups."

"But kids sometimes read it and they should understand it."

Can't argue with that one. "What else should I have put differently?"

"The story with the pumpkin. You said I pressed it up."

"Yes." I imitated the motion. "Over your head."

"You should have said 'lifted.' It wasn't that heavy."

"O.K., but that's already printed. We can't change it any more."

"Just ask me next time before you turn it in."

"Yessir."

****

So I asked. "Say, Chuck, remember when we were at the Hale Farm?"

"Yeah. The basket weaving."

"When I mistook the oxen for cows."

"You said you couldn't see their bellies."

"A grown-up would say 'What a lame excuse.' How would you put it?"

"I'd say '*What an excuse!*' "

"O.K., I'll write it that way."

He gave me a friendly nod. Teachers are always pleased when students accept their advice.

Another time I asked, "Chuck, last year, when you were not yet nine years old, would you have said 'I swimmed' or 'I swam?' "

He grinned. *"Last year* I'd have said 'I swimmed.' Now I say 'I swam.' Well (he chuckled), sometimes I still say 'I swimmed.' You can write it."

142

"What about 'more better?' "

His eyes twinkled. "That I still say. Oh, I know it's not right, but it's just – more better."

Tired Of the Old Swimming Hole?
Let Chuck Show You Dover Lake

The phone was ringing. "Hi, Grandma. When I come to your house next time, can we like go to a different place to swim?"

"I don't know another one."

"But I do. I was there with my dad. It's awesome."

"What do they have? Slides?"

"A huge one and on another you sit on a mat, and you can swim. They have a dog – you know --like a mascot, and it's on all the signs on the road."

"Well, good, but I need better directions to find it."

"Oh, yeah, I know that. If you call my dad, he can tell you. Bye, Grandma, see you Tuesday."

****

Jeff gave me all the needed information. "Dover Lake Waterpark. You'll like the place, Mom. It's right on the back side of the Brandywine ski hill. Can't miss it. You'll have a ball."

Brandywine is an area familiar to me. Once there, Chuck guided me safely through the road repair detours, following the signs with the funny dog.

At the ticket counter I chose the shortest line.

"You can't go there, Grandma. That's only for..." He was studying the sign. "...for season passes." How good to have a person along who can read.

After we had changed into swim suits, we looked at two extremely tall, straight slides. They were at least 70 feet high and very steep.

"Last time, I was on this slide, Grandma."

145

I felt some tightness in my throat, knowing that I'd have to go with him lest he considered me a spoilsport.

"But today I won't go," he said firmly, looking at me to judge my disappointment.

Managing a sad face, I said, "O.K., how about the winding slide with the innertubes?"

"You have to wait forever and then people bump into you. It's much too crowded; see all the kids carrying up the tubes?"

True, people were climbing up the hill, singe file, carrying the large, bright green innertubes, like a string of harvester ants loaded with bits of leaves.

"But we can take a mat," said Chuck.

Only a short line of people was waiting for the ride down a slide where one had to sit on a mat.

"Grandma, watch your step; it's slippery. Dad nearly fell here. And hold on to the mat or you'll lose it."

"Yessir."

The slide with the many curves was just swift enough to be fun but not scary. Chuck waited for me in the splash pool, making sure I was O.K., and gave me an approving nod.

After three more rides, he said, "Let's go swimming in the lake, Grandma."

The beach area was large with ample space to swim and, therefore, was not crowded. After we stayed in the shallow section for a while, we heard a mother say to her young child, "Don't go there, it's deep."

"*Do* go there, it's deep," I said to Chuck. "And you can swim."

He giggled. "Can you still stand, Grandma?"

I tried. "Hardly. So it's over your head. You can swim here just as well as in the shallow. Want my hand to hold on?"

"Don't need it." Pride is a strong motivator.

When we were tired, we had a snack. Then he wanted to go on a pedal boat. You sit and push the pedal as on a bicycle. It is a cumbersome way to move a boat, and the steering is clumsy, but we made it all the way up and down the lake which is about 1/4 mile long.

At one time we found ourselves in the middle of a flock of geese which honked and squawked as if we were in the first boat they had ever seen. Chuck tried to imitate their sounds for communication.

More swimming. Chuck was now interested in doing handstands in the water and diving between my feet. Then he had a great idea. "I'll try to jump all the way out of the water."

I doubted that was possible for humans (whales and dolphins can do it), but Chuck jumped and splashed.

"You try it, Grandma!"

Try, I did. I jumped up and *after* I plopped back into the water, I stuck my feet up in the air. Several times.

"Yeah, but you hafta get your feet out of the water before..."

"Chuck, that's all I can do. Why don't you have your other grandma try it some time?" (She is 20 years younger than I, and Chuck often mentioned that I'm so-o-o much older.)

"Grandma Ella? She can't swim; well, hardly." So I was vindicated.

When the lifeguard whistled for another safety break, we went to a huge wave pool.

"Grandma, sit on the floor and let the waves wash over you. It's fun."

"Nah..."

"Oh, try it."

So I did. After a while I said, "I'm bushed."

"Can we stay till the waves stop? Please?"

What else could I do but agree.

At the car, Chuck was looking once more at the big sign with the funny dog beside the name. "Isn't this Dover Lake a great place, Grandma?"

"It sure is."

"Aren't you glad I showed it to you?"

I gave him a big, happy hug.

The Mysterious Mood of Fog And Rain

Sure, most outdoor summer activities are planned for good weather. We are used to blue skies and sunshine when we think of swimming, boating or hiking. Sometimes, though, it doesn't work out that way. With limited vacation days, one might take on the challenge of less than perfect conditions.

On this year's summer trip with my son Jeff and grandson, Chuck, we spent the first half of a rainy day in an arcade. The two guys asked every 10 minutes, "Grandma, is it still raining?"

"Right now, it's pouring."

More video games. After a while, the thrill of the electronic challenge wore off.

"Why don't we take a drive and look for the place that rents out jet skis?" I suggested.

"Yeah," said Jeff. "When the weather is good, we won't have to waste time finding it."

Uncertain directions and missing road signs delayed us for a while, but then we saw all the wave runners and jet boats at a dock. The owners, not busy on this day, eagerly explained more than we asked for.

When all our questions were answered, Jeff said, "Look, Mom, it stopped raining."

"Well, then let's go now. Just let me change into my swim suit."

"You are going too, Grandma?"

"What did you think? I'd just sit here and watch you guys having fun?"

The modern wave runners are big enough for three people to ride on. They can even pull a water skier, although we didn't try that. Jeff was driving smoothly in big curves, while Chuck enjoyed the machine's maneuverability by jerking it left and right. After a while he slowed down and said, "You know, it's raining again. Do we have to go in?"

149

We had barely noticed when the spray from the lake was increased from above. To be on the safe side, we drove by our marina, checking whether the guy wanted us to come in. No, he just waved us on.

A little later rain was coming down in grey sheets, curtains pulled across the lake. Did you ever take a shower in the middle of a lake? We pushed against wind and rain as if in a struggle. The machine, though, had no trouble. Soon our time was up. When we stepped onto the dock, Chuck and I could hardly walk straight, still trying to balance on the bouncy craft.

Chuck wiped the water off his face and giggled. "Grandma, did you ever have so-o-o much fun?"

****

Another outing in gloomy weather was even more impressive. We were scheduled for white water rafting on a mild section of the river at Ohiopyle in western Pennsylvania. Just when it was time to start the trip, the rain let up. So we went. The river had twice as much water as in previous years, flowing much faster and making paddling easy.

Heavy fog hung in the valley, hovering in fluffy clouds on the hill side. They made me think of laundry, strung out on the clothesline of the mountain crest. A few taller trees were the clothes pins in this picture. At other times the mist reached with fingers into the ravines of the mountain side.

The densest layer of fog, though, was right on top of the water. While it formed only a haze towards the hills, it was impenetrable when one looked along the river. Not to see where we were going was mysterious and spooky. Around a bend the width of the river appeared much narrower, outlined by wet, black trees. The skeleton of a broken down maple, half in, half out of the water, seemed to block the path like a turnstile. Only a few feet of open water? And beyond? Was this the entrance to some netherworld?

Then came an island in the middle of the river.

"Oh, Chuck, the fog makes it look like a rabbit."

"Yeah. See the ears, Grandma? He even has like a nose on that side."

"On the other side are the haunches," said Jeff.

"If the sun had shined, the island wouldn't look like a rabbit," said Chuck. "I can't wait to tell my friends."

By now it rained again, but before we arrived at the take-out, Jeff said, "I've never seen the valley like this. Mysterious, ghostly, gloomy, but beautiful in an unexpected way.

Grandma's Friends – Could They Be Fun?

"So, *where* are we going?" asked Chuck while he buckled his seat belt.

"Marblehead. It's a peninsula in Lake Erie. Friends of mine have a house there, right on the lake, on the bay."

"They are *your* friends?"

"Sure." I explained how I had met Jane and Henry Simko. "One of their boys was a friend of your dad when they were in grade school. He often came with us on trips."

"But that was long ago. Right?" Chuck had a slightly pained expression. Seems, a more exciting babysitter was not available for that day. A bag of cheese Frittos, though, and some library books kept him busy for a while, and then he took a little nap.

"How much longer till we get there, Grandma?"

"We are pretty close. See how the land here is all flat? No hills like in Geauga County. – Oh, there's already the bay."

On the bridge over Sandusky Bay are many high posts for street lights.

"Grandma, there is a seagull on that lamp ... and one on the next light too ... on all of them! Aren't they cool?"

The birds seemed to be part of the light fixtures.

"They all look to this side." He pointed west. "Oops, one sits the other way and here is one missing. But aren't they neat?" He giggled.

I had to laugh, too.

Soon afterwards, we were at my friends' house.

"This is Chuck. – Chuck, this is Mrs. Simko and Mr. Simko." (I don't like it when kids call grown-ups, whom they have just met, by their first names, so I made sure we started out right.)

Within no time, Jane and Chuck were inspecting the beach and the boat. "Grandma, you know how big that boat is? Down

153

here they can like sleep, and it even has a bathroom." He had to check that one out even before Henry had the boat off the dock for our planned ride.

An unusual wind from the south whipped up frisky waves in the bay, but with every bounce of the boat, Chuck's grin became bigger and happier. "Where are we going?"

"That's a surprise," said Jane.

When Henry pulled up at a dock, Chuck's eyes were big. "Going with a *boat* to McDonalds? And look at all the seagulls. There must be like a hundred."

The familiar fare made Chuck relax, and he told the Simkos stories as if they were *his* friends. Being grandparents themselves, they just knew how to listen to a kid.

On the way out the bay, Henry let Chuck drive for a while. The little one was so pumped up with pride that he seemed to forget breathing. When more boats crowded the water, and Henry was again at the helm, Chuck took a big gulp of air. "Wow, awesome. What's that kind of boat called?"

"It's a small cruiser," said Jane.

Although a storm was forecast for later that day, and the lake was getting rough, Henry could still safely drive us to Kelly's Island, four miles away.

On its south side is a rock-beach, no sand, just fist sized smooth stones. The water was clear, green and warm, and the waves, driven by the south wind were three to four feet high. We used some styrofoam rings for floatation which Chuck had brought along. They were not life preservers, but they sure made bouncing in the waves more fun.

"This is the most neatest beach we've ever been to," said Chuck. "Don't you like it, Mrs. Simko?"

"That's why we brought you here," she said. Just then Jane didn't watch, and a huge whitecap doused her.

Chuck laughed out loud, then quickly put his hand over his mouth, afraid he might have offended her. After she caught her breath, Jane laughed too, and that triggered more giggles from all of us.

"How would you like to go now for a ride with a golf cart?" she suggested.

We rented one, and Chuck asked, "Can I drive it, too?"

"Let your grandma control it here where the traffic is heavy, but farther out you can drive," said Jane.

His handling of the cart was not much bumpier than mine. We went across the middle of the island to another beach. Chuck even parked the golf cart, although my hand was never far from the steering wheel.

"This beach is so different," he said. "All sand and so warm, but no waves. Can we come back to this island some time?"

I shrugged. "Maybe next year."

Afterwards, Jane showed us the well known glacier grooves, a unique geological feature, and then Chuck drove all along the shaded west coast which offers constantly changing, lovely views of the lake. In spite of the haze, we could even make out the Perry Monument on Put-in-Bay, the next island.

Later, back at the Simko house, Chuck played at their beach and even had the company of two dogs. They eagerly retrieved the pieces of driftwood he threw for them into the water, again and again.

Time had gone fast, and soon we had to say good-bye. Jane packed some munchies for our trip home. When we crossed the Sandusky Bay bridge again, Chuck carefully counted the sea gulls on the lamps. "Nineteen!" Now they all were looking towards the east. Then he asked, "Grandma, are you gonna write about today?"

"I don't know yet. Should I?"

"Yeah. Your friends are cool. This was real fun."

"You drove a cruiser and a golf cart. Not bad."

"M-hm. And we had the waves and going with the boat to McDonalds. Write it."

Memories Of the Fair

When my kids were young, we went to the Geauga County Fair every year. I have to admit, that event was not my cup of tea. For me the fair meant sweaty crowds, screaming vendors, rides that made me sick when I just looked at them, sticky hands from funnel cakes and chili dogs, my husband giving an expert opinion on each tractor that we didn't need while the youngsters were pestering to sit on all the farm machinery. There were loud speakers droning at a volume so high one couldn't understand the words, and in the evening a dusty tractor pull or a demolition derby where people cheered when cars got smashed. I was very glad when our boys were old enough to drive there by themselves.

****

Now here is Grandson Chuck. That, of course, is a different matter.

"Want to go to the fair?" I asked him on the phone.

"To the Geauga Fair? Yippie!"

"Tonight is the Demolition Derby. Want to see it?"

"Yes, sure!"

"But it's late in the evening. Ask your mom if it's O.K. to come home close to 10."

I heard some muffled conversation, and then Chuck came back. "She said 'Of course.' And can we go to the grandstand? Last time I was there with my mom, we had to look through the fence."

"You've got it, kiddo," I said. "Grandstand."

****

157

At the rides, Chuck asked, "Want to go on the Ferris Wheel? It's slow."

"Sure. That one won't bother me." (I get sick on fast spinning merry-go-rounds.)

The ride was just scary enough, and Chuck was pointing. "Look how far you can see, Grandma. Is that your house over there?"

I craned my neck, but by then the wheel had moved us farther down, and we had a good look at the lemonade stand.

"I can't wait till we get to the grandstand."

"Chuck, it's still several hours before the derby begins."

He nodded. "I know. Can we next go to that ride..." He was trying to read the sign, "Sea-Ray."

"You mean the one that's like a big swing?"

"Yah. It doesn't turn. Can't you go on it?"

"M-m. I better not. Why don't you try it by yourself?"

Chuck shook his head and said very quietly, "I don't want to ride it by myself, but if you can't, it's O.K." With his sad eyes, he won me over.

"All right," I said. "Let's go."

A beaming smile was his answer.

The operator gave me a doubtful look, wondering whether I really wanted to ride. The swing was quite comfortable, and though it rises to the vertical on both sides, I enjoyed it – for a while. Then my stomach became queasy.

"Are you O.K., Grandma?"

Although I wasn't badly sick, I sure didn't feel well. After the swing had stopped, I said, "Let's go to the grandstand and sit in the shade." Chuck didn't object. The breeze was cool, and while I rested, he could watch sky divers descend.

"Why don't you have something to eat, Grandma? That would make your stomach feel better."

I couldn't even think of food, but obviously Chuck was hungry, so we went to the little restaurant under the grandstand.

"Don't worry," he said. "I'll order myself. – Nachos, please and a cherry Coke." He looked at me, and I shook my head. "She doesn't eat," he explained to the server who suppressed a giggle.

The noise level was high, so we could hear only fragments of conversations from other tables. "Mommie-e-e!" "Again? Well, no more Coke for you, young man, or we won't..."

"You feel better now, Grandma?"

"Yes, I do, I'm all right again. Those two nachos I had from you must have straightened out my stomach. I am sorry, we couldn't do anything for a while. I should have known not to go on that swing."

"No, no. It's really like *my* fault. I wanted you to ride with me."

After we both had thus taken responsibility for the mishap, Chuck suddenly pointed his finger harshly at me and said in a commanding voice, "Well, no more rides for you, young lady..."

I needed an instant to comprehend and then laughed out loud.

He watched me. "...or we won't go to the grandstand."

Still laughing and giggling, we bought tickets for the demolition derby.

"Do we go in now? I can't wait."

"We still have an hour and a half to go. Why don't we look at some animals?"

Rows of cattle's hind quarters, hogs in tight pens, chickens with exotic feathers in small cages didn't impress Chuck. "What else is here?"

I looked at a sign on the last tent. "Llamas and Alpacas, it says. See?"

"What's an al-pa-ca?" asked Chuck.

"Don't know. Let's find out."

First we saw alpaca wool in a small bowl, different shades of brown.

"Oh, Grandma, feel it. It's so light and smooth."

The wool really felt pleasant, clean and fluffy, particularly if one had expected anything similar to sheep's wool.

In the big tent I was impressed. There was a pleasant breeze. These animals were kept in roomy stalls, were not tied, could move and turn at leisure and curiously looked and sniffed at visitors. They were about four feet high with a round muzzle, gentle eyes and thick, shiny fur. The owner of the alpacas, a man from a nearby town, explained that they are gentle pets, pleasant to be with and had been introduced to the United States just a few years ago. In their home territory, the South American Andes, they are raised for wool.

Chuck was allowed to pet one. "That's so soft; awesome." He gave me a questioning look.

"No, Chuck, sorry. I won't buy you an alpaca."

"Just asking."

The llamas on the other side of the tent were a little taller, maybe six feet when they held their heads high. We were told that they can carry loads up to 60 pounds, which means they cannot be ridden. They are becoming more popular as pack animals for back packers in the Rocky Mountains, relieving the load of the hikers. They are not as easily spooked as horses or mules, and their soft feet have less impact on the environment, on the mountain trails, than hooves.

"Wouldn't it be nice to go back packing with a llama, Grandma? Can we do it some time?"

"I don't know. Want to go to the grandstand now?"

"Is it time? Great." He took my hand and pulled me on.

****

Not many people were at the grandstand yet, so Chuck could choose exactly the seats he liked. The county fire departments were opening for the demolition derby. Opposing teams were scrambling to connect their hoses and then – with the spray of water – push a ball which was suspended by a ring on a long

160

wire. The crew who could prepare the equipment faster, had the advantage.

When one side was pushed farther and farther back, I said to Chuck, "I'd just pretend to drop the hose and dowse the other guys."

He gave me a disapproving look. "That wouldn't be fair."

"Yeah, but..."

Just at that moment the losing team did exactly that. Judging by how long they directed the water at their opponents, it was *not* an accident.

Chuck grinned. "They are just as bad as you."

Then came the real thing, the demolition derby.

"Why does that truck make the ground wet, Grandma? So it's more slippery?"

"Maybe so it's not too dusty."

"Look, they are already coming out!"

In the first heat, there were three cars.

"Which one do you want to win, Grandma?"

"Oh, how about the yellow one."

"You mean number 23?"

I nodded.

"I hope number 78 wins. He's my favorite."

As luck would have it, number 23 still could move when the other two were disabled.

"Your car won, Grandma. You guessed right." He gave me an approving look as if I had contributed to the victory.

A tractor with a front loader came and pushed the wrecks off the field. The next group consisted of 12 cars.

"Wow, they have hardly space to move. Will that be better for them?"

"Maybe they can't get hit as hard if there's not much room," I said.

One car's engine started smoking heavily, obscuring half the contestants. The tractor came quickly and pushed the car to the side.

"Awesome," said Chuck. "They can do everything." He again urged me to pick a "favorite" car, but this time mine didn't win.

At first I had feared for the safety of the drivers, but it seemed they had crashing down pat, and nobody was hurt. Every time cars crunched into each other, Chuck and the rest of the crowd shouted loud approval.

When the skeletons of this group were pushed or towed off, Chuck said, "Let's watch one more race and then go, O.K.?"

I was surprised that he didn't want to stay till the last jalopy was demolished, but I didn't question him.

In the car, he said, "This was the best day of the whole summer, wasn't it?"

"Well," I hesitated. "We..."

"Oh, I know. But I mean here at home it was the best."

When we arrived at Chuck's house, his mother asked about the fair. He talked and talked. Slowly I drove off while the two of them were still standing in the garage. Chuck mimicked something with his hands and feet, and his mother listened with great interest.

I had a good feeling and could absolutely not remember why I hadn't liked the fair 20 years ago.

"Grandma, We Can Go Bowling!"

Those of you readers who know how to bowl, please skip this story. It would only annoy you.

****

At 7:45 in the morning the phone rang. "Grandma, you pick me up after school today?"

"Of course, Chuck, today is Tuesday, but I really don't know anything exciting to do. It's still raining, the parks are all muddy, nothing new at the museums..."

"Oh, I know what to do; we can go bowling!"

"Bowling? Well, ah..."

"Don't you know how to do it, Grandma? You just roll that big ball down the lane and hit the pins. It's easy."

"I don't even know where..."

"There's a nice place not far from my school. I've been there before."

"You were? When?"

"My mom took me when I was in second grade." (He is now in the fourth.)

"O.K. I guess we can give it a try."

"And Grandma, ask someone how to keep score. I don't know that."

"Yessir."

"Bye, see ya after school. And I'm gonna win!"

****

If you want to be good at any sport, you must have a mental image of yourself completely in control while carrying out the most challenging feats. You see yourself on that steep ski slope just swaying your hips in perfect balance, casually spraying

163

snow at some awkward slowpokes; or guiding a raft over those white water rapids like a cowboy rides a bronco. So, all that morning I pictured myself at the bowling alley like the champions on TV. Concentration in their focussed gaze, they give the ball a spin so it rolls down the lane in a curve. Wow. I've got to try that.

My secretary gave me a crash course in the art of keeping score. I didn't tell my husband where I was going with Chuck, so he wouldn't say, 'I thought you have arthritis in your wrist; how do you bowl if you can't even push the vacuum sweeper?'

In the afternoon, Chuck didn't even care for his snack. "I'm not hungry now." He insisted that I drive down some little side street, and low and behold, there were the bowling lanes. The place was empty, and a guy looking like Santa Claus without the beard gave us shoes and a score sheet, let Chuck choose a lane and, with a friendly smile, resumed his seat at the snack-bar.

"Where are the balls?" I asked.

"Over on the side. See, Grandma?"

Wow, were those buggers heavy. "Chuck, go and ask the guy where they have lighter balls – please."

He went and then skipped back. "He said they are all over; you have to try them."

So I tried. For most of the balls I needed both hands just to lift them off the rack. Then I found one, a pleasant light blue with a swirly pattern, that I could hold in one hand. But the holes were much too small. Was that a ball for a four-year-old? Now I was just looking for holes big enough for my fingers. Ah, there was one – but the holes were so far apart, they'd have fit Schwarzenegger.

"Grandma, hurry up! Let's go." Chuck started. He had to roll the ball two-handed, but slowly it mosied down the lane and knocked over three pins. "Did you see me, Grandma? I got three!"

"Good. Now hit some more with the next ball."

Another two pins fell. "That makes five. Did you write it?" He checked the score sheet and nodded approval. "Your turn, Grandma."

Well, to get the feet and the arms coordinated isn't all that easy. Once I had enough momentum on the ball, even my thumb got un-stuck. I wouldn't really mind a gutter ball so much, but it makes a different sound, so without looking "Santa Claus" and the waitress clearly knew how I bowled.

Both Chuck and I were able to interrupt the monotony of our gutter balls with a few hits, and soon the first game was over. My score was 52 and Chuck's 73.

Chuck beamed. "I won this one!" Then he summoned his best manners and added, "Hope you win the next."

In the second game, Chuck had a spare, and in the fourth frame I had a strike. I have no idea how it happened, but all 10 pins fell down. Maybe a little earthquake? Chuck was so surprised and happy, he shouted "Strike! Strike!" all over so that "Santa" gave me a sideways glance. Trouble was, my glorious strike was followed by four gutter balls, so it didn't do much for my score. Chuck won that game, too.

In the third game, I tried to put a spin on the ball which made it hop into the gutter of the *next* lane. That one wasn't switched on, so the ball didn't come back. Too embarrassed to ask one of the employees to get it, I used another one. Maybe Chuck lost a bit of his concentration, or I was just lucky, but I won game three with a 75 to Chuck's 72. Not a bad score for golf.

"Grandma, if you win the next game, too, then we are even and we have to play a fifth game." His eyes sparkled.

"Nah," I said. "We could quit now, then you'd be sure you are ahead. I'm tired anyway."

But Chuck was already at the next game. By now other people came, apparently members of leagues. They had their own shoes, own balls and own wrist braces. No wonder they were good. They had one strike after another and looked disgusted if they managed only a spare. When the lane next to ours was switched on, a ball appeared out of the return. "Where does this come from?" asked the newly arrived bowler.

"Oh, that's my Gr..." Chuck started.

I quickly put my hand on his mouth and whispered, "Hush!"

Fortunately for his happiness and my peace, he won the fourth game, too. I was bushed. How come those guys on TV never look worn out? "No wonder I'm tired," I said to Chuck. "I had to roll that heavy monster down the lane 80 times, whether I hit anything or not."

"No, you didn't. You had a strike, so you needed only 79 balls."

"All right, you Smart Aleck, let's go home."

After a hearty snack, he didn't sit on the floor to watch Nickelodeon as usual, but lay on the couch and pulled a blanket over his shoulder. His eyes were tiny slits.

I don't remember what I did, but before I blinked my eyes, it was six o'clock, and after the blink the clock showed seven.

Later, on the way to his house, Chuck asked, "Say, Grandma, did you ever bowl before?"

"Hm, I don't remember."

"You once told me you went with my dad and with Uncle Kenny when they were little."

"Oh, that's right. We did."

"Could you then bowl better than you did today?"

"I don't think so."

Chuck smiled. "You'd have remembered it if you had been good. Right?"

How Time Flies

Chuck, nearly 11 years old, is thinking about the future. "You know, Grandma, when I'll drive – oh, I know it won't be for another five years – but I'll go around a curve real fast like with a dune buggy."

"We'll see," was all I said.

One day in early spring, we went to West Branch State Park trying to find out what's there so we could make plans for the summer. After we had found a marina with rental boats and picnic areas, we came to a beach. It had a huge parking lot, big enough for 1,000 cars. At this time of the year, it was completely empty, not a soul in sight.

This gave me an idea. I took the car into the center of a parking lane, stopped, opened the door and said, "Slide over here, Chuck. You drive."

"Me? Now?"

I wished I had a camera to catch his surprise and glowing happiness.

Propped up by his heavy book bag, he could see out and reach the pedals.

Taking the passenger seat, I said, "O.K., put the foot on the brake and shift into drive, here on D."

He did, but nothing happened on the slightly uphill grade.

"Step on the gas."

A big forward-lurch was followed by a dead stop.

"We'd better put on the seat belts."

Chuck grinned, moved about 100 feet and stopped. "O.K."

"Keep going. Take the exit of that lane. Watch out, it's narrow there. Then turn left and go back into the next lane."

"That far?" His eyes sparkled. "I thought till here is all you'd let me drive."

"Oh no. You'll go up one lane and down the next. Look at all the space you've got. Easy now."

To my surprise he could slow down rather smoothly. The speeding up was more jerky, but he managed the left turn and beamed.

"Look where you are going, not at me."

"Which way, Grandma?"

"Now make a right turn."

That one was harder. He couldn't quite judge how far the car was from the gate posts and gave them plenty of room.

At the end of this lane, I said, "When you turn on the drive that circles the entire parking lot, make sure you stay in the right lane. If there were other cars here, you'd run them over being so far left."

"Oh yeah. And you know, you have to go real slow in a curve."

I smiled. "M-hm. – Now, that turn was perfect."

With another happy smile, he stepped on the gas. "Wow, 40! That's really fast. You only feel that when you drive yourself."

"Now park the car nicely," I said.

"Here?"

"Sure. Pick any space and put the car in."

As I had expected, he wound up in an angle, covering part of three spaces. I looked at him questioning.

He giggled. "Not quite straight."

With both of us tugging at the steering wheel, we straightened the car.

"Now put it squarely between the lines."

When he stopped, I said, "Open your door and look how far you are off."

"About four feet."

I nodded and checked on my side. "That's why on the right you are over it."

We backed out again. This time was better. The car was not quite centered, but all in one parking space.

Chuck heaved a deep sigh "Got it. But that's hard."

"Ready to go now?" I asked, and we switched sides.

"Thank you, Grandma," he said on the way home. "I can't believe I drove." An imaginary steering wheel was still in his hands.

"Are you gonna tell your mom?"

"Oh no. She'd get all scared. But Dad will like it."

****

A week later we were in the parking lot of another beach. Chuck drove with more confidence but still with the same big smile.

When he parked neatly, I shook my head. "Where did my Baby Chuckie go?"

His brows went up.

"Sorry," I said. "I know you don't want to be called that, but..."

"That's O.K., Grandma. I know what you mean. I'm big now."

On the way home, he asked, "Grandma, do you remember that park where it's steep and where the tadpoles were and the tree across the river?"

"M-hm."

"Let's go there next time."

"And skip rocks like when you were little?'

"Yeah. Let's."

Part II

The Wonders of Nature

Hertha Binder

Part II   The Wonders of Nature

Contents

Hertha Binder

Survive Winter?

Winter is a beautiful season. If you don't agree, you have not had a chance to experience its wonders.

Yes, in winter it is cold outside, so you have to dress right and move to create your own warmth. There are many winter outdoor activities, each bringing its special joys and rewards: sledding with the kids, ice skating and snowmobiling, to name just a few. Even a snowball fight with your lover or your children can be exhilarating winter fun. The two activities I like best are cross country and downhill skiing.

There are differences and similarities between the two. For both sports you have long boards strapped to your feet which allow you to glide over the snow; in both you feel positive about winter and use the season for your enjoyment.

Cross country skiing can be done any place where there is snow: in a parking lot, on the shoulder of a country road, on a frozen lake or in the mountains. Therefore, there is no need for travel, hotel and lift tickets.

On a crisp, sunny day you may wander with your x-c skis in a quiet valley. It is the more immediate environment you will enjoy: the steam of your breath against the blue sky, the sparkle of the sunlight on freshly fallen snow, the deer tracks preceding your path and veering towards the creek.

You may pause and admire the little hoods of snow covering each rock in the river; the tiny white heaps are always larger on the downstream side. Around the next bend, all is quiet. You wonder why. Then you see the yellow shadow of a coyote on the other side of the brook.

Fog might roll in, putting a blanket over the valley. You feel the moisture in the air you breathe; you suddenly understand how people can imagine ghosts or giants. Suddenly you step back: there is a bear just 20 feet from you! Then you relax; it was only a bunch of logs piled up in an unruly heap. Fog has a way of making simple things look mysterious.

When downhill skiing, the vistas are more grandiose. Looming above you is the craggy top of your mountain. The edge of the glacier seems on the verge of breaking off, and the wind blows ribbons of snow from the overhanging drift, little white flags casting restless shadows. Across the valley you see one mountain top after another. You know them from postcards, but no picture can compare with the breathtaking mountains and the changing mood caused by shadows and light. At one moment a summit dazzles your eyes, glistening in bright sunlight, and an instant later it is oppressive and dark when a heavy cloud drifts in.

Both kinds of skiing cause physical exertion, giving you an awareness of your body and a sense of achievement.

While cross country skiing, which is considered one of the most exhaustive sports, the joy comes from the pure activity. You feel your heart pounding, you are proud of the altitude you have gained and you relish your perspiration. Yes, you sweat in winter!

Downhill skiing gives you a high of a different sort. What affects me most is the awareness of the mountain and its terrain together with the sensation of speed and near weightless gliding.

The mountain becomes you challenger and your friend. Your alertness has to sense a sudden drop in the path, an increase in steepness, or an abrupt flattening. You have to judge the varying conditions correctly: a patch of ice speeds you up and might land you on your behind, or a dip of soft snow seems to stop you in your tracks and throws you on your nose.

If, however, one day everything works just right, if your eyes and your judgement are keen, if your legs and shoulders make the right moves, if your thighs are strong enough to stand the stress of speed and slope, if your lungs are clear and your heart is calm, *then* you feel one with the mountain, with your world, and – if you will – with God.

176

Skiing is not glossy boots and a color coordinated outfit; it's not falling in front of a handsome instructor hoping he'll pick you up from the snow and ask for a date. Skiing is reaching into your soul and rejuvenating your spirit. It is joie de vivre and the contentment of being a fitting part of the universe.

So, please, don't hate winter and withdraw; don't flee winter and go south. Embrace winter, enjoy it, live it!

Outdoors in Winter

About 90 percent of Americans are well adjusted to winter: they hate it. When the first flakes fall in November, this sensible majority looks out the window with hunched shoulders and says, "Oh, gosh, it's snowing already." Then they shoot a disgusted glance at the one co-worker who looks at the flakes with a faint smile. "Well you, you like that snow," they accuse him.

He sees the same weather and thinks (he doesn't dare say it out loud), "Oh, goodie, soon the snow will stay and it will be time to ski."

He belongs to the 10 percent who have an emotional disorder: love for winter. They are the cross-country and downhill skiers, snowmobilers and some other folks who think that white stuff is fun. I'm one of those nuts.

Somehow the normal majority blames us for the fact that it's cold and snowing. We don't really *make* the snow, though sometimes we wish we could. We agree that snow on the roads is bad. But, if it falls on hills, tracks and paths, it just can't spare the roads.

Why do we like to ski? Why are we willing to suffer through long drives on bad roads or a bus pick-up at five in the morning on the other side of town?

Let me give you an example. Not long ago, three friends and I went with two busloads of skiers to Pennsylvania. The pale sun gave the land an eerie brightness, and the Appalachian hills stretched for miles into all directions: forests, fields, farms.

Two days earlier there had been a storm – every tree up to its tiniest branchlets was covered with a layer of clear ice. The sun played in the millions of crystals causing glitters and rainbow colors. Maybe Monet could have caught the shimmering brilliance with his brush. The icicle wind-chimes sounded like tiny Christmas bells.

179

We were part of this wonderland, seemingly in its center, blowing more crystals into the air with our breath, gliding down the snowy mountain side, absorbing the bumps, caressing the slopes with our skis.

Someone once said a skier has a dialogue with the mountain. Skiers often imagine this discussion as they glide down.

The mountain seems to tease, "Look at my north slope, it's a bit crusty today. Are you up to it?"

The skier hesitates. "Well, maybe I'll wipe out, but I'll take you on, anyway." So he accepts the challenge, his heart halfway in his throat, and he makes it. Not very elegant, perhaps, but without mishaps. Then he looks up at the slope.

The shadows seem to sketch a grin on the mountainside.

"I'll show you," the skier thinks. The second time, of course, it's easier. This run is perfect – good speed, nice balance, confidence. Now when the skier looks up, there is triumph in his heart and he proceeds to the next slope taking the mountain's new challenge.

Close to the lodge, at the beginner's slope, there was a little girl. "Yeah," she shouted. "I came down all the way and didn't fall once!" Same sentiment – youngster's variation.

Here on the hill, there is no place in our minds for the day-to-day worries. We can't think of family problems, troubles in business or any other concerns. A true vacation.

Skiing is new every time. Different light – bright sun, fog, clouds. Different snow – hard and icy, soft and mushy, heavy like cement, light and fluffy. Different temperature – biting cold, high winds, balmy sun, starting to melt, bare spots of grass. Different friends – the bold and aggressive say, "Come along on that steep run." The timid and careful suggest, "Let's stay on the easy slopes." The tough and enduring challenge, "Why not take another three runs before the bus leaves?" while the relaxed and restful may yawn, "I'm bushed – let's take a break."

In cross country skiing, the pictures are more intimate. The tracks of rabbits, squirrels or some birds tell us we are not the only ones out there. Others have walked on this path before and are probably watching us now. We belong here, we are part of nature.

That's why we winter-nuts enjoy our paranoia. Want to join us? Try it!

Hertha Binder

Memories of Trees

When I was a child, I thought trees lived forever. Well, yes, after a storm a few trees were down here or there, but generally they did not change. In fall, the same branch on that maple was always the first one to turn golden. That weather-beaten evergreen was every year loaded with cones while its tall neighbor had none.

When we moved to the country in 1959, we had 66 acres. It used to be a farm. I took particular pride in the trees. They were ours to enjoy, ours to nurture and protect. Sadly, I had to learn that trees are mortal and often have an even shorter life span then people.

Two huge sugar maples were beside our driveway, their welcome shade keeping the house cool in summer. At one time we even considered calling our place "Twin Maples." For several years our kids collected sap from them, and we boiled it on the electric stove. That thickened sap wouldn't have won a prize at the festival, but we sure were proud of our harvest.

One winter there was a severe storm, weighing down all the branches with a thick layer of ice, so that they were forced to the ground and froze to it. Several days later they thawed free, but the damage was done. From then on the maples had more dead branches every year until they finally died and had to be cut down. No more Twin Maples.

On the south side of the house stood a Japanese Locust whose lacy leaves let the black bark show through. How I loved that tree! The main trunk was about 70 feet tall, and a huge branch stood nearly horizontal over the lower part of our house. The tree was the landmark of our home and provided a unique silhouette against the morning sun.

As the years went by, the big branch split more and more from the trunk, endangering the house. To my sorrow, my husband had the tree cut down, but he could show me that the entire trunk as well as the thick branch were hollow. They wouldn't have lasted through the next storm. My husband knew, though, how much I mourned the locust and next spring he found a healthy little offshoot from the old roots. He planted it on a protected spot, and by now it's about 30 feet tall, although it lacks the distinctive shape of its parent.

Behind the house was a pear orchard, over 100 years old. One spring an abundance of blossoms floated like thick white clouds over the twenty trees, – a giant bouquet. The following winter my husband's father visited from Europe. He had grown up on a farm, knew "everything about trees" and heavily pruned the pears, so that the long branches wouldn't break under the heavy load of fruit. Next year, the pear trees were all dead. We didn't know whether it was because or in spite of the pruning. The extravagant bloom had been the last joyful breath of life of the old orchard trees.

Of course, we planted new trees: several blue spruce by the road. After many years, one developed into a perfectly shaped cone, taller than the house. Two others by the lamp post achieved gnarled individuality. Then came a twister, broke 15 foot tips of the two knotted spruce and leveled the perfect one. How sad.

In the early years of our stay here, a farmer tilled the land for us. Later we planted 11,000 evergreens. As soon as they were in the ground, a drought set in, and we went with a little wagon, a 30-gallon trash can and a hose and watered all the one-year-old seedlings. Success! They survived, and as soon as the weeds were not cut down every year, the locusts from our cow lane seeded out and created a locust grove of about three acres. On another place, a stand of maybe 200 oaks developed – the offspring of one old borderline tree.

In our back yard stands a big spruce. The farmer's wife had planted a live Christmas tree there many years ago, and it had grown big and strong. I showed our kids how to climb it. Once, Pete and I had come close to the top.

"Can I go up two more branches, Mom?" Pete had asked.

"Try! Just be careful."

"Oh, Mom, the house looks so little."

Just then a gust of wind made the tree sway. "Ooh!" Pete was scared.

"Just hold on," I said. "The tree is rocking you."

The kid's happy smile showed that he had regained his confidence.

My husband helped the boys build a tree house in the spruce, their private summer home for several years. The lower branches were quite smooth from the heavy traffic.

The tornado on the fourth of July in 1969 nearly toppled the spruce. On the west side, the root disc stuck out for a foot. We righted the tree with a heavy steel cable that is anchored in one cubic yard of concrete. You can't buy a tree of that size, might as well save it.

Years later, the big drought of '88 killed the top third of that spruce. We had the dead part trimmed off. The tree lives, but it sure looks odd. I wish it could still be whole.

****

Many people believe in heaven, a place where they meet friends and family who had preceded them. Some folks I know are convinced that faithful pets also await them at the Pearly Gates. "Spot has been with me for 18 years," said a man. "Longer than my three wives together. I trust he'll join me there."

I do hope that I'll also find my trees there: the tall Japanese Locust with its mighty splitting trunk and the delicate leaves; the stately, perfect blue spruce; the maples wearing their buckets, and all our blooming pears. A place without trees looks bare and desolate. Even heaven will be better if our trees live there.

Stories Of the Fog

What comes to your mind when you think of fog? Gloomy day, can't see, driving hazards, depressing mood, damp weather, getting a cold; don't ever want to see it again. True.

Yet fog isn't all woe. Think of a morning just after sunrise. Leaving your driveway, you feel like in the middle of a milk shake. Then the road rises a bit, and suddenly you are in bright sunlight; only half a mile away, over the river, are patches of white fog – little fluffy clouds napping on the valley floor.

You relax now, but the road dips down again, and you can't see past your hood ornament. Headlights on! Seconds later, another rise. Those little clouds are waking up, the wind is moving them. Do they play hide-and-go-seek with you? Now you see them, now you don't.

The river bank had always seemed so even; now all the little fingers of fog show that it is quite scalloped. You never knew that. Fog is a teacher too.

As the sun spreads warmth, the fog lightens. A thin mist makes the colors look faded like the print on an old shirt.

Then the road turns, and sunshine is everywhere. It's now a regular morning, and your thoughts can turn to your daily worries, undisturbed by little patches of fog playing peek-a-boo.

****

Not long ago my husband and I were out for a morning stroll at the Walter Best Preserve. The sun wasn't up yet and thick patches of fog covered most of the lake. Geese and ducks seemed worried. They honked non-stop while they couldn't see, but fell silent once they came into the open.

Just then the sun appeared on the horizon, shining at us as we walked up on a large tree. Between us and the tree was a thin layer of mist, like a scrim on a stage, over a hundred feet tall.

The tree cast a distinct, huge shadow on the mist, every dark branch being much enlarged. It looked like an enormous monster. We stood still and marveled at the display. As the sun rose, the shadow sank, until it finally landed on the ground where shadows rightfully belong.

****

When Jeff was not quite five years old, I stayed with him for a few days on the California coast. One evening we were the only ones at the hotel pool. He jumped again and again from the low diving board but still needed my reassuring presence. Then a huge bank of fog rolled in from the Pacific; we saw it coming, and soon it engulfed us. I could barely make out Jeff from the other end of the pool, I just heard him splash.

"Wait a bit," I called out. "I'll come over to your side."

"You don't have to, Mommie. When I couldn't see you, I found out that I can jump and swim by myself. You don't hafta watch me. Stay there!"

The California fog had taught my five-year-old independence.

****

My earliest memory of fog is from 1946, a year after WW II had ended. In Austria, food was still severely restricted, and no one had a vacation for years. My friend Gerda and I had already logged three semesters of medicine. That summer, our mothers insisted that we go for a week into the Alps. We must have become so crabby, they couldn't stand us anymore.

We had planned several mountain hikes that take about five hours climbing steep trails and three hours coming down again. In the morning of the first hiking day, thick, gloomy fog covered everything. The innkeeper predicted the weather would clear up. Just good P.R., we thought; however, we left.

The moist air was heavy on the lungs, and we couldn't make out anything beyond 10 feet. We wondered if we should have stayed home and slept a bit longer. For about an hour we were doggedly plodding uphill, hair wet, clothes damp, thoughts rehashing the events of the war: her father dead, my sweetheart killed, our homes destroyed. Would we get through medical school? What lay ahead of us? More misery?

Then it became brighter, less gloomy, and as we crested another knoll, we were suddenly in radiant sunlight. The fog was moving and churning below us like a rolling sea, and above it we could see for miles and miles, one mountain top after another. Tears rolled down my cheeks. I don't know why – from the bright light? From feeling free and in the open?

When Gerda saw the tears, she put an arm on my shoulder. "We've made it. The muck is behind us; from now on we are in the sun. Look, the whole world is spread out before us!"

****

Take fog for what it is: nuisance at one time, glory at another. If it were not for the shadows, we wouldn't appreciate the light.

The Mysteries of East Branch Reservoir

A service road runs roughly parallel to the western shore of East Branch Reservoir. It is open to the public with a parking area at the main thoroughfare.

My husband and I enjoy to walk there now and then. In late summer we wanted to avoid the mosquitoes, so we started just before sunrise. The dew would still keep the insects down.

At first, the trail leads through a stand of dark woods with evergreens, deadwood, vines and ivy – poison or not – choking many trees. A flock of crows flushed up and announced our presence with loud and seemingly excited cawing. All creatures were forewarned of our approach.

After a few minutes there were some patches of grass along the road, letting more light in. Behind a curve stood two deer, looking straight at us. We advanced slowly and quietly, walking on the grass so the gravel would not crunch. The does seemed to be an embodiment of tranquility – sisters of Bambi.

I suppressed my memory of two collisions with deer last winter and the damage they had caused to our cars – just within the insurance deductible. But here was peace. The deer finally found us boring and turned away, unhurried, unafraid. We heard dry branches break long after we had lost sight of the animals.

Where the road climbs slightly, there is a wide open field of several acres. That morning it was covered by a patch of thick fog. Everything was blanketed out – no horizon, no beyond. It was spooky and depressing. Uncertain shapes scared me, until I could make out that they were merely shrubs, shrouded in haze.

Suddenly, the sun penetrated the fog causing a dazzling brilliance. I had to shield my eyes. Still, we couldn't see farther than three feet; a white-out in summer.

Then the trail sloped down and within five steps everything was clear. Dew drops glistened like a million diamonds. They hung on all the blades of grass, on the leaves and on the artful spider webs that were strung out between small branches.

A little further, we heard the lake – geese and ducks honking and quacking as if in heated arguments – the swooshing sounds when a group splashed the water while landing. When we reached the water's edge, we observed about four hundred geese and ducks. Some were landing, some were taking off – one flock of geese gaining altitude quickly and disappearing over a hill. Others flew just above the water, their wing tips causing a spray that glistened in the sun.

There was some movement. "What's that?" I asked.

"A crane, probably a blue heron," said my husband.

Ducks were silently gliding into the shadows of the opposite shore, single file. A smaller group swam towards us, the dark green head feathers of the drakes gleaming in the light.

Where the sun warmed the water, small wisps of steam arose, pushed by the gentle breeze towards the middle of the lake – never ending rows of little white ghosts.

The reservoir's waters had been lowered by about a foot. A carpet of water lily leaves covered the dry lake bed by the shore. Walking over them, my husband said, "See, in summer only frogs can walk on lily pads. Now you can do it too." I was quite proud to tread where frogs had hopped before.

On the way back, the sun was higher, the fog had lifted, the dew had vanished. Quiet were the water fowl. The path looked like a common backwoods road on any summer day. Even a few mosquitoes ventured out. The spider webs had lost their droplet jewelry. Unable to see them, I felt quite a few threads across my face when I ventured off the road.

We were quiet in the car, still trying to absorb what we had taken in.

When a Heron Played Tag With Us

Have you ever played tag with a heron? No? We have, and it wasn't even our idea.

One Mother's Day, my two grown sons promised to take me out.

"What restaurant did you pick, Mom?" asked Jeff, the older.

"I hope it won't be too expensive," mused Kenny.

"Hmm," I hesitated. "I don't really want to eat. How would it be if we'd rent a canoe on the Cuyahoga River?"

They readily agreed.

We launched the boat at the Russell Park and started to glide smoothly downstream, finding new vistas at every turn. That river seemed to have a bend every 200 feet.

My two guys were boisterous, hadn't seen each other for a while, laughed, shouted and splashed. I got wet, too. Just around the third curve, there was a Great Blue Heron standing in the shallows between the water lilies. He looked at us for a while and then took off, downstream. We were awed by that large, beautiful creature, its elegant lines, its long bill and neck.

After he was gone, we laughed some more and tried to come close to little painted turtles sunning themselves on half submerged branches. Always, they slid into the water before we could reach them.

Around the next twist of the river, there was again the heron, rising as soon as he saw us, leisurely flying low over the water. I was surprised how heavy herons seem when they take off, as if their wings were barely able to lift them.

"We scared that poor thing," said Jeff.

"Let's be real quiet and go on the other side of the stream." Even Kenny was concerned. "Maybe then we won't flush him out."

This time we could see through the trees where he had alighted. We glided so quietly, not even the paddles splashed, and we hardly dared to breathe.

Our heron certainly was not looking for fish or frogs – he was looking at *us*, just as intently as we were watching him. We nearly got past him, and then he took off again in his heavy way, moving farther downstream.

"This is a dumb bird," said Kenny. "We sure didn't scare him this time."

Three meanders down, the heron was waiting, stretching his neck to look around the tree that had covered us. Again he let us come within 15 feet and then took off.

"Wait a bit," said Jeff. "This guy isn't afraid of us. Look how calm he is. He is *playing* with us!"

"He's teasing us as if we were his toy." Kenny didn't know whether he should be amused or offended.

"I wonder what he'll do at the State Route," I said. "You think he'll go over or under the bridge?"

"Oh, sure, Mom," Jeff laughed. "He'll walk across the highway."

In all, the heron let us come close eight times. (We had counted.) In this game of "tag" we would never catch him, we were always "it."

The ninth time was different, though. He took off before we were even close.

"Look, there is a second bird!" I pointed.

"A female." Kenny has sharp eyes.

The two herons soared high above the tall trees, made a huge semi-circle and headed upstream. As we watched them disappear, I felt abandoned like a discarded toy.

"Are we just imagining that he played with us?" wondered Jeff.

"I don't think so." By now I was convinced. "He never flew far, never looked for food in the water but always watched us and went the route where he knew we'd follow him."

At the take-out, we told the boat guy about the heron.

"Oh, yeah," he said. "The herons aren't shy around here. They like to watch people."

I was very pleased that we had spent our time entertaining a Great Blue Heron.

Hertha Binder

The Many Joys of Rain

"Joys? Rain?" you ask. "She must be nuts."

True, I'm on the weird side, but there are many pleasant aspects of rain. Even we common folks who buy our potatoes and apples in the store instead of harvesting them in field and orchard know that we need rain now and then. We'd have a desert here without it.

Think of all the sounds rain can make. A real downpour swooshes through the parking lot, but if you are in your car, it's like bags and bags of peanuts being dumped on the roof.

Below our bedroom window is an awning. When the murmuring, gentle drizzle runs off the roof, it drops on the window cover like on a drum. "Plop," then a pause and again, "Plop ..., plop..., plop, plop." By now I'm wide awake. As more and more water comes down, it "plopplopplops," till it finally purrs like a sewing machine. After a while, when it lets up a little and reverts to a slow and reassuring "Plop...plop," I can again fall asleep.

Have you ever listened to your lawn after a short, heavy downpour? The dry ground eagerly fills its pores, and as the moisture seeps in, tiny air bubbles are being pushed out. Twenty cans of pop with the fizz coming out would whisper the same way.

Rain can have an unlimited number of appearances, and you probably have seen them all. Just remember: you were sitting on the shore – maybe at a small reservoir or at one of the Great Lakes. A pale sun was still shining, but in the west dark clouds were bulging and rolling like shapeless giants in a wrestling match. Suddenly a grey sheet came down out of the clouds, touching the ground – the rain. It was slanted because the wind has more effect on the heavy drops than on the tiny ones in the clouds; therefore rain always steers ahead of the clouds like a snowplow in front of its truck.

197

As the weather approached, the borders became blurry; you went into the shelter. Nothing but grey all around you. Then it let up, and the sun came back. The dark clouds were moving east, and a huge double rainbow appeared. One end of it was right beside you in the meadow, not 50 feet away as if you could touch it. But when you walked towards it, the rainbow retreated. You can't catch it, ever.

If on another day everything is grey in grey, no sun, just a steady drizzle, watch how your lawn and your shrubs and the trees turn a cleaner, happier green, swelling and filling out their shapes. Even the weeds look healthier.

That fresh scent! The water makes everything smell much stronger: the grass, the soil, the flowers. You feel you have to take a deep breath to get all that clean air into you.

Did you ever have a chance to swim while it was raining? Of course you were all wet anyway, but if you floated on your back and the drops hit your eye lashes, it was as if the rain were teasing you with a gentle, tickling touch. Once, however, we tried to water ski in the rain. With that speed, the drops stung like so many needles, funny, but not real fun.

Emotions seem heightened in the rain. Remember the scene from "Singing in the Rain?" Clearly, Gene Kelly's character was in love with the girl. Otherwise he'd have gone home and looked up the nearest unemployment office or had an argument with the landlord. But he sang and danced, splashed through puddles and felt his happiness much stronger.

When our love was young, before Tom and I were even married, we once went for a day-long hike in the Alps. Although the weather was doubtful, we started out. Midway between two shelter-inns, a heavy drizzle came down. We marched on, getting soaked in spite of our coats. Tom took my cold hand and guided it into *his* coat pocket for warmth. He put his arm around my shoulder and then my waist to shield me from the wind. We giggled when the drops ran off our hoods and down our noses. We tasted the water – on each other's lips.

Had it been sunny, this would have been a regular summer stroll, long forgotten after so many years. The rain made it memorable.

Hertha Binder

When Nature Unleashed Its Fury

Skiing has been my favorite sport for most of my life. In addition to using the local areas, I manage a winter vacation out west every two years or so. Once I went in the third week of April to Mammoth Mountain, a large ski area in California's Sierra Nevada, close to Yosemite Park.

"How can you go skiing now?" asked my neighbor while tending her crocuses and daffodils. "The snow is all gone."

"Not there," I countered. "They still have 19 feet of the white stuff. It was a good season."

She shook her head, imagining me bouncing on my boards over bare rocks and scaring the butterflies.

We skiers – I went with a group of 40 – dreamed of spring skiing: the time when the weather is warm and balmy, when the only concern is how to avoid a bad sunburn and where to leave the clothes you shed. We imagined leisurely lunches on the sundecks with the aroma from the outdoor grill gently nudging our appetites. We looked forward to watching the young folks coming down the slopes in shorts and T-shirts. Skiing would be easy: although the snow might be a bit heavy when the top layers melted at noon, the sunshine would give every little bump a shadow, so that adjustment to the terrain could come naturally. That's what we hoped for.

On the first three days the mountains were beautiful in their white glory – at six in the morning. By 8:30, when the lifts opened, heavy clouds hung halfway down the slopes, the sun was gone, the light was "flat," that means you can see neither the pitch of the hillside nor make out little bumps. Icy winds blew the snow into our faces. It was winter, deep cold winter. Never-the-less skiing was fun, just not the kind we had expected.

On the fourth day, the whole town and more so the mountains were engulfed in a wild blizzard. Howling winds,

201

dense fog with snowing and drifting, a perfect white-out. "What are we gonna do?" asked one of the people in our condo.

I leafed through the prospectus. "They advertise snowmobiling."

"That'd be worse than skiing," said another.

"Horseback riding."

"The poor critters would sink in to their necks."

I went down the list. "A bowling alley is on the main street."

"Did we come all the way to California to go bowling?"

Looking out the window I mused, "Seems to be getting a little brighter. Tell you what. My skies and boots are in a locker at the lodge. I'd better pick them up and see how the slopes are."

The others were still undecided.

On the 20 minute bus ride to the ski area, there was an announcement that all lifts were closed. No one knew whether they'd ever open that day.

"Wonder why," said a man. "In winter we ski when it snows. Why not now?"

"Can't be that bad," hoped another.

At the lodge, the cafeteria was open with, maybe, 20 guests instead of the usual 200. A cup of hot chocolate in my hand, I looked out the window. The storm whipped the snow uphill. How could so much of it accumulate on the sun-porch when none of the flakes seemed to fall down? Clusters of trees – this is near the timberline where tree growth becomes sparse – disappeared in the fog as if nothing were there but a bare white hill. Then suddenly it cleared up for 20 seconds and the visibility was a full 300 feet. Wow, look at the landscape, the trees all encrusted in ice!

A moment later, everything was mysteriously blotted out again. A few spooky figures were visible outside. What did those poor creatures have to do? Hooded and hunched forward, they leaned and struggled against the storm, disappeared in the haze and showed up again. They reminded me of sailors on the ghost ship in the opera "The Flying Dutchman." They too were shrouded in fog, and I thought to hear some the "Dutchman's" melodies in the whistling and droning wind.

Two snowmobiles strained from one side of the base area to the other. After 10 minutes, they returned, and so did the hunchbacks on foot. Were they just marking time to get their pay?

A group of about 10 men caught my attention. Clearing the snow off the sun porch, not five feet from my window, they had piled some tables upside down on others to gain more space. Somehow the wind got under one of them, lifted it up like a sail that rammed into a stack of benches. What a din!

I went to the other side of the large dining room. Here, the window faced right into the storm. The glass pane vibrated from the wind, emitting a hum that changed its pitch with the blizzard's varying force. Two empty flag posts quivered, and their cords clanked incessantly against the metal rods.

Most cars in the parking lot were half drifted over, and I wondered how anyone could find his vehicle without first brushing off the whole row of them.

Only one thing stood firm. The area has a mascot – a mammoth (what else?) – that huge shaggy animal with long, curved tusks. Its life-size statue stands on a high pedestal at the entrance gate, which was right under my window. The mammoth seemed unfazed by the storm. Head lowered, all four feet firmly planted, it was stronger than the elements. I had feared the storm might topple the base, but it didn't budge.

I slowly walked to my locker, took out my skis and caught the next bus to town.

The last day of our vacation was glorious. The storm had blown itself out, the trees glittered with their hoarfrost, the snow was hard and crunchy, and the sky a deep blue. We skied to our hearts' content.

On the long trip home, we all chatted about different ski runs and challenging conditions.

"Which day did you like best, Hertha?" asked the group leader.

"They were all great," I said. "But I was really touched by the blizzard, the day when nature unleashed its fury."

Part III

The Way I See It

Hertha Binder

Part III   The Way I See It

Contents

Beauty Is A Matter of Attitude

Beauty, youth. We all want to have them and to keep them. Good looks and a healthy youthfulness, as they apply to humans, have several aspects.

One I would call *'Static Beauty.'* It is what one can see in the mirror, what a snapshot tells you. Thousands of volumes have been written about its maintenance and improvement. Skin care, cosmetics, moisturizers – hair styles, hair colors, wigs – face lifts, nose jobs, belly tucks, liposuction. All these can enhance a person's picture.

Another aspect of beauty is *motion.* How you walk, carry yourself, bend and turn, reveals a different side of you and will give you a powerful feedback.

Your lively 30-year-old friend has a sore back today. She walks slowly, bends stiffly. If you'd not know her, you'd think she is 50 years old.

The slightly plump 55-year-old neighbor hops on her bike, waves to you and pedals down the block. You mistook her for her daughter.

The woman down the road rides her horse regularly. You've seen her often trotting or cantering across her land. How old is she? Probably thirty. No, wait. Her grandchild is already in sixth grade. Gee, she must be much older than she looks.

Have you ever watched yourself walk? You can do that in a mall, looking at your mirror image in all the display windows. Do you have a good posture or does the weight of your worries make you slouch? You won't solve your problems by hanging your head. Straighten up. Smile, get a bit of a bounce in your step. Now look again: twenty years younger.

Also, take good care of your feet. When they hurt, you look old. If you have corns or bunions, you need larger shoes which then scuff on the floor when you walk. That makes you sound old. Only teenagers walk with untied tennis shoes, and no one will mistake you for one of them.

It's a common saying, 'You are as old as you feel.' I'd like to add, 'You are as old as you act.'

Strike one sentence from your vocabulary: "I don't do that any more."

"Did you go camping this summer?" – "I don't do that any more."

"Still teach your 4-H group?" – "I don't do that any more."

There are two ladies, same age, equally good looking. You ask them, "Were you square dancing last weekend?"

Rose answers, "We don't do that any more."

Mary says, "Yeah, Joe and I, we go twice a week. We won second place at the State Fair last month."

Is it hard to guess which one appears more youthful and, I am sure, feels younger too?

****

I have a friend who came from Europe when she was in her late twenties. She could swim and ski, and bicycle, of course, but many other sports were just beyond her financial reach over there. So when she was thirty, she learned to ride and had a horse for many years. When she was forty, they got a boat and she water skied together with her kids. At forty-five she took up tennis. When she was close to fifty, they went for a week to Hawaii. You guessed it – she tried surfing and had some beginner's luck

At no time did she say, "I don't do that any more." She might say, "No, we don't water ski. We had to sell the boat, but now we go white water rafting. That's a blast."

That woman acts young, therefore she feels young, and many people perceive her as younger than she is.

Now, not all your activities have to be of a physical nature. There are many other fulfilling activities. Call them hobbies, if

210

you want. You can go bird watching, take a course in painting, go to adult education, volunteer at a hospital, learn to swim, be a "Big Sister," or learn how to handle a computer.

Take a class in college. (If you have a high school diploma, you can enroll. If you are a senior, you may be able to attend classes without paying. You won't get a grade or credit towards a diploma, but you probably don't need that anyway. It's free except for the books.)

Learn a foreign language. This widens your horizon immensely, because with every language you'll also learn about the culture, geography, history, living standards and much more of the countries where your chosen language is spoken

****

Equally or even more important than these recreational activities is your *work attitude*. It is generally assumed that young people are full of vim and vigor, ready to change the world. Oldsters are perceived to be stuck in the muck, disgustedly waiting for retirement. Break that mold!

It you are a professional, do you accept or even propose new methods, new techniques, new solutions to old problems, or are you just in a rut? Your clients or patients or customers will be very much aware of that.

Let me tell you about three friends of mine: After Mary raised her seven kids, she went to law school and is now a practicing attorney. Becky, a registered nurse who worked occasionally part time while her kids were young, became a Ph.D. in gerontology. Diseases of seniors had always interested her. She also works now in her new field. Alice was a busy body in local politics. She got a Ph.D. degree in Sociology and has now vastly increased her responsibilities teaching at a local college.

If you are a "middle management" person, such as a nurse, an office manager, a legal secretary, you should bring your enthusiasm to your job, have new ideas about how work could be done more efficiently and more pleasantly. A friend of mine had no special training and no work experience. When her children were grown, she wanted to have something useful to do. So she invented a new job, checking and comparing prices in competitive stores and selling her results to those stores.

If you are a factory worker, do you have a cheerful attitude, a smile for your co-workers and, maybe, even for the boss? Are you proud of the product you help create? It is necessary to find satisfaction in your work. This is often more important than the paycheck

****

You guessed it! Beauty and "Age" are a matter of attitude, how you work, how you carry yourself and, of course, how you look. You've got to be positive in all these areas to be a healthy, vibrant person.

Full of Life at Any Age

Oh, Dear, cheer up! Don't be concerned that you are getting on in years. You sure are not the only one with these feelings.

What are your options? There is the obvious one to be six feet under – but other possibilities exist. Think what activities you liked when you were young and see which of those you still can do.

You liked to go to the movies – why don't you go now? Not all current movies are bad. Get out of the house for a while!

You liked to dress well – stylish clothes are still available. Get some. And don't worry that they will last longer than you. Kids in school chuck them after a year.

You liked to eat out – good restaurants are nearby. Go there and eat something exotic. If your stomach is touchy now, take an Alka Selzer along.

You made plans when you were young. That's really most important – planning what to do next week, next year or in five years. It's characteristic of young folks. Plan! Don't ever say or think, "I won't live that long. Makes no sense to think ahead." Once you quit planning, you are just waiting for death.

Yet it might be another 20 years before the Reaper calls you. What will you do in the meantime? Just sit and rot?

Nobody, at any age, has a guarantee that he'll be alive the next day. Look at the obituaries: lots of young folks die. But they were active and looked to the future. They were alive, vibrant until the end.

Your activities have to include some productive work. Movies, vacations, trips, shopping and clothes are all exciting. However, importance has to be placed on more than entertainment.

You play an instrument well but never used that talent publicly? Check with your nearby church. They might love to

213

have a violin player or harpist with their choir. You'll find recognition and make that ensemble better.

You always dabbled in painting but never had the time to really get into it? Do it now, six hours a day. In a year you'll have enough material for a one artist show. You'll find that your paintings *do* express your character, your views and opinions. If you paint covered bridges, lakes and grazing cows, it shows that you renew your spirits in a pastoral setting. Others will enjoy your pictures (and even buy a few). If you want to state your view about social problems, you can paint that too – the poor, the downtrodden, the decaying cities.

Always worried about the ecology? It's a big problem. Now you have the time to get your teeth into it. Make everyone aware of the dangers to our Earth and how to lessen them. One person *can* make a difference. What you start in your community might spread to neighboring counties and could benefit your whole state.

Actually always wanted to participate in local politics? Go for it! They can use a good mind, a dedicated worker and a riveting speaker. With your help your party can gain at the next elections and this way *you* influence your surroundings.

For years you've wanted to learn another language, but had no time? Start Now! All our local colleges have foreign language courses for beginners and advanced students. Want to know more about that melodious Russian tongue your grandmother often spoke? Learn it! Want to go to Quebec and not be ignored by the locals? Learn French. Want to know what the Mexicans are really saying? Learn Spanish! Want to understand all those Italian operas? You know what to do. It's interesting, stimulating, educational, entertaining and wonderful exercise for your mind.

So – to stay youthful means to do what young folks do. Most important is pursuing opportunities and staying active mentally and physically. Then, once you are gone, they will say,

"She was so full of life." That's how you want to be at any age –
full of life.

White Water Rafting at My Age?

If you can walk, you can raft.

I called my friend, Mary. After some chatter she said, "I thought of you the other day. On TV there was a rubber boat in rough water – people in it. It was a beer commercial. You do that kind of thing, don't you?"

"Beer commercials? No."

Mary giggled. "Oh, you know what I mean. That boating. What's it called?"

"White water rafting."

"Yeah. I've wanted to do that for a long time, but I'm sure I can't."

"Why not?"

"Oh, I'm too scared. It's frightening, isn't it?"

"That depends."

"Can't you fall out?"

"Yes, you can, but it doesn't happen often. Besides, you wear a life jacket that'll surely bring you up in seconds."

"How do you get back into the boat?"

"It's called a 'raft.' The others in the raft will help you in."

"You get wet?"

"Always. In the rapids the water really splashes at you. That's the biggest part of the fun."

"But I'd be afraid I'd make a fool of myself."

"Doing what?"

"Falling out – being clumsy."

"Mary, no one falls out of a raft looking graceful. And coming back in, everyone looks like a squashed toad, even that handsome muscle man or the guide..."

"The guides fall out?"

"Yes, they sometimes do, and nobody cares."

"Then it wouldn't be so bad."

217

"Dear, no one is perfect when he learns a new skill – not a cook, not an auto mechanic, a tennis player or a rafter. You can't get good at it if you don't try."

"Are you going once more this year?" Mary asked.

"Yes, middle of next month."

After some hesitation, she said, "If you'll take me, I'll go with you. I might never get a chance if I don't do it now."

"Atta gal! Last year we had a lady along who was seventy years old. She was the darling of the entire group. Everyone, including the macho guys, was obviously thinking, 'I sure hope I'll be as good as she is when I'm seventy'."

****

In the car Mary asked, "What do you personally get out of it?"

I thought a while. "A lot. There are several aspects. It's a sport that requires your full attention. When you bicycle, you can think of all your worries, but while you are paddling in a rapid, it only matters how you get through. You can't fret what your grown kids are doing wrong, where you'll take the tax money from or how the last argument with your husband went. Believe it or not, you are so busy rafting, you forget everything else."

"That would be a relief," said Mary.

"Then you meet new people, see new landscapes, enjoy the scenery. You'll see, the river bed looks quite different from the interstate. All those huge boulders in the river, as big as houses, are testimony to the tremendous forces nature can unleash. You become aware of what tiny specks we humans are."

****

Mary was tense in the bus to the take-in. But once she saw the rafts, she said, "Oh they are big, they look sturdy."

218

"Best rafts there are," said the guide, a sinewy man of about 30. "The water is great today. We'll have a ball."

Once in the raft, Mary put on a courageous smile and paddled strongly. Suddenly we were in the first rapid, got doused and came through in perfect alignment. Then she relaxed and gave herself to the exhilarating sensations of the trip. "That's fantastic ...Ya-hoo." She couldn't stop grinning.

After about two hours, we ate our lunch of cold cuts. Mary looked at the valley and said, "It's really beautiful here."

"Yes." I took a deep breath. "Here I feel I'm part of nature, a component of the untamed splashing water, an element of the joy that's in its bouncing playfulness. Believe me, I feel ageless, a happy, free spirit. Even if I'm at the end tired, bushed, bedraggled with soaking clothes and muddy feet, the sense of freedom stays with me for weeks to come."

Menopause

Menopause, the scourge of womanhood: vanishing youth and childbearing potential, loss of allure and sex drive, stooped shoulders, pot belly, hot flashes, irrational crankiness, arthritis, bifocals. Decline, the beginning of the end.

****

Really? It ain't necessarily so.

Let's look at some of those *negative aspects.*

The Loss of Procreation, the Inability to give Life.

Do you have all the children you want? How old are they? Probably in their late teens or early twenties. Can you truly say you wanted another one? Get real. Now you won't have to fear another pregnancy, won't have to worry whether the pill/diaphragm / foam / IUD / rhythm method / condom etc. really worked this month. One big concern is gone.

Loss of Allure and Beauty: It has nothing to do with menopause. Watch your figure and your diet, exercise, get your hair done, if necessary get a face lift or get something tucked. Above all, maintain a pleasant, lively personality.

Hot Flashes: What a pain. Some women have them, some don't. They are not worse, though, than morning sickness, pregnancy and childbirth; not more bothersome than PMS and menstrual cramps. It's just a different kind of nuisance.

Crankiness: Yes, that happens. I remember when both my kids were unbearable oafs, my husband an insensitive lout and all of my co-workers sniping bitches. I sometimes sat back and felt sorry for myself. Then I remembered: I had forgotten my hormone pill! So I took it, and the next day all those nasty people were sweet and charming again.

The irritability also has a good side. You feel free to express your opinions. Some things have bothered you for a long time,

221

but you never spoke up to avoid trouble. Now you give everyone a piece of your mind and it makes you feel wonderful. You think you are in control again – most of the time.

Poor Posture: Spinal trouble can cause it, but more often it comes from letting your head hang, heavy with all your burdens, real or imagined. Walk with your head held high.

Arthritis: Everyone might suffer from it. Most people can keep the pain under control with aspirin-like medications and can continue their previous activities such as tennis, skiing, gardening and dancing.

Bifocals: Most folks over forty need them, men as well as women. Vision problems have nothing to do with menopause, just happen about the same time.

Old Age Means Decline: NO. These are the best years, and I'll tell you why.

Let's look at some of the *positive aspects.*

Sex: It's wonderful now, believe me. Before menopause you were either trying to get pregnant or not.

If you wanted a baby, every time it didn't work, you were depressed. Not only did you have the discomfort of the period, you also had the depression of the dashed hope.

If you did *not* want to get pregnant, you were worried every month whether your precautions had worked. If you were a day late, you got frantic.

All these concerns are gone now. Love making, honest, is much more fun, without all those do's and don't's from before. In many families the kids have left home, so you two can make all the noise you want, any time, day and night.

Other Benefits of this time in your life – you can go swimming whenever you want and don't have to plan your vacation according to your personal calendar.

You probably have grandkids. They visit and then they go home. Let their parents fuss with them when they are cranky.

In a more serious vein, you are now more mature and can take on greater responsibilities. You'll probably move into a management position because of your experience and get more satisfaction from your career.

This can be the best time of your life. First you were Daddy's little girl, then you were Joe's wife, then Johnny's mom. Now, for the first time, you are yourself, your own person, not depending on someone else for your identity. You are most importantly yourself, more fulfilled, happier.

You've become a smarter person. Your judgement is better because you can approach life with humor.

Menopause is not a dirty word – it's a time to look forward to and enjoy. Cherish the span of life, live it fully.

A Different Thanksgiving

Not every holiday has to be celebrated in the traditional way. If you can't get the family together, don't mope. Do something quite different and enjoy the day.

****

At the grocery store, I ran into Peggy who used to live on our street. After hugs and greetings, she said, "I'm really afraid of this Thanksgiving. With Gene gone and the kids in Texas, I'll have no one. I'm already depressed."

"This year I'll also be alone," I said. "Tom is out of town, and the kids will be with their in-laws. Want to spend the day with me?"

"What will you do?" she asked.

"I've planned something that's not at all related to the holiday. The weather forecast is good. I'll go for a long walk at Big Creek Park. Want to come along?"

"I'd love to," she said. "That's really something new."

"Good. I'll pick you up on Thursday at eleven o'clock. Pack a sandwich."

****

The day was sunny with patches of fog higher up. We chose 'Chipmunk Trail,' a hike four miles long. There had been a dry spell for nearly three weeks. The maples and beeches were bare – all their leaves were on the ground, blown by the wind into large heaps or ridges. We both liked the rustling sound our steps made and, like kids, tried to kick up the brown and orange foliage.

Then Peggy sat down and pushed her legs into that crackling fluff. "When I was little, my brother, Billy, used to 'bury' me in

225

the leaves." She giggled. "Mom often was worried she mightn't find me any more."

I just watched her.

Rising and brushing off, she examined a tree that looked as though it hadn't caught up with the season yet. "Look, this tree still has all its leaves. Do you know why?"

"It's an oak. They keep theirs until spring."

"Really? How do you know that?" she asked.

"People told a story in the old country: a guy had made a pact wit the devil. The man would gladly let the devil have his soul 'when the oak tree was bare.' The devil wasn't a good botanist, so he agreed. Then in autumn he waited, and waited; it got to be winter, but the oak leaves were still on. Finally in spring, new ones appeared, and only then did the dead leaves fall off. So the oak tree was never bare, and the devil lost the bargain. He got so angry that he grabbed the tree, shook it and tore at it. That's why the oak leaves are so ragged."

"You believe that?" asked Peggy.

I laughed. "No, not at all. But it helps me remember that oak trees carry their brown foliage through winter."

The path led up a hillock, and suddenly we were in thick fog.

"You can hardly see anything," I said, "except those red things here. Do you know what they are?"

"Sumac," Peggy explained. "We have some at the end of our drive. Those fruits also stay on long into the winter."

Descending out of the fog, we decided to sit on a log in the sun and eat our sandwiches. In the valley, smoke rose from a farm house, spreading a haze over the bare trees.

"Look," said Peggy, "they must already be roasting their turkey. But, my ham-and-cheese here is really good, too. Guess I never had a sandwich before on Thanksgiving."

The trail wound down into the river valley where we skipped a few stones over an eddy. "Used to do that too with Billy," she said. "I could get five bounces if I was lucky; he made it seven or eight, that macho guy."

The climb out of the valley on the other side was rather steep and lay in the sun. Peggy got hot, huffing and puffing uphill. "I'm glad this is not August now," she muttered, but she was a good trooper and finished the slope without further comment.

The cabins beside the parking lot came already into view when we heard a 'thud, thud' on the soft trail behind us. We turned. Four riders were overtaking us on well groomed horses.

"Look, where do they come from?" Peggy asked with a big surprise in her voice.

"I'm not sure, but there might be a riding stable on the west side of the park."

"Could we go there and look?"

"Sure. You know how to ride?" I asked.

"We had horses when we were kids, showed them at the fair. I got even more ribbons than Billy did. Wouldn't that be something if I could ride again!"

We took a different exit from the park, and there was a corral with horses. Peggy went into the barn next to it and talked to a man. After a while I saw him take a book and write something down, and she nodded emphatically.

She was nearly skipping when she came out. "Oh, wow, I made an appointment for tomorrow. They'll lead a group for an hour and a half through the whole park. He says there are bridle paths all over."

"I'm surprised they have an opening."

"Someone canceled just an hour ago." She kept on talking while I drove to her home. "That was one of the loveliest days I had in a long time. The beautiful hike, all the memories, your oak story and now I'll even go horseback riding. It couldn't be any better. Why don't you come along riding some time?"

"I might do just that."

When she got out of my car, Peggy said, "You were right. When you can't celebrate a holiday with your family, don't be depressed – do something different! Then your heart won't be heavy and you'll have a great day."

I just smiled.

Life In A Greenhouse

My patient has a bad cataract and needs it removed.

"Schedule Gloria Wilmer for surgery on the left eye," I say to Nancy, my secretary. "No real hurry." I am busy at the desk and can hear the conversation.

"Let's see, Mrs. Wilmer," Nancy is checking the appointment book. "When do you want your cataract out? How would be November 29? That's just after Thanksgiving."

"Oh no, I can't do that," she says. "December is our busiest month. We sell over 3,000 poinsettias before Christmas and once more as many of the other plants."

"Who is 'we?' " I ask.

"It's me, mostly; when it gets too busy, my husband, Frank here, helps me out."

"You work in a greenhouse?"

"We own one," says Frank Wilmer. "Had it for nearly 20 years. Our customers depend on us."

A piece of paper falls off Nancy's desk, and Gloria quickly bends down and picks it up. She is slim and has quick movements, obviously not hindered by arthritis. A full head of nearly white hair frames her oval face.

Nancy checks her chart. In a low voice, so the people in the waiting room won't hear, she asks, "It says here you are 82 years old. Can that be right?"

"She is," says Frank, his hand on his wife's shoulder. "The greenhouse keeps her young." He seems to be in his seventies and is visibly proud of her.

"Who does all the work?" I ask.

"I do," she says in a nonchalant way. "Well, at times he helps out." While Frank Wilmer turns around to greet someone who had just come in, Gloria adds in a whisper, "I like it better if he stays away; he goofs things up."

"I heard that." Frank turns around. "It's true, though. Book work bores me." His eyes are sparkling, and she has a happy smile.

I can't quite believe it yet. "Who helps you?"

She laughs. "No one. Want to come some time and look at our place?"

"I'd love to. Where is your greenhouse?"

"It's on Route 63, about a mile after the school," says Mr. Wilmer. "A pond is beside the driveway, and a red barn across the street."

"Now, your surgery, when do you want it done?" Nancy gets down to business.

"How'd it be if I give you a call after Christmas?" Gloria asks with a hesitant smile.

"We'll come and remind you," says Nancy.

****

These two oldsters who so enjoy their busy life, have pricked my curiosity. I look at their place a week after Thanksgiving. The pond makes the house easy to find. The Wilmers must have seen me drive up because both of them come out and guide me to a small door beside the house. Inside, my eye glasses steam up; it's warm and humid.

After a narrow passage, the room widens to about 25 by 150 feet. There are four rows of potting tables, crowded with plants. What a place. Frank lets his wife give the guided tour.

"This half is now all filled with poinsettias. Over here on the left are the red ones; they are traditional, and most people prefer them. But on this side," she turns to the right, "are all shades from deep pink to white; some are even peach colored; see them? They are for more adventurous customers."

This whole room looks like a painting by Renoir, the blossoms seemingly afloat on a sea of leaves.

"In this corner," says Frank, "we have a few yellow poinsettias. They are new. One of our magazines had an article how to raise them. Gloria tried it and they really turned out yellow." There is again pride in his voice about his wife's success.

"Who buys all these plants?" I wonder.

"Any concert hall will have them in this season. Then think of all the Christmas parties; the churches are our biggest customers. Many people or businesses use them as presents."

"How do you raise them? From little plants?"

"Oh no." Gloria seems close to being offended. "We raise all our plants either from seeds or from clippings."

Beside the poinsettias there are Christmas cactuses. The blossoms pour out of them like little red waterfalls. On the next table are about a hundred hollies with their pointed, oily leaves, sharp thorns and red berries. They seem to spell "Christmas" just by being there.

Gloria adjusts her head-scarf, stoops down and shows me the intricate irrigation pipes. Seems each flower pot is served by a little line. Just then a male voice says behind her, "Hey, young lady, do you already have spring bulbs?"

She rises. "Well, George, what are you buttering me up for?"

He laughs. "Oh, Gloria, I thought it was your granddaughter."

"No," she giggles. "Susie is married now and lives in the southern part of the state. What bulbs do you want?"

"My wife wants some narcissus and hyacinths."

She goes to the far end and brings several pots. They are ceramic with Dutch motifs, filled with soil and apparently nothing else. I can't understand this.

"Will they bloom by New Year's?" he asks.

"That's a little early, but if you keep them in a dark, warm closet and water them regularly, they might come up by then." Gloria gets a paper bag for the cups.

231

"How do I know which is which?"

"Just give them to your wife, and she'll find out." She laughs. "See, I have my secrets: the pots with the children on them, have hyacinths; the ones with the windmills have narcissus."

He takes his pots, pays and leaves.

"What are these?" I ask.

"Bulbs. Many folks like spring flowers early. These can be raised indoors."

Frank brings a pot with tiny blossoms, like out of a fairy tale. "These are miniature roses," he says. "They are for you. And I promise I'll have Gloria call about her cataract just as soon as we are sold out."

"But then comes the spring planting. I have no time for surgery right now," she says with a wink. "I'll just have to use a magnifying glass and hope my cataract won't act up."

"You two are great," I say.

"Oh, we just pretend we are still young, and..." says Frank.

"Yeah, 82 years young," his wife continues. "And when something aches, we try to ignore it."

"Just keep pretending," I say. "I wish more people would do as well as you."

Bridging the Generation Gap

Many elderly folks are upset that their grown children and grandchildren don't visit them often enough. This might be true, and it is sad. *Dear Abby* addresses a similar problem three times a year in her column. Being a grandmother myself, I have a few thoughts on that.

First of all, I don't believe adult children owe their mother and father the same care that the parents had given them. The young adults are obliged to extend concern, love and time to their own children, to the next generation. The parent-child love is not a clear two-way street as between spouses. The parent always gives more. It has been this way since the beginning of time. Observe how a duck or a lioness takes care of her young. Do the little ones ever reciprocate the care? No. They give it to their own offspring.

Think clearly what happens when the younger generations come to your house. What do *they* get out of the visit other than fulfilling a duty?

Are you reporting about interesting events or do you complain about your chronic ailments, about the neighbor's noisy dog and about your loneliness last weekend? Can they look forward to the visit with you?

What about the grandchildren? Do yo offer them anything besides kisses and a cherry pie?

What can you do? Certainly no rule applies to every family. The geographic distance, your state of health and your financial status will all influence your plans.

Let's assume you are in reasonably good health, that is, you can walk half a mile. Let's further assume you have a little money – say, you can occasionally spend $100. Why not invite the family to come with you to Seaworld, or to a deer park or – if you all are so inclined – to the Football Hall of Fame or a similar attraction. That gives everyone something to look forward to.

For a whole day you'll *all* enjoy the attractions and your family. Tell them you'll buy the tickets and the gasoline, they'll have to get the food.

If your budget is more restrained, take them to the beach. You can sit in the shade or splash with them in the water. Don't forget, little kids are a legitimate excuse to do "crazy" things such as going down a slide, bouncing on a swing, playing with a Frisbee. Nobody will think you are weird, just devoted grandparents.

If grandpa can play golf seven days a week, he can skip one day and take the grandchildren fishing. You never fished? It's about time you learned it! So you'll tell the rest of your foursome, "Sorry, guys, from now on I'll take Tiffany and Keith fishing on Tuesdays."

The other three old geezers will first object. Let them. They could do something different once a week, too. Although they won't admit it, they'll envy *you* the little adventures.

If the weather is bad, play tic-tac-toe or checkers and advance to chess. Dominoes, Scrabble, Monopoly or modeling clay are stimulating for young and old alike. See whether you can match or even surpass the pictures on the box of the Erector Set. It might take hours to build that castle or locomotive. The parents don't have time for that, but Grandpa does.

Is there an electric train somewhere around? Dust it off and use it. Let the *kids* throw the switches. You just guide them. (When their father is with them, all they can do is watch *him* play.)

Your grandchildren are in high school and very busy with sports? Go to their games by all means! Keep up with the rules (be it football, basketball or whatever), so you can discuss the events with understanding. The kids will brag, "My grandpa and grandma come to all my meets." And, Grandpa, please don't tell the story how *you* sacked that quarterback 60 years ago more than twice.

I'm sure, you'll be able to find infinite variations of the suggested plans. The important thing is that the kids and grandkids look forward to being with you.

Problems of Retirement

Slowly, I was walking through the mall, watching people. Suddenly, in the middle of the crowd, there stood Irene; she had been a neighbor of ours until they moved a few years ago. Now she looked haggard, more shadows on her face than light. When she saw me, tears were welling up in her eyes.

"Irene, for heaven's sake, what's the matter?" I blurted out.

"Oh, it's Sam, he's retired now; I can't even talk." Her voice sounded crushed.

"What's the problem? Tell me."

"I can't; he'll be right here." She nearly sobbed.

Sam reached us. "Irene, why did you walk away from me? I just about lost you." He didn't take notice of me.

I was afraid something was drastically wrong here, so I grabbed Irene's large package and whacked it against Sam's protruding waist for him to catch it. Then I clutched Irene's arm, doubled-over as in pain and said in a hoarse voice, "Ooh, I'm sick; please take me to the washroom. Quick!"

Irene guided me there; it wasn't far. Sam followed, muttering, "What's wrong with her? What's the matter?"

I pulled Irene behind the door marked 'Ladies' and asked, "Now tell me quickly, what's going on?"

She took a deep breath. "Sam retired five months ago. Now he is home all the time, not two feet from me. He watches me when I cook and knows a better method. He is underfoot when I do the wash and questions every move I make. He *helps* me when I try to sew and goofs up everything. If a friend calls, he sits right beside the phone and even interrupts asking what the caller has said, when he can't figure it out by my responses. He insists that he is the better driver and takes me everywhere: he sits in the beauty salon and waits till my hair is done. He watches my bridge club play.

"You know, I loved this man once. Now I can't stand him any more."

"Have you suggested any out-of-the-house hobbies for him?" I inquired.

"I've mentioned golf, gardening, volunteer work at the hospital, an adult education class, stamp collecting, work at the church ... He accuses me of wanting him out of the house."

"How perceptive. Any luck with part-time work?"

Irene shook her head. "He just gets angry, saying now we have time for each other, and I don't want him. It's not that I don't like him, but not 24 hours a day tagging along with me."

A woman entered laughing and asked in a loud voice, "Is an Irene Benkovic here?"

"Yeah," sighed Irene. "I'm here. Can't he wait any longer?"

"The man out there wants to know whether your friend is all right or if he should call an ambulance?"

I stifled a laugh.

"Please tell him she's better. We don't need an ambulance, and we'll be out in about 10 minutes. He should just sit down," said Irene.

The woman obliged. She was back in a minute. "He wanted to come in because it's an emergency, but I told him he can't. He wasn't too happy." With a chuckle she went to wash her hands.

"Now then," I said. "How would it be if someone else asked him to do some work? Someone who needs him. Then it wouldn't be *you* pushing him out."

"Maybe," sighed Irene.

"Hurry up! Think! We haven't got much time," I worried. "Who could use him?"

"Our church needs a handyman. Since the old guy had his operation, many things have been left undone," said Irene.

"Good. Which church, and who's the pastor?"

"The Congregational Church uptown; the Reverend Richard Minton runs it."

238

"Fine. I'll try to get hold of him."

There were lots of reproaches when we went back outside, "Why do you let me wait so long? Why don't you at least tell me what's going on? Why doesn't someone else help her?" And to me, "What's wrong with you anyway?"

While Irene 'explained' what happened, I quietly disappeared.

****

During the next week, I contacted Pastor Minton.

Seems he has heard such stories before. With a smile he said, "I'll give ol' Sam a call. I agree, Irene needs some time off. We could use help and Sam might like a change of scenery. Thank you for letting me know."

****

Three weeks later, Irene called with a smile in her voice.

"Are you alone?" I asked.

"Yes. I've wanted to give you a call. Within a week the pastor told Sam how much they need him and couldn't he give a few hours a week to the Lord? Sam accepted, telling me he couldn't leave them in the lurch."

"So, how often does he go to help out?"

"Every weekday but Thursday. That day we go shopping together, and then *he* cooks dinner."

"How is Sam taking it?" I asked.

"Great. He's much happier, now that he is needed."

"Irene, I'm glad it worked out. He's lucky someone can use him."

"Oh, dear, I'm lucky too. I have so much to tell you."

"Good. I'll pick you up for lunch next Wednesday."

"I'll be waiting," she said. "I can again make my own plans."

239

The Flowers Of Our County

If people are asked to identify with an animal, a plant or a machine (e.g. a car), they will instinctively choose one closest to their self image, to their goals. Clearly, a man who wants to be a trusty pickup truck is not the same who sees himself as a Ferrari.

Wanting to know how women in my Northeast Ohio county perceive themselves, I posed this question to 100 women: *if you lived in a fantasy land where you couldn't be a person but had to be a flower, which flower would you want to be?* Here is a summary of the answers.

About a third of the ladies wanted to be a red rose because it is beautiful, soft, elegant and has an enchanting scent. Most of them would ignore the thorns or do away with them, but some emphatically wanted to keep them "If someone touches me in a wrong way, I want to scratch back." A minority wished to be a rose of a lighter shade, peach colored, yellow, pink or orange. These are supposedly softer yet and lovelier than red roses.

A touching answer came from a woman who is close to 50. She said, "Absolutely a yellow rose; it was my mother's favorite flower. My father tried to raise yellow roses all his life but wasn't always successful." This mother has suffered from severe Alzheimer's disease for about 15 years and lives in the daughter's home. Unable to recognize anyone, not steady enough to walk, she still has the full love of her daughter who wants to be her yellow rose.

The next largest group are the daisies, marigolds and black eyed Susans. They are cheerful, happy, unassuming, hardy, self sufficient and don't need much care.

Mums expressed the identity of three women. They are beautiful even in autumn's inclement weather and hardy enough to withstand the cold.

I found four sunflowers. They are adaptable – the plant changes its position during the day to face the sun – and tall.

"...so I can look down on all the other flowers and at the end of summer I can feed the birds." One sunflower even said, "I've been short all my life; to be tall would be nice." A friend of mine would be a Yucca plant, a very tall, smooth cactus with a cluster of blooms on top. Again, the height of the plant seemed to be the deciding factor. She also liked a warm climate.

Five respondents wanted to be irises. Their elegance, stunning color and variety of pattern and design made the women think that to be an iris would be the highest achievement. Interestingly, these people raise irises, digging in the dirt, watering the plants, probably giving their own elegance to achieve it for their favorite flowers.

Four chose to be daffodils, the symbol of spring, rebirth of the earth; everything is green again, it'll be warm, and better times lie ahead.

Lilies of the valley were selected for their strong scent and because "it's cool and green where they grow."

Pansies were the choice of four ladies. They are not only beautiful in different shades of purple and yellow, their design reminds of a human face.

One woman wanted to be a white lily, "not because of its innocence or sweetness, but because it makes a statement, it's awesome." There you have it.

I found two carnations and one each of a violet, columbine, gardenia, peony, rhododendron, lilac, tulip, sweet pea, zinnia, gladiola, corn flower and statice. One of my friends wanted to be a Christmas cactus "to have blossoms all over my limbs, but it's good that the plant is tough."

From this collection we see that the majority wants to be beautiful, pleasing, loving, soft, cheerful and hardy. In a word – feminine. As a group, they should be easy to live with.

Naturally, someone asked what flower *I* would be. Well, I'm the country renegade: I'd be a dandelion. Many years ago I saw a parking lot that had been covered with a thick layer of blacktop the previous fall. The pavement had a crack. I looked.

A dandelion! What a tough little bugger pushing its way through the thick layer of goo. Also, in Europe, where I grew up, people are not as fanatic about their lawns as in America. They cut their grass every two or three weeks, so that bluebells, buttercups, clover and dandelions grow in harmony. None of them is an endangered species. The dandelion (the word comes from the French "dent de lion" or tooth of the lion) is not an enemy that has to be killed. The yellow blossoms radiate health, and the stand of seeds, while intact, looks like a little dome. Once the individual kernels take off, they float through the air, each like a tiny Mary Poppins.

Next, let's look at the men.

Hertha Binder

Want To Be A Tree? – Which One?
Wish To be a Bear Or A Puppy-Dog?

What could men identify with? Of course they wouldn't think of being a flower, sure. A machine, it was suggested. Maybe, but while some men know a lot of them, others do not. Or a car? I wondered, might they not think of the one they want to *drive* rather than the one they would be. Better let them choose from living creatures – a tree or an animal.

So I asked 100 men – if they could not be a person – what kind of tree they would be if they lived in some fantasy land. And if not a tree, then what animal would they pick?

The majority, forty-seven, opted for an oak: strong, tall, as hardwood being very sturdy, and good looking. "You can build five houses from one good oak, that's how much wood they have." Or, "The wood is always solid throughout, not rotted inside as in other trees." The oak's fruit, the acorns, impressed others as useful to animals.

Eight decided a Sequoia, or Giant Redwood, fit their personality or the one they'd like to be. Taller than anything else, the trees are imposing, majestic and "lasting forever," resistant to insect pests and even fires. A maple expressed the self image of nineteen respondents. Some of them just enjoyed its good looks, particularly the two crimson maples with their unusual and stunning foliage during spring, summer and fall. A few chose a sugar maple because it supplies syrup and gives of itself, provides and makes itself useful. For the same reason three others identified with an apple tree.

Seven desired an abundance of blossoms which they found in a buckeye; not only is it beautiful but it also proudly represents the State of Ohio. One young man felt he would be an "apple blossom tree." We recorded six evergreens. They are stately and attractive even in winter when the deciduous trees look scraggly. One admired their connection with Christmas, his

245

favorite holiday. Another said, "It's prickly. That's why no one comes close to a spruce, not even the dogs."

Three distinguished gentlemen selected a weeping willow for its dignity and the ability to bend rather than break under stress. They savored the nearness of water and perceived the willow as elegant and impressive. Another pictured himself as a bamboo, also because of its flexibility. Besides, he always dreamed of living in Asia. One fellow figured it pleasant to be a palm tree, "So I'd live where it's warm." One well informed man could imagine himself growing on the Gallapagos Islands where he could develop for long periods without being disturbed by outside influences. Locust trees appealed to my husband for being indestructible. "Look at fence posts," he said. "Even after being in the ground for decades, they are as good as new. They never rot."

Two people thought they resembled a tulip tree with its elegant shape and unique fruit.

Surprisingly, only one of the 47 would-be oaks mentioned that they keep their leaves much longer in fall. Even in winter, oaks still have plenty of leaves. Only in spring, when the new buds have already opened up, do the old leaves fall off. So, the oaks are never bare. I'd have thought that men with a tendency to baldness would have liked to keep their thatch.

Summarizing the favorite trees, most men wanted to be strong, tall, straight and enduring – masculine and virile. Some added productivity to their lifetime goal in addition to supplying sturdy wood after they were felled. Some took care to be flexible, so that the misfortunes of life would just bend but not break them.

Surprisingly, the choice of animals did not reveal the same characteristics. In the fantasy land, the men wanted to live as the following animals: twenty six felt akin to a dog, usually the one the family had owned. He is a friend, a bit protective but mainly has a good life and no obligations. "They have it made," lounging at the fireplace or by the couch, having fun, going for playful walks with the master. They get better food than anyone else, are always taken care of and pampered. No worries, no responsibilities. Only one man wanted to be a Labrador. They are smart and are used as drug sniffers; two would enjoy the life of a German shepherd, reliable, intelligent, faithful and good looking.

Two people saw themselves as a house cat, one for the same spoiled life as the puppy dogs, the other because "nothing fazes them, things roll off their backs."

Sixteen big cats were among the favored animals, such as tigers, mountain cougars, leopards, one black leopard (very rare, different from those that have spots), jaguars, cheetahs, a panther and two lions. All are good looking, even elegant, majestic, sleek, independent, stealthy, cunning, cagy and have no real enemies. When questioned, these gentlemen admitted that being on top of the food pyramid wasn't a bad idea either. One would-be tiger liked to roam. "It's good that he is a bachelor," said his mother who heard him. However, the wife of another tiger said, "You know, tigers mate and then they disappear! They don't take care of their family."

Two polar bears felt imposing, in control, independent, free. They swim and roam and are well adjusted to their environment. Five other bears (brown, black or grizzly – it didn't matter) seemed content with strength, love for adventures and assured respect from others. One brown bear was considered over a polar bear. "It eats berries and honey, you know. It's not just killing other creatures." A pleasant guy, ferocious only when attacked. One father chose the bear for being cuddly and..." "Grouchy," his kids finished the sentence. And one neighbor mentioned, "A bear, so I could sleep in now." The poor fellow returned my call early in the morning; I'm afraid his wife woke him before his usual time.

Four men found nothing wrong with being a horse. They receive good treatment, three seeing themselves as heavy Belgians and one as a thoroughbred. One friendly guy even insisted being a team of horses. (I couldn't understand how he could identify with two animals, but that's what he wanted.)

We gathered seven eagles: majestic, enjoying the beautiful view of the mountains all day long, just leisurely soaring on the updrafts. They "kind of rule." One fancied himself as the symbol of our country. Another appreciated their mating habits: "They stay together for life." One wife, when her spouse named some other animal, said, "I thought you'd want to be an eagle." "Sure," he countered, "but an eagle is not an animal."

I only asked the questions; I did not try to educate.

One of my guests saw ducks as his brothers. He admired their flight and dreamed of joining them in their travels across continents. "They just have to stay away from guys like me," he said.

"Why?" I asked. "Do you shoot them?"

"Oh, yes, I hunt ducks all the time. They are so beautiful."

The combination of admiring and shooting the same creature was a bit beyond my understanding, I admit. From then on I queried the men who voted to be deer (altogether ten), whether they hunted them, and all but one said, "Yes, they are so gentle, are graceful, free and have soft eyes; that's why we stalk them." One allowed that "They are so elusive and smart, they usually outwit me. Graceful and pretty which I never was." The elk impressed another as a grander, more imposing deer.

Dolphins intrigued two people because of their astonishing intelligence and teamwork. They even can kill a shark by ramming him at high speed in its vulnerable neck area. One man thought the dolphins might be the dominant life-form long after humans have disappeared. On the other hand, one person preferred to be a shark: "Then I could bite all the guys who bothered me before I was a shark." At least he was honest. One guest enjoyed the life of a whale so he could see other parts of the world and be the most majestic of the seas.

In their mind, four men could be an elephant: smart, steady, reliable, dependable, strong and beautiful. One added that they are now an endangered species, so nobody kills them. I don't know whether these gentlemen were Republicans. However, I didn't find anyone who volunteered to be a donkey for whatever reason.

A friend of ours would have been an opossum: they have not changed for 70 million years and probably contributed to the extinction of the dinosaurs by eating their eggs. Inconspicuous and unassuming, they are expert survivors. To be left alone, one person elected to be a skunk. He'd sure make his point.

One man perceived a wolf as a family oriented loner, handsome and noble. Two foxes and one coyote were probably chosen for the same reason and besides, they are crafty and wily.

Two fellows felt like a squirrel: cheerful, pleasant, nimble, scampering all over the place without worrying about predators. One of them said he "always hated to shoot them." Another thought he could live as a chipmunk. Saving all those nuts for winter could teach his grown children a lesson about thrift and saving for bad times. We found a river otter. They enjoy life, are playful and always have a good time – or so it seems. One of my respondents even preferred to be a bunny; they are easy to get along with, and one thought it would be fun to be a wolverine with cuddly fur, he said.

The survey revealed one owl. It can fly silently without flapping its wings and therefore can surprise the prey; a hawk was another's choice because of its elegant flight. Among the birds was one robin, a pleasant little guy, always good for a sweet song. One grandpa wished he could be as soft and gentle as a lamb, another loved to be a fawn.

It is interesting that 47 of my guests identified with the strong, straight, long lasting, enduring oak. Yet the animals they picked were puppy-dogs (26), playthings unburdened by worries. If you add all the other carefree creatures (squirrels, chipmunks, otter, bunny, lamb, fawn etc.), you wind up with 36 percent who longed for a life without obligations. And yes, many times the same man chose to be either an oak or a lap dog.

249

Several people who in real, human life are in a managerial, executive position and tell others all day long what to do, would turn into a playful house-dog. Maybe somewhere in their hearts there is a desire to shed all the burdens and trade them for the life of a happy-go-lucky guy.

In any case, I thank all the gentlemen for their thoughts and input. They took the questions quite seriously and possibly understood themselves a little bit better after finding a tree or an animal as an expression of their own character. I am not a psychologist and this was not scientific research, but it was great fun.

Inventing A New Job After the Kids Are Grown

*With Imagination and Hard Work, People
At Any Age Can Come Up With New Ideas*

Donna is dusting the wares in her little souvenir shop. Hardly a customer today. As she works at one of the bottom racks, the door bell gives an energetic jingle. She looks up. There is Jane, a school friend of hers.

"Donna, what are you doing down there?" she giggles.

"Just trying to keep the place clean. It's not easy with all these knickknacks in here and a dusty construction going on outside." She looks at Jane. "You look wonderful, what are you doing these days?"

"You know I'm working now," Jane says. "I'm really happy."

"I thought raising five kids was work enough."

"Oh yes, but now that they're all out of the house, I can do other things."

"Like what?"

"I'm a price checker." Pride is in Jane's voice.

"Aren't we all?"

"M-hm, but I'm checking competitive prices for discount stores. They all sell essentially the same items and they have to know what the competition charges."

"I always thought each store, or each chain, sends its own person to monitor the competitor's prices."

"They had to. Now I'm doing that work and then offer my results to them," Jane explains.

"Isn't that unfair to the consumer?" Donna asks.

"I don't think so. Price checking has been done for a long time. Before I came along, each store had to train a person for the work; it was unprofitable," says Jane.

"What if that one person got sick?"

"That's just it – they were sunk."

"And that's where you come in?" asks Donna. "What if *you* get sick or want a week off?"

"I have two people working for me, have trained them myself and know what they are doing."

"That's wonderful. Wow. Do you use a computer?"

"Oh, sure. We bought a program that fits my needs. Shelley, the younger of my employees, knows how to handle the computer, and if I'm not here, she does that work for me."

"Neat. How many days do you work?"

"That depends on the season. When they change to winter wear, that's in early August, we work seven days a week. We have to go over their entire seasonal inventory."

"What's not seasonal?"asks Donna.

"Housewares, tools, bathroom equipment..."

"I see. So how many days do you work now?"

"Usually three. On the fourth or fifth day, I deliver my results."

"You do that in person or electronically?"

"The four big chains get it electronically – my computer fits right into their system. The smaller stores need their results hand delivered."

A customer is coming into the store to pick up a repaired item. It takes a while. Fortunately Jane has time to wait.

Donna looks at her. "Jane, you are great! You created a service that didn't exist before. That's unique. Who ever heard of anyone inventing a new job – and even after the kids are grown?"

"Not that unique," Jane smiles. "Look at your store here. There are similar shops around, but none is quite like yours. So you have not duplicated anyone's business either. With some imagination and hard work, people at any age can come up with new ideas."

"I started mine as a hobby," Donna says with a happy smile, "but now it's even bringing in some money."

"Hey, look at us gals, fifty-something. We made a new start in life," Jane nearly sings.

"Rah, rah, rah," Donna begins and Jane chimes in as they repeat a cheer from their high school days. They jump up and down, clap their hands...

"Is this the place where I'm supposed to pick up a picture frame?" asks a bewildered male voice. "My wife has ordered one."

As Donna walks to the counter, still a bit out of breath and giggling, the man asks, "What are you ladies celebrating here?"

"Life," says Jane and gives him a radiant smile.

A Second Job For the Fun Of It?

My friend Peggy and her brother Paul like to browse at the farmer's market. They stroll through the aisles, look at the produce, taste samples, buy some exceptional fruit. Inexpensive eye glasses, T-shirts and religious pictures interest them. The scents of strawberries, cheeses, bacon, fresh lemonade and the hot dog stand are so inviting.

At the sausage shop, a mother holds a fussy little boy. While one person weighs bacon for her, an older saleslady gives the kid a slice of salami.

He grabs it eagerly. "More," he demands.

Laughing, the woman hands him another piece. Now he's happy.

"Hey look," says Peggy. "Isn't that Shirley? How come she's selling cold cuts here?"

"Hey, Beautiful, since when are ya working here?" asks Paul. "Didn't I see ya just a few days ago at ChemPro?" (Not the company's real name.)

"Hi, Peggy. Hello, Paul," she says. "I've been coming here for nearly a year now."

"Why, ain't ya working hard enough as chief telephone operator? There must be more 'n 300 extensions at your place."

"Can you wait a bit? I'll take my lunch break; we can go outside and talk."

A little later, all three take a sandwich and a can of pop and sit down under a large umbrella.

"How's your wife and the grandkids?" Shirley asks Paul.

"They're all growing. The little ones get taller and Mildred gets wider." He laughs. "She's babysitting on Thursdays. That's the day Sis and I come here. Now tell me, why do you need another job? You aren't running out of money, are you?"

"No, Paul, it isn't the money, although it helps. The main reason I'm here once a week is to keep my sanity. Then I can stand it there," she points with her head towards the west, "for another few days."

"It's that bad at ChemPro?" he asks.

"Not really bad, at least not worse than usual."

"I thought you liked it there."

She nods. "I do like being a telephone operator and enjoy the contact with people, although I get to know only their voices. But there is a lot of stress."

"What kind of stress?" asks Peggy.

"When customers call ChemPro, they talk to us first and we get most of the complaints. A shipment didn't arrive in time? They gripe at us. The quantity was wrong? We get an earful. No large selection? Guess who hears about it."

"Can't you direct those calls to the people responsible for the error? You don't really know enough about it."

"Peggy, that's just it. People don't want to talk to the person in charge of whatever they need. They just have to let off steam and refuse to speak to someone else. If we do get them to Shipping, they are all sweet and have no complaints. The customers let it all out on us."

"Strange," says Peggy. "Why don't you just hang up on them?"

"It's our policy never to hang up on anyone, although sometimes we put them quietly on 'hold.' When we come back, they still carry on, never aware that for a while no one was listening."

"I always figured you do nothing but connect people," says Paul.

"Wish that were all." Shirley shrugs. "On top of it, they have cut our staff to save expenses, so just two of us work during the daytime. After five in the evening, there is only one operator for the rest of the day and through all of the third shift."

"Only one?" Paul asks. "How can you do that?"

"We get paid for eating on the job, and we are encouraged not to go to the bathroom."

"For eight hours?"

"Can't always do it. But if the only operator is in the washroom, then no one answers the phone."

"And that's why you need another job? Wouldn't just a day off be more restful?" asks Peggy.

"For me it's better if I'm here. At home I'd just stew over the telephone problems. Also, I like this place for several reasons. Although we are under a roof, it's wide open, so I feel free – I see the sky and the grass."

"Oh yeah, at ChemPro you sit in that little cubby hole without windows," says Paul.

"Here it's fun, like that little boy just before," Shirley says.

"You used to farm, didn't you?"

"Farmed all my life till my husband got ill."

"And you are familiar with processed meat?" Peggy asks.

"Sure," agrees Shirley. "I help with the preparation of the sausages, the smoking, the spices and all that. In the morning I set up the counter, wait on customers, chat with them when we aren't too busy, holler for more bologna or corned beef if we are getting low. At the end of the day, I count the money and give it to the boss."

"Quite a change from what you've got to watch for at that phone of yours."

"Yes, Paul," says Shirley. "And the work connects me to my farming past – I love that. Then I can again tolerate ChemPro for a while. When they bug me there, I look forward to my bacon and kielbasa here."

"That's wonderful," says Peggy. "Everybody should have such a 'safety valve.' The other people who work here, are they about your age?"

"Oh no, they all could be my grandchildren. Most customers don't mind. They think I have more experience."

"You do, and that makes you valuable."

"Thanks." Shirley smiles. "I better get back now and see what's going on. Don't you want to try our Dutch loaf? It's delicious."

Paul feels obliged to buy some. "Smells good," he says when she hands him the package. "The wife, she'll like it."

"Tastes good, too. Say hello to your family and next time bring Mildred along." Shirley waves at them.

When they walk out into the sun, Paul shakes his head. "What a woman."

Peggy stops at a fruit stand and carefully thumps a watermelon. "Many people would be better off if they followed her example. Not sit and mope, but get a second job for the fun of it."

Happy In A Nursing Home?

After their kids were grown, our friends, Jane and Henry Simko, had moved to a new home at the Sandusky Bay on the western part of Lake Erie. Her mother had gone with them.

This was my first visit to their new place. On a sunny afternoon with just a few clouds, I turned into the little lane that leads to the lake. Their house is directly on the bay. At the end of the driveway, a Great Blue Heron slowly took off, a stone's throw away. The bay was silvery with just a few little white-caps. The Simko's boat was tied up at the dock, gently rocking.

The back door flung open and Jane rushed out. "Hertha, I didn't hear you coming. You haven't been here long, have you?"

"Just got here. Your Blue Heron there has welcomed me. Is he your personal pet?" I asked.

She laughed. "He hangs around here most of the time and considers us the tenants on his property."

She guided me to the back of the house, to a large patio with a 180 degree view of the bay. In a wheelchair sat her mother, a big smile on her face.

"Grandma Bozic, how are you?" I was surprised to see her so happy.

"Oh, Dr. Hertha," she said, "it has been years since I last saw you." She shook my hand enthusiastically. "You haven't changed a bit."

"Well, you have, and you are looking better than ever." I settled down and we talked about old times, when Jane's oldest was babysitting for my kids.

Jane brought a pitcher of lemonade and joined us.

"What a beautiful place this is," I said.

"Yes," said Grandma Bozic, "and I live just across the bay."

"You do? By yourself?"

259

"No," Grandma said. "I live now in a nursing home. It's just a 20 minute drive from here."

I was afraid I had touched a sensitive subject and didn't know what to say.

"Oh, my section is just assisted living. I'm really happy there," she said.

I looked at Jane with a big question on my face.

"She really is," said Jane. "We are fortunate she likes it there. Since she can't walk at all any more, I wouldn't be able to take care of her. I can't lift her in and out of her chair, in and out of bed, give her a bath. I also work three or four days a week, and she would have to be all alone with nothing to do but watch TV and, maybe, read."

I still felt a little ill at ease. Most old folks fight a nursing home as long as they can, or make their grown children promise they'd never put them there. I admired Mrs. Bozic's silver-blue hair with a rather modern cut.

"Oh, there is a beautician coming once a week. First she wanted to give me curls like all those old women wear, but I found a magazine and told her I wanted that upsweep. Second time around she got it right." Grandma was visibly proud that she had succeeded in making the hairdresser do her bidding.

Jane had an amused smile. "You know, before Mother went into the home, I had to get her a complete new wardrobe; she'd have nothing to do with old bathrobes."

"This skirt and cape look like out of Vogue," I said.

"They nearly are," agreed Jane. "A Penney's variation of a Vogue idea."

"I just want to look groomed when I go to lunch or to one of our socials," said Grandma.

"What are you doing at the socials?" I asked.

"Something different every day," said Mrs. Bozic, and Jane added, "I'll show you their schedule." She went into the house.

Grandma continued, "Every Friday at 1:30 we have poetry reading. A girl from the library comes and reads selections.

260

Last week we had Elizabeth Barrett Browning: 'How do I love thee, let me count the ways.' The week before we had Emily Post."

I sat there with open mouth.

"O yeah," said Jane. "I often take her to lunch on Fridays, but woe be me if she isn't back in time for poetry."

Mrs. Bozic had a coy little smile.

"Is this when Joe Brenner wheels himself over to your side, Mother?"

"We like to discuss the poems afterwards," she said, nearly as an excuse.

"Mom, there is nothing wrong with you having an admirer, someone you can talk to, exchange ideas," smiled Jane.

"He used to teach biology and knows so much about all these waterfowl. We often sit on the veranda and watch them. Joe can name 26 different kinds of geese, 19 species of ducks and all those herons, but he thinks there are some he hasn't seen yet. He is really a bright guy, just can't move his legs."

Jane showed me a schedule of the activities. Church services on Sundays, Bingo on Tuesdays, "Sit and Be Fit" exercises on Wednesdays, 'Sing Along With Kim" on Thursdays, the poetry on Fridays, Saturdays a "Garden Party,' weather permitting; if not, Black Jack.

"Black Jack?" I asked. "I thought they play that in Las Vegas."

"They do," said Jane. "Here they play it for pennies only, but otherwise it's the same. Get to 21 but not beyond. Needs some thinking."

"Well, hello, Hertha," said Henry, Jane's husband. "Sorry to be late."

"That's all right," said Grandma. "This way I could tell her all about Bayview Home."

"Oh yes, she loves that place," said Henry. "Hope I'll be as happy once I'm ready for a nursing home."

****

Jane was preparing to drive Grandma back. Henry was quite handy at getting her out of the chair and into the car, but I saw that Jane couldn't do it by herself.

"See you next week, Beautiful," said Henry and gave Grandma a peck on the cheek.

"Be good," she called back.

I came along for the ride which was short and pretty. At Bayview Home an orderly helped Grandma out.

"I'm so glad I was at Jane's when you came, Mrs. Binder. It was nice to talk to you," she said with a smile and waved.

****

As Jane was driving back, I asked, "Is all that for real? Is she truly happy in that home?"

"Hertha, all that's wrong with my mother is that she can't walk. Her mind works, she hears and sees O.K., and she still has the pleasant, cheerful personality she always had. Over there she feels independent (except for the nurses and aides), has her own life. I visit her at least once a week and usually take her for lunch or for a ride. My brother comes every month. And she is included in all family activities, is with us at all holidays when our kids and grandkids come."

I was quiet for a while. "Then why is there so much complaining about nursing homes?"

"I'm not quite sure, but I believe the main difference between Mother and the unhappy ones is that she is mentally all right. She told you, she's in a section called 'Assisted Living.' People who have lost their ability to think, who can't reason any more, get very little out of all those social programs. These poor souls need some qualified person to take care of them."

"You are actually very lucky. You don't have to feel guilty that your mother is in a nursing home."

"We know we are, but there are several people like Mom who like it at Bayview. It's just like everywhere else. You hear about the folks who complain. The happy ones don't make waves."

We arrived at Jane's house, and Henry was ready with the boat. Before he turned into the lake, he swung around the bay and let us see Bayview from the water. We waved. Maybe Grandma Bozic saw the boat.

Stress – When the Shoe Is On the Other Foot.

While a kid grows up, he provides forever new challenges to the parent: how to calm a colicky baby, how to ease the fear of nursery school, how to hide your own worry when he must stay in the hospital with an injury. Has he practiced the spelling words or the time tables well enough for the test? Might his classmates make fun of his new glasses or braces? Will he feel accepted on the basketball team or in track? How can a mother ease the pain when his first love dumps him?

So many of these hurdles for the youngster are stress for the mother because there is very little she can do to help. She'll rock the baby, she'll talk enthusiastically about nursery school until the kid pulls back at the school's entrance, clings to her and says "Mommie-e-e!" Now what? She has no control whether others are better in sports and is helpless when his girlfriend has enough of him. Whatever Mother then says will just sound hollow.

But there is one event in every youngster's life where he is radiantly happy, and Mother is a nervous wreck, worse than ever before: when he starts to drive.

While he is in the theoretical part of drivers' education, be it commercial or at school, he thinks he discovered truths that his parents can't even guess at. He'll quiz you: what's the speed limit on a freeway, or on a side street in town? What does a yellow flashing light mean, a red one? Numbers on a white rectangular background and on yellow? He'll shake his head in utter disbelief when your answers come promptly. "How come you know that?"

"Hey, I've been driving for 20 years!"

"Does Dad remember the signs, too?"

"Kiddo, every driver is familiar with traffic regulations."

Then come his practical sessions, and he gloats about the mistakes other students in his car had made.

"What did *you* goof up?"

265

"Well, ah, nothing. I did fine." Never was a lie more obvious.

Now a proud possessor of a temporary licence, he wants to drive fast and aggressively all day long. The first Sunday after our oldest, Jeff, had the temporary, my husband sat beside him in the van the better part of the day. When the two of them came home in the afternoon, Tom said, "*You* go somewhere with him. I'm bushed."

"How did it go?" I needed his assurance.

"Not bad," said Tom. "In a few weeks he'll be O.K."

Oh yeah?

Full of apprehension I climbed in on the passenger side.

"Where do you want to go, Mom? The farther, the better." Jeff's eyes were sparkling.

"We could get some milk in town." I had promised myself to keep my mouth shut except for a true emergency, but a gasp escaped me every few minutes.

When we arrived at the store, Jeff gave me a triumphant smile. "See?"

Never in my life had I felt so old. Many of my patients are up in years, a bit incapacitated, and their grown children drive them to my office. Now I was one of that old generation, chauffeured by my young guy.

Of course I thought he drove too far right or too far left, too fast (most of the time) or too slow (at an entrance to a freeway), was sitting too close on the bumper of the car in front or didn't pull up enough at a red light. My stomach hurt, and surely my blood pressure was up.

Gradually, as the weeks went on and there was no accident, I accepted Jeff's driving. You can get used to anything, I guess, but it was a few years before I could relax with him at the wheel. Only when our younger son started to drive, did I feel safe with the older one.

****

One summer, though, our roles were reversed. When Jeff was 18, we visited friends and relatives in Austria. They drive crazy over there. Many Europeans have underpowered cars, so they try to prove their own worth by passing any vehicle, often with only a mile per hour difference in speed. It takes forever. They also habitually pass in blind curves, and cuss all the time about other drivers while making the same mistakes themselves. I had been there before, so I was not surprised.

It was Jeff's first experience with that kind of traffic. "Mom," he said after the first ride. "They can't drive. Did you see ... ?" My aggressive Jeff was scared. So was I, by the way, but I knew what to expect.

But what could we do? Our plans included many trips by car.

"Jeff, if it is our fate to die here in a car crash, we can't change it anyway. So we might as well relax."

We never got really used to the European drivers. (They also have a much higher accident rate than in the United States.) Once my friend's husband, Norm, let Jeff take his car on the Autobahn (similar to our four-lane interstates).

While Jeff was beaming, Norm shook his head. "I didn't think a young guy would drive so slow, staying most of the time under 65 mph. This car does 90 easily." (There is no speed limit on the Autobahn.)

Back in our room, Jeff plopped on the couch. "You know, Mom, it's scary when you see what mistakes the driver makes and you can do nothing about it. I feel stressed out just watching them."

"Oh yeah?" I had to chuckle. "Tell me about it."

"What do you mean? You had no control when I started to drive?"

Putting my hand on his shoulder I said, "Well, dear, the stress of *your* driving is over now, and as far as the Europeans go – we'll be out of here in a few days."

Be A Volunteer!

So you sit in the living room of your new apartment, unhappy to the core. This place looks so cold. The walls are just painted, in light tan at that. No pattern. You miss your nice blue wall paper with the roses on it. And the window sills! They are aluminum. Ever heard of that? Why couldn't they be some comfortable, worn, brown wood like in the old house?

Your Early American rocking chair and your paisley drapes are as out of place as you are.

You miss your garden. They said you couldn't take care of it any more; you were sick from the heat and got a sore back from weeding. Your own kids, both grown now, said you couldn't keep up the house after Bob was gone. What did they know, living two hundred miles away?

After two years of discussions and arguing, you had given in. The kids were very helpful in moving you here, even eager to get you out of the old place. Now you sit here and have nothing to do. No one needs you. Life isn't worth living any more. It couldn't be much worse.

"Senior Haven" they call this place. Yeah. Those folks are seniors all right. But you are not, darn it; soon you will be though, with nothing to do and nothing to look forward to.

Well, what's the use? You decide to go out for a few groceries. At least you can still drive your car and don't have to go on that dumb bus.

When you want to cross the lobby, they are all sitting there, some social gathering, with big labels "Hello, my name is ... " sticking to their chests. You can't even get through. Someone corners you, "What's your name?"

"Adah Kostic."

"Oh, I live just two doors down the hall from you. I'm in 615. You are in 611, aren't you?"

"Yes, I am," you admit. How does she know?

269

That 615 lady sticks a label with 'Adah' in big letters on your coat. Now you are being branded.

"Why don't you sit over here with me," says 615, "so we can chat. My name is Mary."

You don't really want to be here at all, much less chat.

Mary, however, talks and talks. About her grandchildren, about her quilts and most of all about her volunteer work at the Hillside Hospital. "Why don't you come and volunteer, too? They are so short on help," Mary insists.

" ... ?" You don't quite know what to say, so Mary grabs you by the arm and nearly pushes you out the door and into her car.

"But how do I get started?" you finally get in edgewise.

"We'll first go to Carol Hudac; she's the director of volunteers."

"What do you do as a volunteer?"

"Some of us transport patients, take them in a wheelchair to X-ray or wherever they have to go."

"What else?"

"Some are at the information desk. You'd probably want to know the hospital a bit better till you do that."

"Oh sure."

"We are needed in the cafeteria and some of us are water ladies."

"What's a water lady?"

"Patients need fresh drinking water every day. We take care of that, fill their pitchers with ice water. The head nurse will give a list who shouldn't get any."

"No water?" you wonder.

"Yeah; before surgery or before certain tests they can't have it."

You have arrived at Carol Hudac's office. She seems to be a person who loves the whole world, bubbling over with contagious eagerness. She gives you a form to fill out. Name, address, work experience. It's not hard to do. "Adah, could you start today?" she asks. "We are short three people." With a winning smile she hands you a pink apron.

You feel shanghaied, but – be honest – you didn't really object much either.

After a few more introductions and instructions, there you are, pushing a cart with water pitchers from room to room, checking that the name on the bed matches the one on the jug. Patients are either asleep or talk on the phone or look too sick to be bothered. Not much contact.

In room E 26, though, there is a 10-year-old girl with a leg in traction. That looks awesome.

"Doesn't that hurt?" you blurt out.

"No," she says. "It's better when the leg is up." She seems quite brave. "You are new here, aren't you?" she asks.

"Yes," you admit. "I was kind of pushed into doing this. Here's your fresh water. Want me to fill your cup?"

"Yes, please," she says. "What's your name? You don't have a name tag yet."

"Adah. What's yours?"

"Beth Streszynsky. It's written there at the end of the bed." She points to a label.

You study the spelling and then look at her. "How did your leg get hurt?"

"I fell on the ice and slipped under a car. It just started. He didn't see me, so he rolled over my leg. It's broke into seven pieces."

"How much longer do you have to stay here?"

"Only one more week; it'll be four weeks altogether."

"My, that's a long time." You straighten up the water pitchers on your cart. "I have to take this water now to all the other patients ..."

"Come back again. I have no one to visit me," Beth says in a whisper.

"No one?"

271

"My dad comes twice a week, but the other days he visits my mom. She needs him more."

"Where is she?"

"In the University Hospital downtown. It's the best place."

"Why is your mommy there?" Aren't you digging too deeply into people's private lives?

"She has a lump in her head, in her brain. Dad told me it's that lump that makes Mommy act so weird. But she'll be better when they cut out that lump tomorrow. Maybe like she was before."

"Where do you live?"

"In the pink house, right after the light on Route 69. I bet you've seen my house."

"I don't know. I've just moved here."

A nurse comes in. "That's a good girl," she says. "You finished your whole lunch." Then she arranges the pillows.

You quietly leave the room and go to the rest of "your" patients.

Mary takes you home. "I'm so glad you came along. We need all the help we can get."

****

Next time at the hospital you distribute your water with a friendly smile to each of the patients. There isn't much conversation.

Then you come to E 26. You have thought a lot about Beth the last two days. Today she is out of bed and has crutches. She carefully takes a few hops. "They'll take me to physical therapy now, so I can learn how to walk with these things."

"I bet you'll be really good with them," you say. That leg looks so short, and you wonder whether the kid will ever be able to walk again. You take a bag from the bottom shelf of your cart and hand it to Beth. "For you."

She takes it with hesitant surprise, looks in and then squeals with delight. "A Raggedy Ann! Oh, I've always wanted one. It's lovely! Thank you so much." She quickly turns, bangs you on the shin with her crutch and nearly falls over. You catch her. That's almost a hug, you think, and Beth presses her head to your shoulder.

You hesitate, want to ask about her mother, don't know how to. "Beth, do you have any brothers or sisters?"

"Yes, Jim. He's much older than me. He's in the Air Force. Last Christmas he was home, but I haven't seen him since."

"Did you hear from your dad?"

"Oh yes, he was here last night. He told about Mommy. She can already talk a little, he said. And she and me will get home about the same time."

"That'll be great," you say. "Then I won't see you again, Beth. I wish you and your mom get well real soon."

"Oh, Adah, please come and visit. Please!"

"Your dad and mom might not like that; they'll be too busy."

"Oh no; they'll like it, I know."

"All right then, I'll visit you next week," you say, but you don't think you will.

"Promise?"

"Promise." You can't remember that you have ever lied so deliberately.

Beth gives you a radiant smile. "See you next week at my house. Remember, the pink one after the light on 69." She hugs the Raggedy Ann.

****

At home you wonder. Beth's family clearly has troubles. Mrs. Hudac had said, don't get involved. You don't even know Beth's parents. The mother is probably very sick, and the father might be grumpy with all his problems.

273

When you go for an errand, you take a detour over 69. Which traffic light did Beth talk about? Oh, there is only one, and right after it is a pink little house. That must be where Beth lives. You drive slowly past.

****

Next time you do your water run, Beth is gone. You hurry today with your duties and leave an hour earlier. As if a force were guiding you, you find yourself on 69. What are you doing here? Then you stop in the driveway of the pink house. An old pickup stands there. The grass needs mowing; the porch could use some paint. Slowly you get out of the car. Do you have the right to be here? Then you see Beth smiling in the window.

"I knew you'd come, I knew it. I told Dad about you." She turns to the back of the room, "Dad, Adah is here; I told you she'd come."

A man, about 40, comes from the kitchen. "Hi," he says. "Kid told me a lot about you."

"Will you stay, where are you going?" Beth is all excited.

"I'll pick up some groceries," you say. "Just wanted to see how you are doing."

"Can I come with you, please?"

You both look at the father. Will he agree?

"It's O.K. by me if you get the crutches in your car. I won't be here when you get back; have to work second shift this week."

As you and Beth are already in the door, he says, "Here's two bucks, Beth; bring some orange juice. Mom is supposed to have a lot of it."

Beth is surprisingly good at getting into the car. You are both quiet.

The shopping goes rather easy. Beth holds on to the shopping cart and hops along swiftly. "That's fun," she grins.

You pick up your things and help Beth with the orange juice.

At the checkout counter the crutches get stuck, and someone asks concerned, "How did your granddaughter get hurt?"

"She isn't ... " you start and see Beth's earnest, big eyes. "I mean, she wasn't paying attention, and a car ran over her leg."

In the car Beth whispers, " 'Your granddaughter,' he said."

You gently put your hand on hers.

When you get to the pink house, you hold the door open and help Beth carry in the orange juice. Then you look and freeze in your steps: on the couch rests a woman with a shaved head, a pale face and big dark circles under half closed eyes.

"Hi," you say, unsure of yourself.

She doesn't answer.

"Oh, Mom, Adah took me to the store. Here's your juice."

The mother says in a monotonous voice, "Come back again; Beth likes you."

You promise you will and gently close the door behind you.

****

Next Thursday you are at the Streszynsky house again.

Beth is waiting for you. She hops towards you and gives you a hug. Just like that. "I knew you'd come," she says.

Her mother's hair has grown a little, but that's the only improvement you can notice. She seems paler and thinner than last time and has trouble breathing. You wonder how a 10-year-old can stand the depressing atmosphere.

Beth picks up fifty dollars from the kitchen table and a piece of paper.

"What's that?" you ask.

"Dad said maybe we could pick up some groceries for us, too, if you don't mind."

"Take rye bread and two percent milk," the mother says feebly.

"O.K., Mom."

"Well, let's go than," you say, glad to be out again.

When the shopping is done, and you are back in the car, Beth asks, "Where do you live?"

"In that tall building; many people live there."

"Do they have a playground?"

"I'm afraid not; the place is mostly for old folks."

"Like you?"

You hesitate. "Yes. Even older than I am."

"Could I come with you and see it?"

"Now? Won't your mother worry?"

"She doesn't know time. It makes no difference when I get back."

"We can't stay too long, though, or your groceries will spoil."

"No. Just a little while."

Beth is impressed by the building. She's delighted with the elevator.

"Haven't you been on an elevator before?"

"There's one in our school, but we're not supposed to ride it."

Once in your apartment, Beth is amazed. "It's so high up, and you can see so far! And look at these beautiful windows. Are the frames silver? I didn't think windows can be that pretty." She strokes the walls. "They feel smooth like silk in a fairytale. Not like ours with all those old flowers on." Beth takes it all in as if it were a dream castle.

"We ought to go now," you say softly, "but I hope you'll come back."

Another hug is her answer.

****

Next Tuesday at 10 p.m. you get a phone call "This is Stan Streszynsky. Are you Adah?"

"Yes, I am. What can I do for you?"

"We got your phone number from the hospital. First they didn't want to tell us. Only when I said we need you, did they give it to me."

"You need me?"

"You see, you can't go for groceries with Beth this Thursday."

"Oh?"

His voice is wavering. "Her mom, she died this morning, and the funeral is on Thursday. Beth wants you to come to the wake." He clears his throat. "You don't know us, hardly; maybe you don't want to come. It's a closed casket, ... " He blows his nose. "... just a few people. Beth has taken such a liking to you; hope you could come."

You are glad he is rumbling on, so you don't have to speak. But when he stops, you say quietly, "I'm so sorry for you all. Where's the funeral home?"

"It's at Kelly's. Just two blocks from the hospital."

"I'll be there. Give Beth my love."

"You know," he says, "Beth and me, we don't even know your last name. That's funny, ain't it?"

"Kostic," you say. "Adah Kostic."

"So you are from the old country too," he says.

"My parents were," you agree, "and my husband."

****

The service at the funeral home is simple and dignified. Interment will be at a later time, after the cremation.

You put your hand on Beth's shoulder.

She blinks back tears as she looks up to you. "The preacher, he said Mom is in heaven now. Do you think her hair has grown back again, and she can talk and smile?"

You nod. "Yes."

"And he said she'll be happy there. She wasn't happy here since the operation; I know that."

When nearly everyone has left, Stan Streszynsky says, "Mrs. Kostic, you've been so good to Beth. I wonder whether we could ask you ... "

"?" You raise your brows.

"You see, school starts in two weeks. When she gets home, I'm still at work and I don't want her to be no latch key kid if I can help it."

"The bus could drop me off at your place," says Beth.

" ... and I'd pick her up when I get off work."

"When's that?"

"I'd be there 'bout 4:30."

"What if you work second shift?"

"I won't be on second shift no more. Talked already to the foreman. He has kids too; he understands."

What should you say? There stands this man, stricken by his fate. There is Beth, her eyes fixed on you without wavering. What else can you do but agree.

****

Soon the first day of school is here. You wait for the bus in front of the building. Beth hops out, swinging her crutches in triumph. "You didn't have to wait down here. I could'a come up the elevator myself."

"Tomorrow you can do that. I just wanted to make sure everything went O.K. today."

Beth again takes in the "beauty" of the apartment. "Now I can be here for an hour and a half every day we have school," she says in a whisper. "And all that because I broke my leg."

You just smile.

Then she says, "You know what? Miss Kellner, the bus driver, she said they wouldn't let me out at a stranger's house, so I told her you are my grandmother."

"You did?" What else is that kid all going to do? "Want a glass of milk?"

"Yes, please," she smiles. "Yes, Grandma."

****

Next week you bump into Mary in the hallway. "Who comes on the school bus every day?" she asks.

"Beth. Her mother just passed away, so she stays here till her father picks her up."

"She has a bad leg?"

"That's how I met her in the hospital on my water rounds. I'm so glad you talked me into that. I feel needed again."

Mary smiles. "It's good for all of us who work there."

Enjoying A New Game

The ping-pong table was my husband's idea. He got it for our eight-year-old grandson, Chuck. Of course, the kid is at our house only once a week, so the rest of the time Tom and I are whacking away at the little balls. The last time we played was probably 15 years ago, when our kids were at the ping-pong age.

Never having been particularly good at it, we are pretty pathetic now. However, we find it a lot of fun. Tom tries "trick-shots" all the time, while I am satisfied if I can place the ball out of his reach. More often, I'm happy if I just get it properly over the net – that is on a good day 50 percent of the time.

You might wonder what's so great about that ping-pong, or table tennis.

This little activity has many features. It is something that we can do together. Sure, we consult often in our professional as well as personal life. But here we both laugh about funny shots; say, he still gets the ball to my side after it hit the ceiling. That requires a giggle-break. Ping-pong is a very fast game, even if you play it slowly. You really have to react fast. It also keeps you moving quite a bit. The heart rate clearly goes up, so it can be considered an aerobic sport. Yes, I know, other activities require more exertion, but this one is not for slouches either.

Ping-pong is quite stimulating. In the morning, we can skip our cup of coffee in exchange for half an hour of table tennis. The activity wakes us up just as well. If we play in the evening, it does not keep us unduly awake afterwards.

Now, my husband never wanted to play any games with me where one wins and the other loses, such as tennis or chess. He says I compete enough with him in medicine and claims that I always want to win. I have no comment. This is the reason, however, that in ping-pong we do not play games or sets, we just hit the balls back and forth enjoying any skillful placement.

Another factor of table tennis is the need to pick up the balls from the floor. Stooping down after every one of them makes me dizzy, so we fill our pockets with balls and then play. When all the balls are used up, we pick them up – a different exercise.

Why do I tell this? It is not to brag that two grey-haired folks play some lousy ping-pong. It is to show that we have fun with rather simple and modest things. The folding table can be stored in a utility room and does not interfere with our daily activities.

Of course, when Chuck comes, we all play, sometimes as a foursome with his dad. To encourage the child, we try to play the balls right to him. That turns out to be just as difficult as placing them out of reach of another partner.

In short, table tennis gives us a chance for another physical and mental activity, revs up our heart rate and "clears out" the coronaries. It makes us laugh a lot, a fact that should not be underestimated, and it is a new "toy" for Chuck – *his* ping-pong set.

Do *you* have an old ping-pong table in the basement or in the barn? Why don't you drag it out, dust it off, buy new paddles and balls and use the thing? It is neither immoral, illegal nor fattening – just an activity that gets you off the couch and the TV for a while. Don't worry, you'll catch up with the gossip in plenty of time. You will be surprised how good it feels to be laughing about such unimportant things as a missed ball.

Go to it! Have fun!

Don't Get Frustrated

Two years ago you were on that long awaited Caribbean cruise and although you had enjoyed it and admired the many sights, you had been a bit disappointed that there was not enough time at any one port. This applies to all vacations: there is never enough time.

This year, you've planned to fly to Nassau and stay there all six days. You want to take it all in, the night-clubs, the shops, the market, the restaurants.

You want to stay on the beach and get a tan, or relax with a drink beside the pool. Of course you want to sample also all the beach activities, rent a gentle pedal boat and watch the crazy guys water skiing, parasailing or windsurfing. Maybe you are in good enough shape to be "crazy" yourself and try one of those sports again.

Tourists can take a ride in a glass bottom boat from which one can see the famous reef and at the same time watch people snorkeling.

As long as you can remember, you have wanted to go deep sea fishing. This is the year you'll do it. You can already picture in your mind that snapshot with you and an eight-foot-long sailfish.

You know that you can rent a bicycle, a tandem or a motor scooter. What a wonderful way to explore the island. There are tennis courts right beside the beach with a refreshing breeze, and the brochure from your hotel shows a well-equipped weight room.

Of course you can't miss the casino a short walk or bike ride over on Paradise Island. You won't risk too much money, you are not a gambler, but for a while you'd like to try it. Maybe you are lucky and win back what you've spent there.

Before you even leave home, sit back and think a bit. All those activities are interesting and fun, but you won't have enough time to do them all.

In no other six days of the year have you tried to cram so many activities. And why do you expect to accomplish all these things? Because the brochures of the island list them in an alluring way. Many things will have to remain undone. You'll be frustrated again.

So, you'll have to decide (best before you leave home) what your priorities are. If you want to partake vigorously in all the beach activities, you ought to cut out much of the partying; if you crawl out of bed at 11 with a hangover, you'll get seasick when on a boat fishing or watching the reef.

If you want to enjoy the nightlife, fine. But don't plan on the vigorous sports. Maybe shuffleboard will suit you better.

You get the drift.

This doesn't mean you can't change your plans as you go along. If you meet a congenial couple and want to join them, fine. Drop one of your planned activities and enjoy the company of your new acquaintances. But be aware that you've changed your plans.

****

If you are on that vacation with your spouse or significant other, remember that your companion might want to do different things. Discuss what you plan to do, and consider that you don't always have to be together. Maybe one wants to do some shopping, and the other goes deep sea fishing. So you go your own ways for a few hours. Later, you'll have dinner together and a walk on the moonlit beach.

Contributing to the charm of these islands is the easy going, laid back attitude of the locals. They have a soothing, balmy attitude.

Should you be in a hurry, though, such as signing in or out at the hotel or wanting to get to your safe deposit box, and there are six people in front of you and only one leisurely clerk, you with your northern rush-rush attitude, might not enjoy it so much. Be prepared, it goes with the territory.

****

The same principles of planning too many activities for the limited time apply of course to other vacations as well. When in the mountains, there is climbing, rafting, horseback riding, swimming, taking a cable car, sight seeing, you name it. Or a winter vacation with downhill or cross country skiing, snow boarding, NASTAR races, snowmobiling, demo skis, sleigh rides and ice skating.

A vacation in the city poses the same problems. Can you list all the possible sights to see in Washington, D.C.? It takes you half a day just to write them all down.

****

Your vacation can be all you have hoped for if you are aware of your time limits. Plan your days, change your schedule if needed, know what you'll do should it rain for a few hours. You'll come home with memories that'll last you for the rest of your life, and there will be no feeling of frustration. It was just a wonderful week.

You Don't Have To Be A Kid To Fly A Kite

Two weeks ago, my husband brought home a beautiful kite. Made of woven nylon, it had two wide wings and an extra piece reaching down, like a rudder on a boat.

I had never been able to get a kite into the air. Our grandson Chuck and Tom, however, with their masculine traits, knew just how to make it fly. For about an hour, they were in the backyard, proudly watching it soar.

When they took the kite down, though, a sudden gust of wind yanked it towards the trees, and in spite of excited running and yelling, the kite got hung up on a tiny branch. No way to reach it. After a while of strategic considerations, Grandpa cut the line. He and Chuck came sadly into the house, just before a downpour started.

"Bye, kite." Chuck waved at it when he left.

****

For a week the kite didn't move. However on Sunday, I saw that it had slipped quite a bit. With a ladder Tom and I could get it down. It wasn't even damaged.

"Chuck will be happy," I said.

Tom nodded. "It's such perfect weather today – sunny and a light breeze. I'd like to fly it now." He was tying the string back on.

"Hey, neat."

Twice he tossed it in the air – twice it fell back down. The third time, though, it went up with a big lurch, rose erratically until it was above roof and trees, and then soared steadily.

"Just hold on." Tom handed me the spool with the thin nylon string. "I'll get some gloves. If you like, you can let out more rope."

287

I was a bit hesitant at first and just held still. Then I felt the steady pull and let out a few feet of line. The kite rose more sharply when I pulled hard. Soon I got the hang of it and sat down leaning against a tree. There was a teasing give and take between the kite and me. Supported by the air current, it seemed to assume a personality of its own. It was as if I had found a new friend.

Suddenly tires squealed on the road, loud voices at the neighbor's, slammed car doors. I turned and looked. Lots of laughter. Someone had missed the driveway.

When I turned back to my kite, it bounced and wiggled. I held a loose piece of rope in my hand. The long line was dragging on the ground, the spool spun like crazy. I ran frantically after it, nearly caught it, lost it, stumbled. Finally the rope got tangled in a shrub. I freed it and yanked on it to make sure the kite behaved.

When I looked up, it waved in the sunlight, changing reflections as if it were winking at me. Pesky little piece of nylon!

Flustered, I walked back to my tree and sat down again.

Tom came back out. "Here are gloves so the rope won't cut your hands."

I only grunted.

"How come you are out of breath just sitting here?" he asked.

Not wanting to admit my fumble, I just said, "How quiet the kite is now."

"Always is when it's high up. Look, you can see the whole length of the rope when it gleams in the sun."

After a while I asked, "Want to take it down?"

"Might as well." Easier said than done.

We couldn't just roll up the spool. The pull of the kite was much too strong. So I reached up as high as I could, four feet at a time, pulling down the thin rope with my gloved hand. It was quite an exercise to haul all of the 250 feet back in. Tom got sore wrists winding it onto the spool.

When we had it halfway down, a neighbor stopped by. "Beautiful weather to fly a kite," she said. "Is Chuck with you today?"

"Oh no," I said. "Today we dared to have fun without the excuse of a kid."

She laughed. "You are getting independent now, aren't you? More power to you!"

Thoughts On the Death Of A Young Man

Betty's 19-year-old son, Jack, was killed last week. Now the funeral was over, the flowers had been sent to hospitals, the crowds of relatives and friends have dispersed. His class mates were stunned. He was one of them, how could he be gone when they were still here?

Jack's father called me, "Hertha, could you come over some time? Betty needs you. You have gone through the same ordeal, so we thought you could help."

I promised to be there tomorrow.

What could I tell them? How could I ease their agony?

****

Slowly, maybe in a year, the pain will lose its sting, will become more dull. It won't be a knife in your heart, rather a lead brick on your chest, forever. When you think of it, it will always be there, but at times current events might block it out for an hour or half a day. The wound will heal, the scar will stay forever.

****

We all dream at times what our future will hold and worry what life will bring. The death of a child is never included in these thoughts. Oh yes, others have lost a child, but that can't ever happen to us. Not at the end of the 20th century with vaccines, antibiotics and seat-belts. No. That possibility does not exist.

Therefore, we are so totally unprepared for this blow. We all know that we'll have to bury our parents; that's the course of life. We have a 50 percent chance to mourn our spouse. Tough, but it can't be helped. But a child – never. It's against nature.

291

Where would life be if children died before their parents? There would be no future.

****

But some children do die; look at the statistics. Read obituaries and see how many are survived by heir elders. The reasons are many – the numbers are high.

****

Imagine you had met a fairy 20 years ago who said, "I'll let you decide your own future. But after you have chosen, you'll forget that I had ever asked you."

"What choices do I have?" you asked trembling.

"You can have a child, healthy, bright, the joy of the entire family who will grow up to be a fine young man. But when he is 19, he'll die. This will bring you great sorrow."

"What other choice do I have?" you asked.

"Not to have the child," said the fairy. "No joy, no pain."

"Oh, I want the child, dear Fairy. Nineteen whole years of happiness, who would want to miss them?"

"Your wish will come true," she said.

****

If you can cry, then cry. If you want to talk, grab someone and tell him all your sorrows. Let your woe pour out, it's better than to hold it in.

Avoid places that will remind you of Jack, find a new vacation spot. If in years past you went sailing and swimming, take up a new hobby now, learn to play tennis. On the lake you would always see his face surface from the water or his figure rig the sails.

****

In the more distant future, you'll be able to look at old pictures with love, show them to friends like the ones of your parents. This is my mother in her garden. This is my son before a canoe trip. Both will be cherished memories without a sting. But that time is yet several years away.

****

If your daughter should have a child, DON'T let her call him Jack. The grandchild will anyway remind you forever of your son, because family resemblance will be strong. It would be cruel to put the burden of the same name on you. Tell your daughter that as soon as you know she is pregnant.

****

Be aware what you are mourning now. It is the end of a young life, the dashed hopes of a future. But don't forget to be thankful for all the joy and happiness Jack has brought you. All life has a beginning and has an end. The timing is not ours to decide.

****

The wound will heal, the scar will stay forever.

Hertha Binder

The Joys And Pains Of Motherhood

*For the sake of clarity, I'll call the child "he" and the
mother "she." Benjamin Spock did this in his book
on child care. In no way does this imply that girls
are less precious, less welcome or less troublesome*

Being a mother is a life-long commitment. The mother's
love is boundless, self-sacrificing if the need arises and lasts
until her death. Our children can never fully make up for the
endless hours of toil and worry, but we didn't repay our mothers
either. The continual encouragement we give our children
borders sometimes on the inane. Have you ever watched a little
kid jumping into a one foot deep pool? After the first hop, he
looks at his mother for approval.

She beams. "Wow, you jumped! That was really brave.
Want to try it again?"

The mother's enthusiasm coaxes him on. Another little
splash. "Did you see me, Mommie?"

What else? "Sure! You were great." She smiles and claps
her hands, absorbed in watching him. The kid's performance is
repeated 30 times. His eagerness increases, he splashes now
more, so the mother gets a bit wet. She plays scared, and he is
delighted as if he were getting even with her. For what? For
overcoming his fear?

Finally, the child stumbles a bit and for a moment dips his
face in the water. Instantly, mother is there, picks him up, pats
him on the back, caresses and reassures him. An onlooker might
have judged the mother's enthusiasm excessive, but she knows
that for the little one an emotional basis has been formed to
become a good swimmer or diver later on. He has learned that
water is to be enjoyed and mastered, an important lesson for life.

While the child is young, the relationship includes much busy work such as feeding, cleaning, washing, playing and listening to a whiny "Mommie," a resolute "No!" and an insistent "Why?" a hundred times a day. The mother's reward is a happy smile, a sleepy snuggle or a sweet smell after his bath.

Animal mothers are known for their patience with the offspring, their endurance and sacrifice in defending the young. A mother bird will imitate a broken wing making her appear helpless and easy prey for a marauding cat. This way she'll lure the aggressor far from the chicks and keep them safe. A mother goose will scare away an approaching fox. Wings flapping, hissing, neck stretched forward, she'll protect her brood while risking her own life. The patience of a lioness seems inexhaustible as she lets the young ones tumble over her while pulling her tail and ears and then she licks them affectionately.

But mothering does become wearisome. The Carners, our neighbors, live about 300 yards away. Their pleasant dog, Penny, had one litter after another. The two youngest Carner children often came over to play with ours, and their dogs came along to romp with our pets. I remember one summer's day. All the kids, our dogs and the male Carner dog had gone with my husband to the woods for some adventures. I stayed behind, sitting in the quiet yard with a good book. It was so pleasantly still. There came Penny, slowly walking up to me.

"Oh, you missed the others," I said. "They are in the field now, probably chasing a rabbit."

She seemed to understand me, but didn't run after them. Slowly she sat down in the shade beside me, sighed deeply and put her head on the front paws. In no bouncy mood, she just needed a rest. We two mothers were glad to be left alone for a while. After about 20 minutes, we could hear one of her pups squeak. Penny didn't move. When the squeals became more frequent, she raised an ear and turned towards me.

"Yes," I said. "They are calling you. Hungry again."

She stood up in slow motion as if not able to raise herself and with hesitation walked toward her house. By the edge of our yard, she stopped, turned and gave me one half-hearted wag of her tail.

"I know," I said to her. "They wear you out."

As the squealing became louder and more insistent, she left without turning back. Five minutes later, the pups were quiet. Mother had arrived.

As a child grows older, he wants to assert himself. In theory, the mother likes that. In practical terms, it means that mother and child disagree. If she says, "Time to go to sleep," he protests, "I wanna play." If she suggests, "Have a bath," he objects, "Me not dirty." But should she have the presence of mind to say, "Let's play," he might counter, "Read me a story," and snuggle up. – "Tonight, I'm too tired to give you a bath," – "Whaaaaa! I wanna play with my rubber ducky and the boat." Aha; success.

When Pete, our oldest, was about five, the Kennedy-Nixon debates were on. While sitting sideways in the bathtub so as to face me better, he asked, "Mom, which one will you vote for?"

I wasn't convinced that either candidate would be a great president. Neither did I want the kid to tell the whole school about his parents' political preference.

"Well, Mommie, who?"

"Oh, I guess I'll vote for Nixon."

"And who'll Dad vote for?"

"I suppose, he'll do the same."

Pete braced his feet against the rim of the bathtub and said with conviction, "Well, I want Kennedy!"

I was sure he would have "wanted Nixon" if my husband and I had voted for Kennedy.

As the youngster grows, he doesn't need as much of his mother's time, but he occupies her thoughts just as much. Now come confrontations about hairstyle (don't worry, it'll grow out again or can be cut), about clothes and the choice of friends.

297

Instead of saying, "Clean your room," have you ever tried piling your own trash in front of his door? Old magazines and discarded clothes might do. Maybe he'll show his difference by keeping his side of the door orderly. You never know. Still, the mother's love is there, maybe not as visible as in earlier years. It bursts forth if the child becomes ill or gets into trouble. Any note from a teacher that he's not doing well will make the mother think that the teacher is no good. Must be so.

Then he is grown up. If everything goes well, the mother basks in his success as if it were her own. (In a sense, it is.) She is proud of the responsibilities he carries at work, grudgingly acknowledges the good sides of his spouse, adores and spoils the grandchildren. The mother's love is easy now.

But what if things don't go well? What is he dies of a disease? Might he have inherited it from her? What if he is killed in a car accident? Should she have offered another cup of coffee, loaned him the money for a better car?

What if he turns out to be a less than perfect person? The bright kid can't hold down a decent job. The youngster who had been taught morals with so much care, committed a crime. What is his mother to make of that? Don't forget, every criminal has a mother who had the highest expectations for him. Even after bitter disappointment, there is still love in the mother's heart, a longing that things will get better and that she'll have another chance to put her arm around him. A hope for a smile that says, "Hi, Mom. We've been through a lot. Thanks. I love you."

Then the mother's heart can rest in peace.

Part   IV

Long Ago

Hertha Binder

Part IV   Long Ago

Contents

An American Wedding

You are upset about the little glitches at your daughter's wedding? The pews didn't have matching flowers, and the organist started much too late with "Here Comes the Bride ... ?" Let me tell you about our big day; that was one big glitch in four acts.

After a six year engagement over in Europe, Tom left for the United States – alone. Once he found a place for me to work (no visa in those days without your own financial support), I came over. That's why some of our friends call me a mail-order bride.

Seasick and worn out, I arrived in New York on Columbus Day, October 12, 1954. One day later, we got our marriage licence in Manhattan, where Tom lived. There was no family here at all, just the two of us. We had to find some witnesses.

During the months before I came, Tom had a friend and co-worker. Helga was her name – tall, blond. I guess she wasn't too interested in him because she was all enthusiastic about being my maid of honor. She lived in Hoboken; that is on the other side of the Hudson River, in New Jersey. Tom had gone to church there with her. He planned that we would get married in the same church by Pastor Norden.

As best man, Tom had lined up a guy from the lab where he worked, I think, but on the morning of the wedding day the man told Tom that he had an exam in some evening class. If he didn't take it, he would lose the whole semester. Tom told me he wasn't sure whether he could find another best man. I cried about the problem to our landlady, Mrs. Rehfeld, who catered kosher food for Jewish social functions. Her husband worked in a pawn shop in the next block, a stocky man with a round face; he was just home for lunch. Mr. Rehfeld offered to come along as a witness.

"You can't do that, Moshe," said Mrs. Rehfeld. "How can you go to a Christian service, you, a cantor in the temple?"

"That won't matter. They want a witness, not my religion."
So it was settled.

The ceremony was set for six in the evening because Tom had to work. About two in the afternoon the pastor called. He couldn't marry us in his church because it was in New Jersey, and our licence was from New York. We thought the United States was one country and the laws were the same all over.

Pastor Norden knew a way out, though. He'd drive from his church to Staten Island, part of New York State. There he could "borrow" a church from the pastor, a friend of his. We should follow him.

Helga had a car and drove. Tom was on the passenger seat, Mr. Rehfeld with a skull cap and I were in the back. When we got to Hoboken, there was great excitement. Norden wanted to take his family along to Staten Island to visit friends, but one of his three kids was missing. They couldn't find him, and his mother was all upset.

The boy showed up after about 20 minutes – dirty, grinning, surprised. They had to clean him up which took some more time.

Now I was getting nervous! But then I thought I had waited six years – another hour would not make any difference. Or maybe fate wanted to tell me that this union was not supposed to be.

We were following the Nordens from Hoboken to Staten Island, probably fifteen miles. This was in New York's evening rush hour, even going over toll bridges. Helga had no idea where we would wind up.

Our only connection were the three Norden boys. They were looking out the back window – that was long before seat belts – and told their dad when he was about to lose us.

We did make it. Norden's family drove off. I got out of the car with as much decorum as I could and slowly walked towards the church. The others had gone ahead. Big surprise. The church was locked! Back door too. So Norden took Helga's car and went to his pastor-friend's house for the key.

We didn't dare to think what would happen if that guy wasn't home. Tom checked whether we couldn't get in through the windows, but they were closed too.

Mr. Rehfeld shook his head and mumbled, "Those goyim aren't very organized, are they?"

I forced a smile.

The pastor finally showed up, triumphantly waving the key, but our troubles were not over yet. The key fit, but nobody could find a light switch in the whole church. There was light in the basement; we could get married there, someone suggested. Now, in Europe most churches are about 900 years old, and the basements are like catacombs, old burial places with spider webs. I did not want to get married there, but Helga explained that this basement was a friendly room used for social functions. "O.K.," I said, but just then someone found the light switch behind the altar.

Tom and I got over our memorized words of "plight thee troth ... " all right, and we were man and wife. Mr. Rehfeld took a few snapshots of us.

Afterwards, I was anxious to see what the witnesses were signing, but I thought it improper to look. Only in the car, on the way to a restaurant, did I see the certificate. It had the wrong date! The date from the next day! Now was I married or not?

At this point, Helga was very helpful. She said emphatically that she had witnessed the wedding, so it was legal.

Mr. Rehfeld claimed he had to get to his temple. He was probably afraid he'd have to eat something not kosher. Without further ado, we let him out at the next subway station. When we had finished dinner (Helga had even brought a cake with candles), the three of us went to Radio City Music Hall for a show. Afterwards she drove us home.

In the stairway of the apartment building, I found that I had forgotten the keys. We did not think the Rehfelds would hear the doorbell at two in the morning, so we sat down on the steps. Would we have to spend the night there? After a while I rang the bell anyway, and the door opened instantly. Mr. Rehfeld said with a big smile, "We had seen your keys on the dresser, so I waited up for you."

It had been a long day. We both were quite bushed. Tom thought we still had to make love because "What would people think?"

I said, "If we won't tell, nobody will know," but ...

This was 46 years ago. We are still married to each other, and things are running just as smoothly.

Boy, What A Funny Talking Klutz I Was

Those awkward immigrants, who are they and why do they act so clumsy, you might ask.

Obviously, an immigrant is a person who came from another country. Each one is an individual and has characteristic traits; each has a different fate. Every foreigner who comes by choice to the United States is happy to be here and is prepared to encounter difficulties, but some of those problems are just weird.

I felt stupid when I came from Austria, a small country between Germany and Italy – NOT the one with the kangaroos. Why? Everything was different. My cultural background was pulled from me. Past experience counted for nothing. When you turn a door knob in Europe one way, it opens the door. Here it closes it; same with a key. The hot and cold water faucets on a sink are reversed and you feel klutzy burning yourself when you think you turned on the cold.

In the old country, milk was bought in a bottle or filled by the store keeper into an open can. In a restaurant, you got it in a glass. I had never seen a milk carton. When I bought milk in a cafeteria, I had no idea how to open it. A woman at the next table saw my puzzlement, came over, showed and explained where to pull it apart and where to press to make a spout. I was so thrilled, I bought some more milk and opened the carton by myself. Success! I was on the way to become an American.

In Austria, there is no such thing as a rural mailbox. The postman carries the mail to the house and sticks it into a special container that's fastened to the front door. When I went for a ride with friends, I saw a row of mailboxes on a road that also had a sign "Radar controlled, 60 mph." I thought the mailboxes had the controlling radar in them. My companions kidded me about that "radar" for a long time.

When you see a display for the first time, you have no idea whether you look at something typical or unusual. I had arrived in Richmond, Virginia, in October, and a large department store was already decorated for Christmas. In one window were winter coats in white and pink, in another ladies' lingerie with a pattern called "mink," that is the underwear was black and brown. Wow, I thought, in Austria they have dark coats and underwear in white and pink, but here ...

Proper behavior is another problem. Customs are so different. In Richmond (and maybe in other places of the States) it was customary to wink with one eye at a familiar person as a quick greeting. In Austria that would have been understood as an invitation to have sex. If a man had winked, it would have been a gross imposition. Had a woman done it, she would have established her ill repute. But in Richmond, all people happily winked at each other: the cleaning woman at the doctor, the "housemother" of the dorm at passing male and female students, the department chief at the new resident doctor – me.

And table manners, oh my! Every half educated person knows how to eat properly, or so I thought. In Europe, you keep both hands on the table during the entire meal, you permanently have the fork in the left hand, the knife in the right. You cut off a piece of meat and, with the left hand, put it into your mouth. Never does one lay down the knife, be it on the plate or on the table, never does one put anything into the mouth with the right hand. Only uncouth people, woodcutters or such nature men, would hold the fork in the right hand and – worst of all – put the left hand on the lap.

As you know, in America it's just the opposite. Of course no one had ever mentioned that to me before I was invited by the boss's family to a Thanksgiving dinner. I was embarrassed when the lady of the house gave me a quizzical look, and I was klutzy when I tried to imitate the others.

Food is totally different. I found that only scrambled eggs and black coffee were the same, but even that was not quite true. In Austria we ate eggs for supper, not breakfast. Everything else was strange. In Austria one keeps sweet things sweet. Salty and sour foods are left that way. So, Italian dressing on lettuce and tomatoes was O.K., but on pears and peaches? Yukk. And French dressing with its partly sweet taste – double yukk. Pork was fine, but with raisins? It turned my stomach. Raw onion rings on cottage cheese? My digestive system wasn't as eager to adjust to the New World as I had been.

Static electricity was another surprise. Many years ago, I had learned about it in physics class where we had to rub a plastic rod, touch it, and our hair would stand up, but I had never encountered it naturally. My shoes with crepe soles, together with the metal locker in the clinic, gave fire works.

"W-wow, what's that?" I stammered when I got my first shock.

"Honey," said my locker-neighbor, "it's just a little bitty static. Don't make a fuss. You'll get used to it."

It was even worse when I touched a patient's eye and produced a visible spark.

Manual labor had been rather cheap in Austria. Regular visits to a hairdresser were affordable even to a poor student like me. Therefore I had never set my own hair and hadn't even heard of home permanents.

"Oh, it's easy. Any klutz can do it," said my room mate. "The explanations are all on the box. I'll give you a perm if you do my hair."

I thought about that. My Hippocratic Oath had included "... do no harm to those who trust you." I didn't dare to pour chemicals on her head, so I didn't get a perm either and had my hair cut short like a man's. However, the beauticians in those days weren't used to short cuts, so they just chopped my hair off. My self esteem sank another notch.

And then there were the many problems with the language. I had studied English in school for six years and then with a private tutor before I came to the United States. Therefore, I thought to be fairly well prepared. Wrong!!!!

309

Memorizing "Friends, Romans, Countrymen..." from Shakespeare's *Julius Caesar* doesn't prepare you to ask at an airport for a washroom or for food. Neither the Bard nor my English teacher talked about chili dogs, double burgers, apple fritters or a doughnut. A Coke – dispensed in Europe in an identical bottle is there called a "Cola," but nobody here knew what a Cola was. "Coke," I had thought was that black stuff that's made from coal after the gas has been removed. So you go hungry or find something you can point at and say, "This, please."

When I first arrived in New York, I heard a joke which rang so true: an immigrant had eaten coffee and apple pie for a month because he didn't know anything else. His friend suggested he should order a ham sandwich: that's not difficult to say.

So the next day the man asked for a 'hem sahndwich.'

"White or rye?"

"A hem sahndwich."

"O,K., white or rye?"

"Oh, please, give me coffee and apple pie."

You'd think the waiter could have guessed the man's trouble and said something like, "Yeah, buddy, what kind of bread do you want it on. White (and held up a slice of white bread) or rye (and showed that, too)?"

Of course, people speak in phrases, not in single words. When I was asked in the cafeteria, "Morninwhatyahavetoday?" I gave the guy a helpless smile. So he repeated it, louder because he considered me deaf and dumb. "MORNIN WHAT YA HAVE TODAY?"

The person behind me in the line was helpful and translated for me. "Good . . . morning. What . . . do . . . you . . . want ... to. . . eat . . . today?" He said.

What a relief. "Oh, two pancakes, please."

Some words are the same or very similar in the old and the new language. For me, station, house, father, mother, machine were simple to understand. Just a slightly different pronunciation, but the same meaning. No sweat. But there are many words which are also the same, but have a different meaning. A "toilet" in German is a ball gown or a vanity, that stand with mirrors for grooming. A "commode" is a chest with drawers. A "closet" is a lavatory (you close the door when you are in it). A "bathroom," as many of you will know, is a place with a bathtub or a shower, nothing else. A "Cabinet" is a small bedroom or a group of ministers, such as the Secretary of State, the Interior, Education etc. One could go on and on.

Then there was the difficulty of improper pronunciation which the Americans often could not understand. I worked at the Eye Clinic in Richmond, VA. In a small room at the far end of the department, I checked patients for glasses. Towards the end of one day, only one man was left in the waiting area.

There remained also one record, and I read the name. "Mr. Webb," I called out.

The man looked at me, but did not respond. He seemed resigned to more waiting.

I repeated, "Mr. Webb." Still, no answer. Going to the other side of the clinic, I looked for patient Webb, but there was none. One chart without a patient, one patient without a chart. Finally I had an idea "What's *your* name, sir?"

"WA-E-B."

Oh boy, I had a long way to go.

Another incident at the same hospital, was even more embarrassing. A man came back furious that he couldn't read with the glasses I had prescribed. One of my colleagues took over trying to appease the guy. It turned out that I had put some lenses on him, had shown him a chart with small print and apparently had asked, "Can you see that?" which he said he did. Then he had wanted to know, "Will I be able to read with them glasses?" and I had agreed. However, the man was illiterate. My assumption that he could read what he could see was of course wrong. I had not caught on to that. There are no illiterates in Austria, and therefore, I had never been in such a situation.

The foreign accent is another problem. For our younger son's 10th birthday we invited eight of his classmates to go roller skating. We had a van, and when Tyrone, one of the boys, was getting on, I said, "Hi, come on in."

He stopped halfway into the vehicle, stared at me, giggled and said to the others, "She talks funny."

When I was already in practice in our county and people knew that I was a physician, the accent was occasionally of benefit. At that time, scientists in cartoons on TV spoke with a German accent. A-ha! One elderly grouch shook his head and said, "With that brogue a' yours, you must be smart."

And one teen-age girl said in a swooning voice, "Oh, I wish I had an accent like yours. It's so sexy."

There you have it. Even talking funny can have its good sides.

Of Chickens And Puppies

My husband and I had grown up in city apartments in Europe and also lived in several flats in Cleveland. You can smell the neighbors' food, hear their arguments, wake up at two in the morning when college students beep the car horns at each other. That's no place to raise a kid. We wanted more space!

Because both Tom and I were then working at University Hospitals, we looked at houses in the eastern suburbs. Wow. They were way out of our financial reach. "Look farther out in the country," suggested one realtor with a condescending smile. "Prices are much lower there."

We bought an old farm with 65 acres of weeds and scrubby trees. So much space! In the east, our own woods lined the horizon! And it was all ours – we personally owned all that land! Well, it belonged to the bank, a minor formality. Our enthusiasm was boundless. Only a few years earlier, we had come to this country with four suitcases and about $2,000. Now we were $30,000 in debt. What progress – we had arrived!

The land gave us a sense of freedom we had never felt before. Our kid, Pete, could run around without my worrying every second about cars or other dangers.

And people were so friendly here, so cordial, so caring. Can you imagine, the folks who sold us the house even left 12 chickens and a rooster, free of charge (or, maybe, included in the sales price of the property).

"You'll have good eggs," said the man.

"I'd like to take the hens along," said his wife, "but we're moving to Arizona, and the trip takes too long."

During the next weeks, Pete's main activity was chasing chickens. The unusual exercise must have increased their egg production, and we had about 10 eggs per day. Pete collected them from the coop where he often had to fight off the rooster who didn't like intruders.

We ate eggs for breakfast and supper (that was before the age of cholesterol awareness), hard or soft boiled, sunny-side up or down, scrambled or as omelettes and, my favorite, deviled. But 10 eggs per day meant 70 per week. With all our rustic appetites we couldn't eat *that* many. We even fed quite a few to our eager puppy dogs and found customers among our neighbors. A roadside stand with a sign "Fresh Eggs – Free" didn't coax any takers.

Big bowls with eggs filled our fridge. We ran out of space. Then Tom had an excellent idea: he and Pete lined up some eggs on a fence in our back yard and used them as targets for B-B shooting. What spectacular effects!

But we just couldn't handle that much of a good thing. Also, there was not a square foot in our yard where the chickens hadn't left their mark. We could not safely step anywhere. So, at a family council, we all agreed to use the chickens for meat.

"How will you kill them?" I asked.

"Oh, I helped my aunt when I was a boy," said Tom. "You just twist their neck. It's easy."

"Don't you first have to catch them?" I asked.

Before Tom could answer me, Pete asked with a sparkle in his eyes, "Dad, can I wring the rooster's neck? I want to get even with him."

Now, twice a week, there was much excited cackling with feathers flying all over the place. I never watched how my two heroes slaughtered the chickens, but I saw them several times in the backyard with bow and hunting arrows.

Tom presented me with the corpses. "You take care of the rest, O.K.?" He had an engaging smile.

It seemed to me, buying meat in the grocery store was a good idea after all.

****

Of course, other animals came to share the country life. Within our first week, the Carners, neighbors to the south, said, "You need a dog when you live out here. We have friends who would let you have one of their puppies. Nice dogs!"

"Oh, Mom, a puppy. I can't wait." Pete was hopping with excitement.

"We'll have to ask Dad first."

But before my husband was home, the Carner kids brought two puppies. "So you can pick one," said Mindy, the 10-year-old.

One little dog was grey with pointed ears, the other tan with round, floppy ears and very short legs. They overwhelmed Pete and me with their puppy-charm, and when Tom came home, he had to agree to keep them both.

"The grey dog will be Kyon and the tan one Canis," he said.

"Funny names." Will, the seven-year-old Carner boy, shook his head. "How come you call them that?"

"Kyon is Greek for dog and Canis is Latin," lectured Tom.

"Wow," said Mindy. "Now I know a Greek and a Latin word."

"Will you keep 'em both?" asked Will.

By now the dogs, Pete and the chickens were one happy melee. We couldn't send a puppy back, but I'll never forget the sly look Mindy gave her brother when they hugged the pups before they left. Had the dogs' owner bribed the kids to get rid of both of them?

Of course the pups were not yet housebroken, but most of the place had at that time no rugs, so we learned to manage. Our home life had become one happy, noisy blur of activities.

But then tragedy struck. Canis ran into the road and was killed. Pete cried for a while, and in the evening he and Dad buried her.

Just when they were done with the sad task, Mindy walked up, a light brown puppy in her arms. "You won't miss the dead one so much," she said. "I got this pup for you."

315

Pete cuddled the new dog. "He looks just like Canis."

"It's a she," corrected Mindy. "And she's from the same litter. What are you gonna call this one?"

"How's Candy?" asked Pete.

Dad agreed to this less sophisticated name, and happiness was restored.

****

One morning Tom pointed outside. "Look at those patches of fog. Aren't they cute?"

"They are only on our land," I said. "The neighbor doesn't have any. Isn't that strange?"

Tom put an arm around my shoulders. "Our own private fog." For a better look he moved to the side, which resulted in a loud yelp because he had stepped on a puppy.

"And our private pups and chickens," I said.

"M-hm, and lady bugs and mosquitoes ..."

We were quite happy then.

My "Horsemanship"

One of my favorite operas is the *Valkyrie* where supernatural warrior maidens ride through the air. As a teenager, I always wished I could join them.

In Austria, where I grew up, there was not a chance to ride a horse, not even on the ground. Only farm boys, bareback, took their draft horses to water or across a field. On the other hand, rich folks rode English style with proper hunt caps, jodhpurs, polished high boots, sitting on well groomed horses from expensive stables. I didn't belong to either of these groups.

But in America, the land of boundless opportunities, Tom saw an ad for a riding school. Hey, the lessons were affordable. I quickly signed up. Tim, the owner of the place, brought out a beautiful dark brown gelding with shiny fur.

"First, you have to get on the horse," he explained.

That seemed self evident, but it wasn't as easy as I had thought. He was on the horse's left side, so I went to its right.

"No, no, no! You *never* mount a horse from the right! Always from the left." He didn't explain why.

Being a rather short person (some of my friends call me "the runt"), I just couldn't get a leg high enough for the stirrup. So, Tim placed two wooden steps beside the horse, and then I could get on. Wow. A quick thought of the Valkyries flitted through my mind. Now I hoped the horse wouldn't fly through the air.

"His name is 'Spud,' " said Tim. "Pet him."

How unique, I thought. I had never heard that name before. Gingerly I leaned forward to touch Spud's neck.

Tim hadn't let go of the bridle yet, guided Spud into a corral and carefully closed the gate. "Hold the bridle here loosely and gently kick him. Then he'll go."

I kicked, and nothing happened.

"Harder," encouraged Tim. "He barely felt that."

When I kicked harder, Spud made a hop that nearly threw me off and then walked once around the corral stopping in front of Tim.

"Don't ever hold on to the saddle," admonished Tim. "That's not proper horsemanship."

I wondered about horse-womanship. Sure, it would have been braver to fall off than to hold on, but ... ?

As the lesson continued, I could make the horse go and stop, but I wasn't quite sure whether it was really I who communicated my intentions to the mount. Maybe he and Tim had a secret code, and the horse obeyed him and not me. While I received instructions, Tom and little Pete watched. They did a lot of giggling.

Anyway, I was exhilarated but afterwards I could hardly walk. (I am naturally knock-kneed, so the bow-legged position was really strange to me.)

When I told my friends about my beautiful horse, they laughed. "Spud? Is he lumpy?"

I gave them a blank stare.

"Spud means 'potato,' don't you know? It's slang."

How shocking. This stunning horse – I thought he looked better than the famous "Man o' War" – why would they call him a lumpy potato? And in slang?

A month later, we moved from Cleveland to Geauga County, and the weekly riding lessons stopped. We were too busy with our new place, but our neighbors, the Carners, had a pony. When they left for a week's vacation, Mindy, the 10-year-old, said, "You could have Jumper while we're gone. Can ride him too, he's very gentle."

Those Carners, not only had they supplied us with pups, now they even loaned us a horse. Such nice folks; what a great place to live.

The pony was installed in our barn together with a wagon full of hey and straw and a small box with oats. Mindy brought saddle and bridle.

Will, the youngest Carner, gave us all the instruction he thought we needed. "Only one cup of oats a day."

"Why?"

He shrugged. "That's what my dad said. Guess oats cost too much."

In the afternoon we saddled Jumper, and I got on. (That was easy. I wasn't too short for a pony.) He stood still like a statue.

"Kick him, Mommy," urged Pete.

I was afraid the little horse might gallop away, but no-o-o. He didn't budge. So I kicked harder. Now Jumper moved in slow motion as if he had to figure out at every step how to untangle his legs. With much effort, we made it half-way down our cow-lane. How would I turn this stick-in-the-mud? Oh, but turn he did and went home even in a slow trot.

O.K., I thought. He had caught on to it. As a reward, I gave him two cups of oats.

His spirits became more lively every day; we fed him all the oats he wanted and bought even more from the feed store. Towards the end of the week, Jumper was so spunky, I didn't dare ride him any more.

When Wills entered the barn after the Carners' return, Jumper reared up as if he'd want to break through the roof.

"What did you do to him?"

I explained that he liked oats, so we let him have as much as he wanted.

Wills looked at me with open mouth and then shouted to his sister who just entered the barn. "The Binders fed him nothing but oats!"

Mindy shook her head in utter disbelief, and I felt very guilty.

A few days later, though, we heard that Jumper, on a strict diet of hay, had calmed down to his stoic self again.

"Well," asked Tom the next day. "Are you ready for your own horse?"

"You mean, buy one? Let's wait a bit and study up on how to handle them."

A Snake As Teacher

Before I had my first child, I dreamed like all mothers-to-be of the bonding with the infant and the many cute stages he'd go through. Having grown up as an only child without the company of little boys, I was not prepared for the masculine fun my husband had with our five-year-old.

One Friday evening they found a snake behind our house. Tom came into the kitchen holding the wiggly critter in his hand. I let out a little squeak and backed away.

"Oh, Hon," he said, "you don't have to be afraid. This is just a little garter snake. Look at him. See, his head is slim – that means he is not poisonous."

"Ah-hum," I said with an unsteady voice. Then I cleared my throat and said with more conviction, "Ah-hum."

"Mom," said Pete, hopping on one leg with excitement, "we need to put him somewhere."

"Yeah," I said, "way back by the fence."

"No, no," said Pete. "We have to keep him, Mom."

"No, we don't," I said firmly.

"Look, Dear." My husband smiled at me. "If you find us a large jar, about a gallon, we can keep the snake for a day or two."

"You mean he'll be in the house overnight?" I stammered.

"Pete, help Mommie find a jar."

"Oh, I know, the apple cider." Pete opened the fridge door.

"Just empty the rest in a glass," suggested Tom.

"You hold that thing firmly." I glanced at my husband and the snake that tried to climb up his arm now.

After the jug was cleaned, I watched with fear and awe as the two stuffed the animal through the narrow opening. They put a piece of aluminum foil with air holes over it and fastened that with a rubber band. Seems the snake was glad to be left alone, so it curled up and kept still.

Pete carried the jug with him the same way he had until then dragged his teddy bear along. While he had his bath, the snake was placed on top of the toilet tank.

"You give Peter his bath tonight," I said to Tom.

"I will, I will, Dear. Don't worry." He gave me a pat on the shoulder.

I busied myself in the kitchen for a long while, heard some doors being opened and closed, some whispered words, and when I walked past Pete's bedroom door, I heard is father read, "Do you like green eggs and ham?" It was Pete's favorite story by Dr. Seuss, so I assumed the snake had lost importance.

A while later Tom came to the living room. "Fast asleep," he said.

"Who?" I asked.

He chuckled. "Why, Pete, of course, who else?"

"What about the snake?"

"Oh, come now." Tom shook his head. "Since when are you such a scaredy-cat? The snake is in the closed jar on the porch, the porch-door is locked. Need more protection?" He put his arm on my shoulder, and we settled down on the couch to watch TV.

****

The next morning was strange only in that my husband got up earlier than usual, must have been very quiet because I didn't wake up when he dressed, and was on his way out the door when I came down.

"What time is it?" I was half yawning.

"Have to be at work early today." He blew me a kiss.

I fixed my breakfast and looked at the paper. Why was he avoiding me? Seems he didn't want me to find out something.

It was so pleasantly quiet in the house. Saturdays I didn't go to work and often had some special times with Pete; a trip to the zoo or a park, a visit to the library or a museum. No cartoons on yet. He must still be asleep, I thought.

The porch door opened slowly, and in came Pete, snake jar in his arm. "Look, Mommie, doesn't he look nice?" he asked innocently and put the jar on the kitchen table.

I had considerably calmed down since last night, so I looked at the snake with him. A pocket book "The Snakes of North America" lay on the kitchen counter, and Pete found the picture of "our snake."

It was a garter snake, as Dad had said. The sleek, dark grey body had lighter grey stripes along the head. The scales were smooth and glossy. His forked tongue looked funny when he stuck it out in characteristic fashion.

After a while I said, "O.K., when do you let him go?"

"Mom, can I let the snake out in the living room?"

"Are you nuts?" I wasn't so calm any more.

Pete took the jar to his room. Five minutes later he was back. "Mommie, this snake can't hurt you. Can I let him out?"

"Take him outside and let him out in the grass."

Quietly Pete went with his snake into the living room. I heard him switch on the TV and watch cartoons. When I looked, he was lying on his stomach, the snake jar cradled in his arm. The snake seemed to watch "Tom and Jerry" with interest.

Pete looked at me with such theatrical sadness in his eyes, that I had to laugh.

"Are you sure you can catch him again?" I asked. "I don't want him to hide in a closet or in the couch where we can't find him."

"I'm sure, Mommie, don't worry." Instantly he had the cover off and laid the bottle down.

A minute later the snake came out and slithered along the living room wall.

Pete sensed my fear, grabbed the snake and stuffed him back into the bottle. "See?' was all he said.

There was a knock at the door. Will, the neighbor's boy, two years older than Pete, was looking for excitement. "Hi," he said to me, and "What have you got?" to Pete.

Together they let the snake out, caught him and put him back into the jar at least 20 times. I began to feel sorry for the snake and wanted to interest the boys in something else.

We had then a little wading pool in the back yard, one foot deep and six feet across. "Why don't you guys go into the pool for a while?" I asked. "It's warm today."

"I'll be right back," said Will. "Got to get my swimming trunks," and he was out the door.

Pete wanted to take off towards his room, but I grabbed him by the arm. "Where's the snake?"

"Look, Mommie. Right here and the lid is on. See?" My five-year-old had a tone of voice as if he were an adult calming a stubbornly frightened child – me.

For a while they made a ruckus in the pool, squeaking, screaming, splashing. The snake was in the jar in the sun. I thought the situation was under control and went into the house for towels. When I came back out, the boys were bent over the pool, watching the snake swim.

"Look, Mommie, how pretty he is."

"He didn't need to learn, he can swim naturally," said Will.

Both boys watched me out of the corner of their eyes. The snake swam with so much grace, beauty and elegance that I couldn't help but admire him. I kneeled by the pool and watched him. What a wonderful animal. How lively, how alert.

The kids picked him up, stuffed him into the jar, dropped him back into the water, caught and squished him, let him swim again. Then they lost interest and went into the house.

I watched the snake for a little longer. That poor thing couldn't get out of the pool because the rim was too high and steep. Soon he'd get tired and drown, I thought. I called Pete – no answer.

So **I** bent down and gently grabbed the snake. He seemed to relish the warmth of my forearm and wrapped his body around it while I held him just behind the head. He didn't struggle or wiggle, so I was not afraid. I carried him to the shrubs at the end of our lot and let him go. I hoped he'd survive the hassle he had suffered at our house.

Pete and Will stormed out again. "Where's the snake, Mom?"

"I let him go," I said quietly.

"You? How did you do it? Did you catch him with a sieve?"

"No," I said, hardly containing my pride. "I picked him up like you had shown me so often and carried him to the bushes. The poor thing was so cold, he could hardly move."

Pete shook his head. "You never know what *my* mom's gonna do."

When my husband came home, Pete raced to the car. "Dad, you know what Mom did?"

"She had a heart attack because of the snake?" he asked waving at me.

"No, much worse. She took the snake ... "

"... in her hands?"

"Yes," said Pete, "didn't you, Mom? And she carried him to the fence and let him go."

They both had walked up to the house. Tom gave me a hug. "Well, old girl, you are growing up after all," and to Pete he said, "Guess we have to find another snake." They looked at me, but I was totally unconcerned.

****

I know you can be a career woman, a women's libber and a good wife and mother without handling a snake. But this adventure boosted my self image, freed me from irrational fear and let me appreciate grace and beauty in motion where I had not expected to find it. A snake and my five-year-old had taught me that.

For days I boasted to everyone who would listen how I had carried the snake to its safety.

With A Camper, You Never Know What Happens

A few years after we had come to the States, my husband developed severe ragweed allergy. Conventional remedies as well as shots didn't provide much relief, so a vacation in a ragweed-free area was the solution. We chose northern Maine, where the plant doesn't grow.

Since we planned to be out of town for a month, we aimed for thrift. It was decided we would camp. At that time we had a van, and Tom, always a do-it-yourselfer, fitted it out for camping. He built a wooden platform behind the front seats and bought two air mattresses to cover it. Underneath was space for cooking utensils, clothes, blankets and pillows. A board with some padding could be placed across the two front seats for Pete, then age five, to sleep on.

Tom was careful we'd be protected from the summer's heat. He had a huge mosquito net that fit tightly over the open back door. To be sure that everything worked well, we spent a night in the van in our back yard.

"Isn't that great?" Tom asked in the morning. "We can really sleep well on those air mattresses."

Pete was all enthusiastic, and no one asked for my comments.

On our first night of the trip, we were at a campground high up in the New Hampshire mountains. It was chilly, so we put on longjohns and sweaters. I wished for earmuffs, too. In spite of all the clothes, we were still too cold. So Pete came to sleep between us for more body warmth, and we shut the windows. Tightly stacked together, we dozed off. But an hour later, both Tom and I woke up again.

"I can't breathe right," I said. "Gosh, I need fresh air."

He opened the side windows. "There isn't enough oxygen when the windows are closed. I didn't think it'd be that bad."

We had to keep one window open. Pete snuggled up a little tighter to me.

"Is the mattress all right?" asked Tom.

"Not really," I said. "With Pete and me so close together, we push all the air away. I'm lying on the wood here."

"Want to come over to my side?"

"That would squeeze out more air," I mumbled.

Soon it started to dawn, and the birds began to sing. I got out and walked around a bit. The evergreens smelled so refreshing. If I had slept well, I'd have liked it there.

Tom came back from the camp office. "Guess what. It's 34 degrees. No wonder we were cold." He expertly cooked breakfast. It was good and warm, reviving our spirits. Before we took off, he shoved the dirty dishes under our platform. When he hit the brake, all the stuff underneath it slid forward and when he stepped on the gas, it rumbled back, happily mixing clean underwear with dirty pots.

The next night wasn't much different, but we were already at a campground in Maine near Rangeley Lake, where we planned to stay.

In the morning Tom rented a little boat. "I'll go fishing with Pete," he said, "so you can have some time for yourself."

For a while I watched them. No catch yet.

"Those fish just laugh at us," Tom called to me.

With a chuckle I went back to our van and tried to establish some order.

It was warm now, the sun was shining, the lake glistened, and a family of ducks swam near the shore. The parents were teaching the ducklings how to dive for food, sticking their tails up into the air, while squirrels were playing hide and go seek between the trees. At that time I was four months pregnant with our second child and thought I felt the little one stir in me.

My two guys came back. "Mom," said Pete, "I stepped into the water. I need new socks."

"Dear, I don't know where your clean socks are, but I just found one from yesterday. Put that on. At least it's dry."

Tom smiled at me. "Just imagine, next year we'll have two little kids."

"Next year," I said, "we'll rent a cabin with beds, a clothes hamper, a kitchen sink, shelves and a bath. You don't think I'll spend four weeks with a five-month-old in the van."

He was surprised. Then he gave me a kiss. "I have to do some errands," he said. "Be back in two hours."

What errands? I wondered. Pete and I went to feed the ducks and the squirrels and then explored the camp grounds.

Less than an hour later, Tom was back. "Let's go!"

"Go where?" I asked.

"It's a surprise." He was beaming.

After ten minutes he pulled into the driveway of a lakefront home. Two smaller cottages were on the other side of the lawn.

"What's here?" I asked.

Tom pointed at one of the cabins. "I just rented this for a month."

The owner came out and showed me the little house: two bedrooms, a dining-living area, a kitchen, a bathroom with tub, and central heat.

"Oh, Tom, this is great!" I put my arms around his neck. "What does it cost?"

"We can afford it." He picked up Pete for a three-way hug.

Then I rushed into the van and started taking everything into the cabin.

"Let me give you a hand," said Tom. "You are eager to get settled here."

"Yes, Dear, and this is the end of my camping."

After that, our days fell into a comfortable routine. In the afternoons, when it was warm, we swam in the lake. Pete even got a one-child raft which he could row and over-steer in our little cove where Tom and I could wade out and turn him around.

During the nights we heard and sometimes watched the raccoons banging the garbage cans, no matter how tightly the lids were fastened.

In the cool mornings we usually went for a long hike. Well-marked trails led to various mountain tops or over a ridge to the next lake. Pete held up quite well.

Every local person warned us about the bears. "If they get startled, they'll attack," said the landlady.

"Don't get between the mother and her cubs," advised the mailman.

"If you have to run, make it downhill and get into shrubs," said the guy at the gas station.

There were even posted bear warning signs. But we never met a bear. We didn't see a deer or a fox or a badger either. Nothing bigger than a squirrel. Why? Our five-year-old was happily yapping all the time. If we told him to hush, he was quiet – for two minutes. Then he kept jabbering and thus warned everyone a quarter mile in advance, and all the ferocious and gentle animals went into hiding, probably watching us.

Only once did we encounter bears. We were in the van, on a paved road, and a mother bear was sitting in the middle of the lane, playing with two cubs. Seems our vehicle was quieter than Pete. Only after we had stopped, did she slowly get up, pushing the first little one with her snout and shoving the other with her paw off the pavement.

The town of Rangeley was at the other end of the lake, easily reached over a state route along the north shore. We went there every two or three days. Once, Tom stayed home while Pete and I went for groceries. I had seen on a map that there was another road along the south shore. We tried that one on the way back. It was not well graded and went up and down, up and down like a roller coaster.

Pete was thrilled. "Go faster, Mom!"

"Hee, hee. Faster, Mommie, faster!"

So I stepped on the gas and the next bump was steeper than I had expected. "Whe-e-e-e," we sailed through the air, all four wheels off the ground. You can't mistake that. Then the shocks bottomed out. Yikes! To my surprise, the van behaved as if nothing had happened.

"Mommie, that was great." Rarely had I seen Peter so happy. He looked in the back of the van. "Do you think Dad's gonna help with the groceries?"

"He might. Why?"

"Shouldn't we put the apples back in the bag?"

I laughed. "Yeah, and – oh – what happened to the eggs?" Carefully I opened the box. Only one was broken.

At the cabin Tom did come out and opened the side door. "How come the platform is tilted?"

Pete and I tried to look innocent. "With a camper," I said, "you never know what happens."

New Fun At Summer's End

It was one of those lazy August days, hot and humid. Our two kids were bored and had enough of amusement parks, zoo, fishing, swimming, boating and bike rides.

After revving up his go-cart for an hour in the parking lot, seven year-old Peter came back into the house. "There's nothing to do, Mom."

"Nothin' do," echoed Jeff, our two-and-a-half year old.

"Were you already in your tree house?" I asked Pete.

"Yeah." He switched on cartoons on TV. "Reruns," he mumbled and switched it off again.

"Want to go to Mike's and ride his pony? His mom invited you."

"Nah," said Pete. "I don't like the horseflies."

"Pony step my foot!" said Jeff.

"Really?" I looked at Pete.

"Well, not quite, but Jeff got scared."

"Then you guys will have to invent something new to keep you busy," I said giving each of them a popsicle, and they wandered out again.

After a short while Pete rushed in, full of eagerness. "Mom, does the builder still need that plastic?"

"Which one?"

"The big black roll."

The floor of our barn had been redone in the spring. Before the workers had poured the concrete, they had used heavy gauge plastic as a moisture barrier. Some of it was left over.

"The builder is done. What do you want to do with the plastic?"

"We'll make a slide." He was hopping on one leg with excitement.

A slide? I wondered. Whatever it is, it'll keep them busy for a while.

333

Just then Will, the neighbor's boy, came over looking for action.

Pete tried to move the roll of heavy plastic into our slightly sloping back yard but had a hard time with it. "Come on, Will, help me move that thing."

Together they dragged it onto the higher part of our lot and unrolled it, three feet wide, over 50 feet long, and still folded in layers.

I was curious. Perched on the back steps, I was rocking Jeff on my knees, as we both watched the construction of "the slide."

Pete and Will sat on it and tried to skid downhill, but their feet and behinds would not move.

"Let's try water," suggested Will.

The two boys went for the garden hose and let water trickle on the slide.

Pete took a running start and shot down with enough speed to carry him the entire length. "Yikes, here we go! Come on, Will."

They went down on their stomachs, on their backs, head first, feet first, sitting up, lying down, forwards, backwards and sideways.

"Jeff too." The little one pulled my hand.

"Go ahead and try it," I said.

He made it to the top, plopped down, slid a little and started crying, "Mommie, cold!"

"You gotta go fast, like this. Then you don't feel the cold." Will showed him, but Jeff was too scared.

"Tell you what, Jeff, Mommie will get warm water from the kitchen." I filled a large pail with it and splashed him gently with a few drops.

He smiled and then yelled, "Mommie, go!" as he yanked on the handle.

I switched off the garden hose, put Jeff on top of the slide and poured water from the pail behind him. He barely moved.

Pete came to the rescue. He jumped on the slope shoving Jeff all the way down, and Will followed. They squealed with delight as they landed in a heap on the grass.

Jeff looked for the pail. "More!"

I went into the house, but just then the phone rang, and I was delayed for a few minutes. When I brought out more warm water, the garden hose was again in service, and Jeff slid down with the same enthusiasm as the older boys, just a little slower.

Then he saw my pail. "Jeff no need that. Jeff big boy," and whooped it up with the others.

Before long, there were somersaults, backwards and forwards, and Jeff was riding on Pete's shoulders going down with a scream.

When they started to chatter and get blue lips, I turned off the water. "That's enough for today." I scooped up Jeff, dried him off, and gave him fresh clothes.

****

The next few days were hot. The slide was in daily use. A roll of heavy gage plastic from a builder's supply store had been the cool attraction for the rest of the summer.

Fishing For Our Sustenance On the Florida Keys

It had been a difficult and busy year for me, so my husband said one day, "Why don't you go on a vacation over Christmas? Take Pete along and relax."

The kid, at that time 10 years old, was hopping with excitement. "Oh, boy, Mommie, do we go where it's warm and we can swim?"

Figuring that it'll be warmer the farther south we go, I picked Sugar Loaf Key in Florida, near Key West.

"Will we fly to that island, Mom?"

"No. Only to Miami and from there we'll take a rental car."

"Do you know how to drive one of them?"

I didn't answer such a silly question.

****

In those years, we had a Volkswagen and some other tiny car. The rental was a Fairlane, the biggest model they had, twice as wide and twice as long as my little beetle at home. Well, I thought, no problem. They had wide lanes there.

Once the "Overseas Highway" lead over causeways and bridges between the islands (I don't know why they are called "keys"), the lanes weren't wide at all.

"Mom, watch out! We won't fit through there."

I shared Pete's concern and hit the brake. But then I considered, "The car in front of us made it; we should too."

"Yeah, but look. It says 'Wide Load' on the truck that's coming at us."

While I slowed to a crawl, the car behind us gave me the horn. All right; I held my breath and resumed normal speed.

A little further, many fishermen were standing on a narrow sidewalk. One kid cast with a big back-swing. "Bang!!!"

"Yikes! What was that?" Pete looked at the roof.

337

"I think he hit us with a sinker. Better close your window, or another one catches you with his hook."

Minutes later we approached a bridge. It was quite high, maybe 70 feet above the water, and the top of the bridge formed the horizon. Nothing beyond, just the end of the highway and the sky.

"Mom, does the road stop there? Won't we fall in?"

I wasn't sure. "Oh, look, there's a car in the other lane. He must be coming from somewhere."

From the top of the bridge the view was breathtaking, unique. Beneath us lay the ocean, several keys connected by bridges, and the Gulf.

When we arrived at our motel, Peter said, "I didn't know just riding in a car would be such an adventure."

The small island of Sugar Loaf Key had private homes and one motel with its restaurant, the social center of the community. One man, Jim, owned a 16-foot powerboat with a 100 hp outboard motor. He took guests fishing and water skiing.

On our first trip out, he showed Pete how to hold the fishing pole, how to cast, "Watch you don't hit your mom," how to let out the line. There was a wiggle. "Gentle now, let him get a good bite – now you snag him." Jim showed with his hands the needed movement, and Pete snagged.

"Now reel in slowly," Jim coached.

A sudden tug. Pete fell against the side of the boat. Jim grabbed him. "Let out line!" He flicked the little lever on the reel, and the line whined as it was pulled out.

"You've got a strong one." Admiration was in Jim's voice.

Gradually Pete reeled in, and Jim explained the rules of the Fishing Tournament. "I'm not allowed to help you, but I can net the fish once you've brought him to the boat."

After about 15 minutes we could see him. A barracuda.

"Must be four feet long," said Jim when he scooped him out.

"Cool," said Pete. "Can I enter him in the tournament?"

"You could, but they've already got bigger fish."

338

"So I wouldn't win?" Pete's voice was small.

"Why don't you have him mounted?" Jim said to me. "He's a pretty one."

"Do you know a taxidermist?" I asked.

"Sure. I can take the fish to him as soon as we get in."

"Groovy," said Pete. "Where will we hang him?"

"The waiting room might be a good place. Many people can admire him there. Underneath, we'll write your name and the date you caught him."

"Neat."

****

As a form of PR, being friendly to fishermen, the restaurant – without charge – prepared the guest's catch.

This day Pete had caught a little grouper, maybe 10 inches from head to tail. "Mom, tonight we'll eat my fish. Right?"

I hadn't thought of that, but I agreed.

"Will you cook my fish?" he asked at the kitchen. "We want to eat it."

The chef's assistant came over. "This?" he asked. He gave the fish a long look and daintily picked it up with two fingers. "I'll try to filet it."

We went to the dining room and first ordered each a bowl of soup and salad.

The waitress asked, "Do you really want that little fish?"

"It's a grouper," said Pete. "And it's not that little."

Soon our filets came. Each was about as big as the slice of an apple. They looked quite lonesome on the large dinner plates, dwarfed by a sprig of parsley.

Pete managed to divide his into three bites. "Good, isn't it?"

"Delicious," I said.

The waitress came back. "The gentleman with the blue shirt over there caught a big swordfish today. He'll let you have some of it. They can't eat it all."

Mr. Blue Shirt smiled and gestured his offer to us.

I nodded acceptance.

Soon the waitress brought one inch thick swordfish steaks, so big they hung over the rim of the plates. She patted Pete's head. "There you go. A little boy's got to eat."

Pete pouted. "My fish tasted better."

"Sure it did," I said. "It was younger and more tender."

"Yeah. And today you didn't have to pay for the supper because I caught it myself."

****

"So, when can you teach me to waterski?" I asked Jim in the morning.

"I wouldn't go this time of the year," he said. "Brrrr. It's too cold."

"All your pamphlets advertise it for the winter vacation. I've wanted to waterski since I was a kid. Now I'll do it, cold or not."

"Let's wait till tomorrow. I'll take along my boy, Ben. He can go in the water with you."

Next day, 15-year-old Ben helped me put on the skis, positioned them properly, handed the rope to me, got ready himself and then yelled something to his dad. To everyone's surprise, I got up, and we skied for quite a stretch. When my legs and arms started to hurt, I wanted to quit but didn't know how. Trying to ask Ben, I looked at him and wiped out.

The boat came around in a few seconds. "You did great," said Jim. "Don't remember anyone getting up the first time."

"That's because I showed her," said Ben. "Pete, you want to go next?"

"Tomorrow," said Pete.

At the motel, someone said, "I saw you skiing out there."

I expected some compliment, but she shook her head. "You must be frozen stiff. Crazy."

340

A soak in the hot tub for half an hour did feel good, indeed.

Next day it was Pete's turn. He was ready.

"Ben has to work today," Jim told me. "But you could go in the water with Pete and help him."

By then I was an expert with half an hour's training, so I agreed. We skied in a bay on the gulf side of the island, an area about a mile long and half a mile wide bordered by several tiny keys. They kept the big waves out.

"When Pete gets up," advised Jim, "you just stay there. We'll pick you up when he's had enough. The bay's only four feet deep, so you don't have to worry."

I helped Pete with the skis and the rope. He fell once, but the second time everything went OK. The boat took off and – since I didn't have my eyeglasses on – soon disappeared. I didn't quite know what to do. Walk in chest-deep water? Stand still? I swam a little, but in that vast area it seemed senseless.

When the boat came back, Pete was yapping with excitement. Jim helped me in. Then he pointed into the water. "Look at this big stingray. Must have a wing span of 10 feet. They can hold still for hours while waiting for prey to come along. Quite poisonous."

"Hey, I've just been standing there!

"Groovy, Mom. We should'a taken a picture of you with the stingray."

****

Our vacation time was over. We had visited the Key Deer, these very small, cute creatures, on Big Pine Island; had enjoyed the unique ambience of Key West, part old fashioned charm, part commercialism. Now we had packed and were dressed for the flight home.

On our way to the airport, Pete wanted to stop and watch some dolphins, one of them supposedly "Flipper" of TV fame. The rather primitive place had large pens, maybe 200 by 75 feet.

The partitions barely reached above water level, and I was surprised that the dolphins didn't jump out and escape into the open. Apparently, they didn't want to. Many of them playfully dived and jumped, while I took picture after picture. Then there was a little show. At the end, the trainer asked for a kid to step into a tiny boat and hold on to Flipper's back fin. Pete was feisty enough to be picked for that honor. The dolphin pulled the boat several times around, Pete beamed, and I used the last exposure on my roll of film.

"Now, who wants to jump in the water with Flipper?" asked the trainer. "He'll pull you around."

"Mo-o-o-om?" Pete's eyes were big and insistent.

"You don't have swimming trunks here."

An elderly man sat beside me. "Doesn't he have underpants on?"

Pete already took off his clothes, gave me one more questioning look and hopped in. Now it was even easier to hold on to the fin than it had been from the boat. When Pete had a firm grip, Flipper swam faster and faster, far out, turned around, swam circles, splashed with his tail, but – well trained as he was – did not dive.

"Take a picture," yelled the man beside me.

"I'm out of film."

Then the two approached the shore at about 20 miles per hour. I was scared that Pete would fall off, but Flipper slowed down so skillfully that everything went smooth. Pete gave him a gentle pat on the snout while the dolphin squeaked and nodded his head. Seems they were friends for life.

"Pete, we've got to hurry, or we'll miss the plane."

"Mom, I'm all wet."

"In the car, take off those underpants and put the other clothes back on."

"But I don't have dry underwear."

"So you'll go without. No one will ever know."

At the airport in Miami, we ran and reached the gate just when they were about to close it. Breathless and disheveled, we dropped into our seats with the misgiving looks of other passengers on us. Within seconds the plane took off.

"I'm still sticky from the salt water," said Pete. "But boy, was that groovy. I'll never forget Flipper."

A Less Than Perfect Mother
Part I

One of my patients was a scared little girl, Kaitlyn. She clutched her Cabbage Patch doll. The mother worried that I wouldn't be able to do an exam, but with a few "fish" crackers and a colored flashlight I could keep the little one calm. At the end of the check-up, she even gave me a smile.

"You are good with kids," said the mother. "Must have been very caring with your own children."

"Well ... " I smiled faintly. "Sometimes."

After they had left, I saw that Kaitlyn had forgotten her doll and put it on our "safe-keeping" shelf.

My next patient had canceled, so I had half an hour and sat down in a recliner. Memories of old times came back to me.

... there was our first child, Peter, about two years old. By then he could walk quite well on level ground, but that day we were at a little park with a plowed field. Pete was intrigued by the deep furrows and with effort crossed them, surprised how hard it was to step on those ridges that came up higher than his knees. After a few stumbles, he made it. Happiness and pride sparkled in his eyes. I scooped him up, carried him to the car and handed him to the babysitter who was already waiting. Then I slammed the car door shut – on Pete's finger.

How could I!

His screams could be heard for a mile, and during the whole ride he snuggled up to the babysitter and gave me dirty looks. At home, I put a Bandaid with colored stars and stripes on the finger.

The next day he showed me his hand. "Boo-boo all gone."

I was forgiven, but for years I felt guilty when I looked at his hand though it showed no damage.

... worse came when he was on the eighth grade wrestling team. After practice one day, he said, "Mom, this finger hurts."

345

"How come?"

"It was straight like this when Keith rolled over it. That guy must weigh a ton." Pete seemed to plead for sympathy.

"Well," I said soothingly, "I'm sure in a few days it'll be much better."

A week later, he mentioned, "Mom, that finger still isn't good."

"Can you bend it?"

He tried. "Ouch!"

"Really? If it still bothers in a few days, we'll have to get it checked. Just don't bump it again."

Another week later, we saw an orthopedist, a friend of ours. On the X-ray the finger was visibly broken – not just a hairline crack."

"Do I get a cast?" Pete asked.

"You don't need one anymore," said the doctor with a chuckle. "Your mom waited long enough. It's mostly healed."

Peter had a smug expression with an "I-told-you-so" smirk.

Wow! I, a physician, had waited two weeks! Surely, I had flunked "motherhood" this time.

... when Pete was twelve, we visited my husband's parents in Austria and spent some time with them in the Alps. Grandpa had a lung condition, so he could not stay at high altitudes, and therefore we chose a relatively small ski area at a lower elevation, frequented by the locals. The top half of the mountain – above the cliffs – was snow covered. We planned to ski in the mornings and spend the afternoons with the grandparents. This was our first big winter vacation. Before that, Peter had skied only at a local area near us.

He needed new boots, and we bought them in town under Grandpa's "expert" advice. The sales lady seemed very concerned that they would fit comfortably and be big enough for a few years. The skis we just rented.

With the new gear, we excitedly rode the cable car to the top and admired the scenery. I let Pete go ahead, so I could be right with him, should he need help. After a few minutes, the gentle slope became suddenly much steeper. In a ski area catering to tourists, such a drop would be clearly marked, but here the natives knew their mountain without signs.

I didn't yet see the drop-off. Pete misjudged the slope, skied too fast on the steeps and fell pretty hard. The binding didn't have to release, because he slipped out of the *boot*, and the ski with the boot still on it cruised down the slope and into the woods.

This was awful. What was I doing here, half a world from home, taking my kid into deep snow with a ski on only one foot and nothing but a sock on the other. How would I get him down the rest of the slope and then back up a T-bar lift, where one has to slide on the snow? Would he get frostbite and lose his toes? How irresponsible could I be?

To my great luck, the Austrians are not only good skiers but also friendly folks. Within a minute a young couple who had seen the mishap caught up with us. They were Sepp and Helga as I heard from their conversation.

"Don't worry," said Helga. "Sepp is good. He will find the ski." She helped Pete up, steadied him and let him rest his foot on top of *her* boot.

Sepp was already in the woods, 200 feet down.

"We just bought the boots this morning," I said as an excuse. "In the 'Ski House of Tyrol'."

"Oh, I know them." Helga nodded. "Who fitted him?"

I shrugged. "A middle-aged woman, plump, talkative ..."

"Must have been Frau Klammer, the owner. She fits everyone too large."

That eased my guilt feelings a little.

Sepp was already hiking up the slope, waving the ski at us.

Then the two helped Pete back into his boot. "I will adjust that buckle, right?" said Sepp. "There you go. That feels better, no? Now you won't any more lose the shoe." He gave Pete an encouraging smile.

"And look over there," said Helga, "see that trail? It's easy and leads you around that steep part here. Good luck!" They were gone before we could thank them.

For the rest of the week we skied with an instructor and on the last day of our vacation we were able to master that steep slope without losing anything. Sweet revenge.

Even now, more than 30 years later, I still feel ashamed. What an irresponsible mother. But did I only have troubles with Pete? Oh my, no. Poor Jeff, and poor Kenny.

****

I heard some commotion in the waiting room. Kaitlyn had returned for her cabbage patch doll. I took it from the shelf and handed it to her.

"Thanks again," said her mother. "You are such a caring person."

M-hm.

A Sailboat In the Living Room?

Some people are extremely neat. Everything has to be in its place, not one water spot on the kitchen table, not one toy on the floor; you know what I mean. My husband's mother was such a person. Others are just plain sloppy, and order seems to be painful to them. Most teen-agers fall into this category. As for myself, I'm somewhere in between. As long as things are clean and sanitary, it's fine with me. I have to be accurate enough with my patients' eyes and don't want to be fussy in the home, too. My husband usually agrees with that viewpoint.

Once, however, the constant clutter got on his nerves. "Say, can't you see to it that the kids are more tidy and put their toys away before they go to bed?"

"Probably," I said. "It would of course mean that I have to be always after them. 'Pick up the ball, put those cars away, the teddy bear belongs on the shelf, do this, don't do that ...' "

He thought for a while. "Nah," he said slowly. "That sounds like my mother. I hated our perfect home and her nagging. Just make sure the path from the door to the kitchen is clear." Then he gave me a hug. "A friendly atmosphere is more important."

One year, though, this attitude was really put to the test. Peter, then age 13, wanted to build a sailboat from a kit. After he and his dad had studied many catalogues, they chose a model and ordered it. Soon after, two huge boxes arrived.

"Mom, what's that?" asked seven-year-old Jeff.

"It's my boat!" shouted Pete. "See, it says 'Sunfish' on the box. That's its name." He gave the package a hug. "Isn't it great? Look at it!" In his mind, he saw already the finished product. To me, these were two heavy crates with something rattling inside.

Soon Dad came home. He and Peter put sawhorses in the backyard and placed the long pieces on them. All special things, such as the mast, the sword and its sheath, various cleats and some odd-shaped parts of the hull were in the kit. For other sections, wood had to be bought at the lumber yard and then carefully sawed according to a pattern, a real father-and-son project.

"That'll keep him busy all winter," said Tom. "He won't have time for much TV."

The material had arrived early in the fall when it was still warm, but now it often rained and got colder.

"Where will you work on your – ah, Sunfish in winter?" I asked.

It seems, my two ship builders hadn't thought about that. "I could do it in the basement," suggested Pete.

"The door's too small to get the whole boat back out," said Tom. "You could try the barn."

"In winter?" I asked. "With no heat?"

We all mulled over that question for a few days.

"Would the whole mess fit into the living room?" I asked.

Pete and Tom gave me a surprised look.

"It would fit," said Tom. "The boat will be 13 feet long, and our living room is 20. But do you really want the sawhorses and those boards, the dust and the noise in here for months?"

"Well, if this is what he'll do all winter, better here than in the barn. We'll walk around it," I said. "No noise while anyone wants to sleep, and no painting, O.K.? That'll have to wait till you can take it outside."

So, the two sawhorses and parts of the boat moved into our living room. Of course, Pete wasn't there all the time, and then we found the half-boat quite handy. One could nicely spread out the Sunday paper on it, Jeff's hot-wheel cars had a smoother surface for racing, and the Sunfish proved "shelter" when Jeff sat under it while watching cartoons. That year we put our Christmas tree, surrounded by the presents, on top of the new structure.

One day, while my husband was busy with patients in the office, Bill, our accountant, showed up. I had to take him into the house and apologized for the mess.

He spread his IRS forms on the hull and smiled. "Biggest desk I've ever had." After the tax work was done, he carefully inspected our set-up. "This is actually quite neat. My kids would like that, but my wife? I'm not sure about her."

"Look," I said, "it's our son's home, too. Besides, he won't build a boat every year."

"Can I make an airplane next year, Mommie?" Jeff had his own ideas.

Just then Pete came in and eagerly explained the details to Bill. "I had to drill all these hundreds of little holes, put the screws in and then spread on the caulking."

"Did that smell?" asked Bill.

"Not bad." Pete gave me a quick glance. "Then we bought that large sheet of plywood and sawed it like the pattern. And these pieces, see them? I had to soak them in the bathtub so they would bend. Now I still have to sand the whole thing before I can paint it."

"You are quite a guy." Bill put his hand on Pete's shoulder. "Next time I have to work with your mom, you'll be done."

One night I went downstairs when I heard a moanful, creaking noise. What was that? Then came a loud "Popp," followed by something like "Trepp-epp-epp" and another groan. I switched on the light. Oh my! The boat's sides were all straight, the bow had come apart.

Pete and Dad took it in stride. "We'll have to take bigger screws," said Pete.

"I didn't think those dainty nails would hold it together," said Tom with good hindsight.

By early May the Sunfish was finished. Bottom, sides and deck looked perfect. The sword and its sheath were in place, the well for the mast was installed. Even the bow stayed together

351

after Pete had applied more glue and extra clamps. "Now we'll take it outside for painting," he announced.

It took Dad and Pete only half a day to get the boat around a few corners into the open. They had to remove the front door and take the hinges off the frame. I think the two of them would have done away with the whole front wall of the house rather than disassemble the craft.

Finally the boat was outside. Pete and Dad raised the mast and hoisted the red-and-white sail which then happily luffed on our front lawn.

On Memorial Day we took the Sunfish to a nearby lake. It didn't leak! Pete and Dad tried it out and found it was quite easy to maneuver. Then Jeff got a long ride while Pete was tacking near the causeway giving his father a chance to take lots of pictures. The slim boat really was pretty with the colorful sail against the blue sky. After Jeff's ride, it was my turn. Pete ventured into the middle of the lake, where we caught a strong breeze. Exhilarating! Where had the kid learned to sail?

When we finally came back to shore, Jeff was playing with a little boy while Tom talked to his father.

"Hi," said the man. "Beautiful clipper you've got there. Your dad told me you've built it all by yourself."

"M-hm." Pete beamed. "Well, Dad helped some when we needed the power saw."

"How long did it take you?" the man wanted to know.

"All winter. And Mom let me build the boat in the living room."

The Chosen Child

"I'm glad you could come right away," said Mrs. Banker, the adoption agent at our Welfare Department. "I think we found a little boy for you."

Tom and I were all excited. "Where is he, when can we see him, how old is he ...?"

"Reddish blond, blue eyes, four and a half years, a repaired cleft palate. You agreed to a handicapped child, didn't you?"

We nodded.

"He lives in a little town outside of Korby, Kentucky," she said. "You didn't want a mentally handicapped child."

"No, we didn't," my husband said.

"It's a question here." Mrs. Banker opened a folder and closed it again. "He got poor scores on all evaluations ..."

Our faces grew longer and longer.

" ... but there is a report from a psychologist that Kenny did above age level work the first 80 percent of all tests and then he quit. No one could make him finish his work. They don't quite know what that means. I don't either."

"How about if we drive there and take a look at the child, meet him, talk to him ..." I said.

"I wanted to suggest that. Let me know when you can go. His social workers in Korby said they'll make all the arrangements for you, hotel reservations, meeting time and place. Take your son along. He's important.

****

When we got to Korby, we all were tired, more from emotion than from the drive.

A bellboy helped with the luggage. "Hey, this suitcase is empty," he said.

353

"M-hm."   My husband nodded.   "We're getting a new child."

The porter looked at me quizzically. "And you'll put him in here?"

"No," I said, "but his things."

The man clearly thought we were nuts and left quickly, not even waiting for a tip.

****

Next morning we met the two adoption agents from Korby, Mrs. Warner and Miss Snellen.

"He is eager to meet you," said Mrs. Warner. "Talked about you yesterday. He wanted to know how old Jeff is, but I didn't know."

"I'm nine and a half," said Jeff. "I'll be the older brother now. When Pete was alive, I was the younger one."

"You'll be very important," said Miss Snellen. "I think of all your family, Kenny will like you best, so you'll have to make friends with him."

"Yeah," said Jeff. "I'll try."

While Mrs. Warner went to pick up Kenny, Miss Snellen took us to a state park.

Soon Kenny arrived – a cute little boy with a slightly crooked nose.

We all greeted him and Mrs. Warner told him who everyone was.

Kenny had a pleasant smile, but held on to Mrs.Warner and didn't say anything.

"Hey, Ken," Jeff said. "Look at those swings. Wanna try 'em?"

"Been here befo'," said Kenny and ran to the swings, getting on one seat. "Gimme a poosh," he said to Mrs. Warner.

She motioned me to do it.

"Higher," he said.

I pushed harder. "That enough?" I asked

"No. Higher," he hollered with a loud and surprisingly deep voice. A little kid with a baritone sound.

"I don't want you to break your neck first time I see you," I said.

"Look at me," Jeff called out wanting to show off.

Dad and Miss Snellen motioned to him that he should hold it down and not out-do Kenny.

"Let's race over to that tree," said Jeff.

Kenny started before Jeff was off the swing, so the little guy reached the tree first. "I won, I won," he shouted. "Race ya' there." He pointed to the table.

They did. Jeff was way ahead but then slowed down to let Kenny win once more.

Kenny knew how the merry-go-round worked. He showed it to Tom.

"Jeff," said Miss Snellen, "we all know that you can run faster. It was kind of you to let Kenny win. He needs to feel good now."

Jeff just smiled. It's not easy to be a psychologist at age nine.

****

In the car Kenny pulled on my hair.

"Let him," said Mrs. Warner. "He's trying to make contact with you."

"Is there a big fly sitting on my pony tail?" I was trying to shake it off.

"Yeah, there is," said Kenny with a big grin, playing "fly" again and again.

"Better than if he'd ignore you," Mrs. Warner whispered.

At the motel Kenny inspected our room. He didn't know what the TV was. When Jeff switched it on, Kenny started to

355

cry and hid behind the bed. "Boogey-man will get me." He was quite afraid.

"Oh, I understand," said Mrs. Warner. "His folks belong to a fundamentalist religious group. TV and toys are considered a sin. We should have told you that."

"Makes no difference to us," said Tom.

I thought not watching TV for a while would be refreshing, but I said nothing.

To cheer up Kenny, Jeff unpacked a few toy cars. For a while the two played happily and checked who could imitate an engine sound louder.

"Brrrrrrrrrrrrrr," made Jeff.

"B-U-RRRRRRRRRRRRRRRRRR," countered Kenny.

Both cheered when the cars crashed.

After a while Mrs. Warner was ready to take him home.

"Want to take these cars along?" Tom asked.

Kenny hid behind Mrs. Warner's skirt and whispered, "Boogey-man."

"All right," she said. "These cars will still be here tomorrow, and here the Boogey man can't get them."

As she walked to the car with Kenny, he turned and looked back at us.

****

Next morning when Kenny came with Miss Snellen, I played catch with him. He let out a boisterous laugh whenever he got hold of me. Then, without any provocation that I could see, he scratched me on the face, bit my arm and tried to choke me.

He didn't really hurt me, but the sudden turn from happy play to hostility stunned me. I slapped him on the cheek before I could think.

He slowly stepped back, held his hand to his cheek and looked at Miss Snellen, at Tom, and at Jeff. None of them said anything.

Then he looked at me for a while, climbed on my lap, and fingered the collar of my dress. When I put my hand on his shoulder, he held still. Seemed we were friends again.

"Let's take a ride," said Tom. "Kenny, Jeff and I will go. Mom and Miss Snellen can stay here and rest.

****

"What is his foster family really like?" I asked. "We don't know much about them."

"His mother, Mrs. Meynard, is about fifty-five," she said.

"That's rather old to take care of a child so young," I mused.

"Right. She can't quite keep up with such a lively boy."

"Is there a father?" I asked.

"Mr. Meynard works in a factory and is quite withdrawn. I feel he is a 'non-person' to his children as well as to his wife. Of course, that's just my impression."

"What other kids are there?" I asked.

"The Meynards have two teen-age boys, their own, and two foster children. Billy, who is 12, and Kenny," said Miss Snellen.

"How do they all get along?"

"The two older boys have outgrown their mother's influence, and Billy hangs around with them. Hunting seems to be their main source of fun. The father minds his own business."

"So Kenny is the only one close to her?" I asked.

"Right. And you know, you are the eighteenth set of parents willing to adopt him. All the others came and then declined. I could never figure out why."

My husband and the kids came back, loaded with toys. There were balls in assorted sizes, a big teddy bear, a pail and shovel for the beach, some picture books, more cars and trucks.

Kenny's favorite toy was a wooden duck on wheels. When pulled by its string, it made a ratchety sound.

"Isn't that a toy for a much younger age level?" I asked.

"Don't forget," said Miss Snellen, "he hasn't had any toys at all."

"Oh yes," I said. "I'll have to adjust."

****

Next day Kenny came with several shopping bags, filled with his clothes and a blanket. "Here," he said and handed them to me.

"Oh Kenny, we brought an extra suitcase for you." I took it out of the closet.

"You brung that one for me? How'd ya know I come along?"

"We hoped you would," said Tom. "Let's put your things in here."

Meanwhile I asked Mrs. Warner, "How did his farewell from the foster mother go?"

"Surprisingly smooth. He and his mother both smiled as if they had a secret pact. Not at all as if he were leaving forever. I can't explain it."

****

Life at our home was hectic. Kenny was in constant motion, restless, fidgety. He was extremely loud, shouting in his deep voice and making a ruckus even if he was in a good mood. He often had bouts of bad behavior, spitting in the babysitter's face, hitting the dog, spilling food and being contrary any way he could.

Once a helicopter circled over our house. "That's my maw! She's looking for me." He was convinced.

"Kenny, that's a patrol copter. Your old mommie isn't in there."

"Oh yeah. She tol' me she'd come and git me!"

He waved at the helicopter. When it finally disappeared, Kenny was sad. "She'll come back?" he asked in a very small voice.

For a while he stayed pensive, but in the afternoon he and Jeff were whooping it up with water pistols. At night Dad took them both target shooting with a BB gun and Ken did better than either of them.

"Bull's eye, I hit the bull's eye," he shouted. "Every time."

I didn't quite believe it.

"This kid is a fantastic shot," said Tom. "Must have experience."

Kenny's bedtime was prolonged today. He kept bragging about his marksmanship.

****

Two weeks had passed in this raucous, hyperactive way. The household revolved around Kenny. Most of the time he was boisterous and happy.

Today was a difficult day. He had fits of crying and got upset about little things. Finally he flung himself onto the couch and cried quietly. When I approached, he turned his head away.

"You are homesick and miss your old mommie, don't you?" I asked.

He turned towards me, surprised that I knew what was bothering him.

"You miss your brothers, too, can't go hunting with them."

"They wouldn't a took me 'cause I'm too little." He pouted.

"Did they play with you?"

"Showed me how to use a sling shot. We'd shoot blackbirds."

I tried to stroke his head, but he pulled back.

"I want my maw!" His tears welled up again.

"I know how you feel."

"No, you don't," he nearly shouted.

359

"But I do," I said. "We've told you that Jeff had an older brother. He's dead now."

"Pete?"

"M-hm. He died last summer. I know how it is when you want someone but can't have him back. How it hurts."

We both said nothing for a long while.

Then Kenny got up and leaned his head against my shoulder. I put my arm around him and he snuggled his sticky little hand into mine. We shared our grief.

****

"Say, Kenny, remember you had many tests before you came here?" I asked.

"Tests?"

"Yes, like puzzles and questions. You probably had to put things in order."

"Oh yeah. At Miss Hawkins' and at that man. That what you mean?"

"That's probably it. What did your old mommie say you should do at those tests?"

Without a second's hesitation he said, "Told me 'Say nothing.' "

"What if you had to say something? They knew you could talk."

" 'Say you can't. Always tell 'em you can't' she said. 'Don't finish it.' "

That's strange, I thought. Why did she want him to appear stupid, unadoptable? "Did she say what would happen if you did well and finished your work?"

"Yeah. They'll take me away from home."

"Oh." Now I understood. She wanted to keep him. Out of love?

"But now I'm here anyway."

"Is that bad?" I asked.

360

"No," he said with a smile. "Now I like it here. I didn't right when I got here." He looked at me as if to check whether he had hurt my feelings.

When I didn't get upset, he said, "And when I was bad, you didn't send me back, neither."

"Is this why you are so nasty at times?"

"Yeah. My old mom, she said, be real bad. Then they'll send you back."

****

After his bath, I wrapped Kenny in a huge towel and carried him to his bed where his pajamas were waiting.

"When Jeff was a baby, and Pete," he asked, "you had to keep 'em, didn't ya?"

"Why, yes." I didn't quite know what he was aiming at.

"But when you got me you could 'a not took me. You could 'a wanted another one."

"We picked you."

"I picked you too, from all the others."

"Were there many others?" I asked.

"Oh yea. They got there and looked and then they went away again. But that's O.K. 'cause I didn't want 'em neither."

"We wanted you," I said. "You are just right for us."

When I pulled the pajama top over his head, he put his arms around my neck. "My mommie," he whispered. "My new mommie."

This was a badge of honor. I had graduated. A lump was in my throat, and my eyes were wet. The chosen child had now accepted *us*.

Hertha Binder

Adventures in Hawaii

When Jeff was 11 and Kenny six years old (and I was pushing 50), my husband wanted to attend a medical course in Hawaii and take the family along. We planned that I wouldn't go to lectures, just sight-see and have fun with the kids.

On a vacation, I like to *do* things in addition to admiring natural wonders, architecture or art. The kids also want to be active, maybe learn new skills.

The first morning on Waikiki Beach, we admired the palm trees, the deep sand and the huge waves. Later we bounced around in the surf, enjoying the warm water. Then we saw how a few native Hawaiians were taking guests in an outrigger canoe. Two or three boats made the trip together, 10 guests and one guide in each. These boats are real narrow canoes but can't tip because a floating timber is rigged out about eight feet from the hull. This provides stability to make them seaworthy.

Of course, the kids wanted to try that.

In our canoe was a woman in a yellow blouse who didn't look too athletic and was visibly scared. "Won't this thing break apart?" she asked Mike, the guide.

"Lady," he said, "the first Hawaiians used these boats 1,500 years ago. They came all the way from Samoa, 2,000 miles away. These boats are sturdy." Pride was in his voice.

"The boat is that old?"

Her husband hushed her and apparently explained.

Mike gave each of us a paddle and instructions. "When we go out, we'll paddle slowly, you can look around, like there to Diamond Head. Pretty, no?"

"Does he own the mountain?" whispered Jeff.

I laughed. "He's just proud of it."

"Out where the water gets dark and deep," Mike pointed, "we'll turn around. When I say, you have to paddle real fast and hard so we catch the wave."

363

Most of us nodded with obedient disbelief.

"If you don't paddle hard, we won't get fast like the wave and just bob up and down out there for the rest of the day."

Just before the deep water, he turned the canoe around and looked over his shoulder for a suitable wave. Our neighboring boat took off. "We'll get a bigger wave than that," said Mike and then he shouted, "Now paddle hard, stroke, stroke, stroke, harder, stroke ... that's it; stop, relax."

The water made a strange, swishing sound, and we found ourselves on the down-slope of a huge wave. What a surprise – we stayed on the same part of the wave all the way in. An odd sensation.

"Yahoo," "Wowee," "Great," "What a ride," "Terrific." Our group laughed and whooped it up.

"Now we turn around and do it once more," said Mike. "You've paid for it. But if someone wants to get off, you can do it here." He looked at Mrs. yellow blouse. She ignored him.

We all wanted to repeat the ride. The second trip out was even better. Everyone knew what to expect and was relaxed.

"You are a real good team." Was the compliment included in the price of the ride?

On the way in, a surfer was riding the same wave we were on.

Mike pointed at him. "See," he said to Jeff, "same thing, only he stands up."

Jeff's eyes were big. "Mom, can we try it?"

I pretended not to hear.

When we met Tom for lunch, Jeff was hopping with excitement. "Dad, you know what, Mom said we take a surfing lesson if Kenny can stay with you."

"I didn't say that!"

"Well, you didn't say no." Kids are such diplomats.

Having finished lunch, Tom said, "Come on, Kenny. Let those two athletes ride the waves."

On the beach was Allen, a middle aged man with typical Hawaiian features. He looked at Jeff. "He's a bit young, no?"

"I can swim real good." Jeff was emphatic.

Then Allen looked at me. "And you ...?"

I ignored the implication that I was too weak or too old for a first time surfing.

He took two boards from a rack, huge, heavy things. Just then a surfer walked by with a much smaller board.

"Why do we get such big ones?" asked Jeff.

"So you won't fall off," said Allen. "Big ones are more steady, don't tip." He put the boards on the sand, had us lie down on them, nicely in the center, and made us practice the strokes with our arms.

A few tourists, strolling on the beach, stopped and watched us. One lady laughed out loud.

Allen came to our defense. "You want to try too?" he said to the onlookers. "Can't surf if you don't first get out there."

And then we were in the water. I am a fairly good swimmer and always felt I did most of the work with my legs, but on this board, I couldn't use them at all. So I slid back until I was to my waist in the water and tried kicking.

Whoa! The front of the board rose up, and the next wave flipped it.

"What you doing?" asked Allen. "Got to stay on board."

Embarrassed, I scooted back on.

We made it all the way out, and Allen got off his board.

"You can still stand here?" I was amazed.

"M-hm," he said. "But a little farther out is deep."

I understood. Here was the edge of the "continental shelf." (Maybe "island shelf" would be more correct.)

While Allen turned us around, Jeff looked as if he regretted his courage, but I had no time to worry.

"We let Mom go first," Allen said to Jeff. "You watch."

"Now you paddle real hard to catch wave," he commanded me.

365

I did as I was told, but the wave just bobbed me up.

"You not fast enough." Allen explained. "Come back again."

Doing that, I slid off the board and had to struggle back on. What a slippery thing. This was exhausting.

Allen pointed me in the right direction. "Now go," he shouted and apparently gave the board a strong push.

This time I made it. There is no mistaking it when you catch the wave.

"Get up," I heard Allen yell.

Gingerly I raised myself on my hands and knees, and finally I did stand up for a proud 30 seconds. What a feeling! Then I fell off. By the time I had shaken the water out of my ears and retrieved the board, Allen and Jeff were there.

"You did good," said Allen, "but you must stand up quicker."

"Did you see me, Mom?" Jeff was beaming. "I could stand on it longer than you."

Of course.

Allen looked at his watch. "Let's go out again. We have time for two more rides."

Now he showed us how to avoid getting dowsed by the waves while paddling out.

Less tense, we could ride easier, but at the end I still fell off, shooting the board 30 feet in the air.

For the rest of the day, Jeff and I were jabbering about surfing. My husband listened patiently while Kenny ignored us.

From lying on the surfboard I had a terrific sunburn on my back and particularly on my thighs.

Next morning, I bought a pair of cheap jeans at a 5 & 10. I wore those with a long- sleeved blouse. Allen nodded approval to my outfit. He was much friendlier on the second day; seems he wasn't worried any more that we'd drown.

We went out five times, caught the wave, got up quickly and rode it all the way it. I even learned to pick up the board before I fell. Smooth.

"Did you see me, Mom? I turned once all the way round. Did you?"

"No, Jeff. I'm glad to just go straight."

In our room, my husband and Kenny were all excited.

"You were real great," said Tom.

"How do you know?"

"We watched you with the binoculars."

"You could recognize us?"

"Sure," said Kenny. "You're the only surfer with long pants. And I saw Jeff spin around before he wiped out."

"Dad, how long is the stretch we ride?" asked Jeff.

"About a third of a mile."

"No wonder I'm bushed." I sat down.

Tom gave me a squeeze. "You're doing pretty good for an old chick, Dear."

****

On the last day of our vacation, we flew in a little plane to the "Big Island" of Hawaii, a short hop from Honolulu. The largest island of the group has two extinct volcanoes, Mauna Loa and Mauna Kea, each more than 13,000 feet above sea level – and the sea is right beside those giants. An active volcano, not as high, is Kilauea (keel-how-A-uh), the center of the Volcanoes National Park.

"You've seen pictures of volcanoes before," said Tom as we drove to the park in a little rental car. "Can't be too much new stuff."

"We'll find out," I mumbled.

A road leads along the rim of the Kilauea crater, and from secured observation points one can look inside. A footpath winds down the extremely steep walls. The ground on the bottom of the crater, about 500 feet below, looked cracked, crumbling. Although we saw a group of tourists in the depth, we quite happily stayed on top. Even to me it seemed that one of those cracks could suddenly open up and swallow a reckless visitor. Opposite us, steam or smoke escaped in little puffs. The mountain was exhaling.

When we continued in the car around the crater, we saw, close to that smoke, signs advising people with heart or lung problems not to proceed because breathing might be too difficult.

"We all are healthy," said Tom.

"Hey, neat," said Jeff. "Wonder why some people can't breathe there."

Hundred feet later, we found out: a concentrated smell of smoke mixed with sulfur, like rotten eggs, and something pungent that gave us a suffocating feeling. We quickly closed all the windows. Didn't make a bit of difference. The intensity of the stench was overwhelming. Maybe hell smells like that. Although we could see that about half a mile later visitors would be out of this zone, we all agreed to turn back, the sooner the better. Again in a more pleasant environment, we took in deep gulps of air as we looked back at the spot where the volcano shows how alive it is.

A little later we had lunch in the elegant "Crater Rim Restaurant," with another stunning view across the crater. Binoculars were mounted on a deck to let people observe details.

The nearby nature center showed a 15-minute sound movie of the last eruption. To have as foreground parts of the restaurant we had just visited, drew us right into the events.

"Hey," said Kenny, "we were just there."

"Look!" Jeff was all excited. "There are the binoculars!"

Glowing lava was flowing down the mountainside, gurgling, steaming, bubbling.

"Can you imagine that smell?" said Jeff.

At the end of the movie was a shot with the restaurant's deck burned down. We all were quite shook up.

"Any questions?" asked the ranger.

"How could the guy breathe who took the movie?" asked Jeff.

"The whole crew wore gas masks. They couldn't have stood it without them."

"And the porch," said Kenny, "it burned in the movie."

"Yes, it did," said the ranger. She showed Kenny a picture of the smoke-stained building with only a few charred timbers left of the deck.

"Why do they build it again on the same spot?" asked my husband.

"Kilauea erupts every few years, but the buildings – this here as well as the restaurant – are not always damaged. It depends which direction the lava flows. If they are scorched, we build them up again. It's well worth it for the many thousands of visitors."

Next, we went to a lava tube. We learned that towards the end of an eruption, when the lava flow slows down, the outside cools, gets hard and forms a crust. The inner parts are still liquid and run out leaving an empty tube. We had seen the process in the movie. The one we visited was about 100 feet long and four feet high. In a crouch, we all walked through it.

"Hey, Dad, what's that funny looking plant?" asked Jeff outside.

"By golly, it's a fern."

"They grow as big as trees?"

"Look," said Kenny. "It has no shadow."

"Probably because the sun is straight above us," said Tom.

"It's now early in July," I said slowly. "And as far as I know, we are here at about 20 degrees latitude. That would fit."

"It's called 'the sun is in the zenith,' " stated Jeff.

"Wise guy," muttered Kenny and then he said to me, "Look, Mom, I have no shadow either. Can you take a picture?"

"Sure can."

Then we piled back into our little car.

"Where do we go now?" asked Kenny.

"Back to the airport," said Dad.

"Can't we first go to that black beach?" asked Jeff. "I want to see it. Don't you, Mom?"

I wasn't too curious about a black beach. One could get dirty, I assumed, and we had no change of clothes along. To please the kids, though, Tom drove there.

The beach is not very large. About a third of a mile long and 50 to 70 feet wide. The sand is intensely black (of course it's lava that has been ground down by the pounding surf). I had never seen such a mass of black before, except large heaps of coal beside railroad depots, when I was a kid. That stuff was dirty. If you touched it, you couldn't brush it off your hands or your clothes.

Therefore I guessed the black sand would also leave smudges on us. But even after we had walked on it, our tennis shoes were still clean. Cautiously, I picked up a handful of that unusual stuff.

"Oh, it's light," I said. "Weighs much less than regular sand."

My three guys tried it, too.

Then, opening my fingers gently, I blew softly on the sand like on a dandelion in seed, and ever so lightly, the little grains flew off. They seemed to float. What a delight.

We sat down at a picnic table and took in the scene: I couldn't get over the shimmering, saturated blackness of the sand. Nowhere was it less black or a bit grey. Not where it was wet from the waves, not where it was dry, not when the sunlight reflected off it, nor in the shade. Velvety black. The foam of the waves rhythmically washed over it – a brilliant white. The sea was turquoise, and the coconut trees rimming the beach were a dark, luscious green.

I had seen pictures of this place before and had thought that the colors were exaggerated. They were not; actually they were pale compared to the strong hues of the real thing. We sat for a long time. Even the kids were quiet.

The next day, on the long flight home, I reviewed my impressions of the Hawaiian Islands. Beauty is everywhere, in the steep, green, fluted mountains, in the turquoise sea and the huge, white capped waves, each majestic in its quarter mile width. Three things impressed me most: the awareness of the force that a wave exerts when you surf it, the smell of the volcano and the ethereal beauty of the black sand.

Hertha Binder

Without the Kids, I'd Have Missed That Fun

When Jeff was 15 and Kenny 10, we went skiing to Big Sky, a resort in Montana, south of Bozeman. Chet Huntley, the newscaster, was instrumental in its growth. The ski area was well developed with a beautiful lodge (our room even had a loft), well laid out trails and efficient lifts. The weather was agreeable, and we had a great time skiing, same as on other places before.

"Mom," said Jeff one afternoon, "they have snowmobile rides advertised. Can we go?"

Most skiers don't like snowmobiles. They are annoyed by the gasoline smell, the noise and the fact that one has to control a machine which is huge and heavy compared to a pair of skis. I share this view, but to please the kids, I agreed.

We signed up for an "all-day" trip, 10 a.m. to 4 p.m. Jeff would take me on the back of his sled, so I didn't have to drive that thing.

"Oh, no," said Tim, one of the guides. "In this rugged country, we can use only small machines, every rider for himself."

Oh boy. Jeff gave me a questioning look, worried I might back out, but Tim was already explaining how to start, steer and stop the machine, what to do when crossing a slope or when it goes steeply up or down.

"Don't worry," he said. "I'll be in front and Jill here, our second guide, will bring up the rear, so we won't lose any one."

Jill gave me an encouraging smile.

Our group was small. Besides the three of us there was only a young couple, Dan and Susan. They were obviously familiar with snowmobiles and didn't need instructions.

So we took off on a narrow back-road, Jill right behind me. After a few minutes, we had to cross an avalanche that had come down just two days earlier. The snow seemed unstable, the trail across was not well packed down, and therefore the sled leaned heavily downhill. To say that I was ill at ease would be an understatement.

"Hey, Mom, I nearly flipped," bragged Kenny. "Did you see me? This is real fun."

"M-hm," was all the agreement he could get out of me.

Back on the road, Tim stopped when his machine belched out black smoke. He and Jill fiddled with the motor for a while.

"You'll have to wait," he said. "We'll go back and get another sled."

How encouraging.

While we waited, it started to snow. Big heavy flakes were slowly floating down.

After abut 15 minutes, Tim came racing back. "Let's go!" He revved up his engine. Jill had not come along, and my confidence sank another notch. However, the trail was not too difficult, and in spite of more wind and snow, I was warm from being so tense.

"Let's have lunch now," said Tim a few miles into the valley. "There is a storm supposed to come in later today." He had chosen a spot where overhanging evergreens shielded the trail from wind and snow. It was dark, though, as if dusk were setting in before noon.

Tim broke a few dead branches off the trees, piled them up beside his sled, poured some gasoline on and lit them. Soon the spooky red flames contrasted with the surrounding dark grey. A spark of life in the stillness of winter. Tim had brought along different sandwiches, nicely wrapped in aluminum foil: Reuben, ham and cheese, corn beef. When heated in the fire, they were just perfect. No sauerkraut has ever tasted as delicious as the one in my Reuben. After a while, he even produced hot coffee; I hadn't seen how.

During our leisurely lunch, the fire warmed some of the snow on overhanging branches. A big gob fell on Jeff, just inside his collar. While I tried to brush it out, another lump of snow hit me on the head, and one plopped on Susan's sandwich.

"It was too hot anyway," she said with a giggle.

By now it was snowing heavily and the visibility was down to a few feet.

"We better head back," said Tim. "You guys don't want to be out here if this turns into a blizzard."

We didn't argue.

The return trip was easier; downhill, the machine didn't struggle as much, or – maybe – I was used to it. Strange enough, as we approached the ranch, the snowing stopped, the sky became much lighter, and in the distance the sun peeked through a small hole in the clouds.

"Hey," said Tim. "That storm passed us by. Tell you what, we still owe you some riding time. Let's go there." He motioned with his head to a trail leading south.

By now I felt pretty comfortable, "vro-o-o-ming" it up with the rest of them. After a while we reached a ridge with a surprising view. Mountains and valleys were spread out before us. Steam billowed behind small stands of trees, coating them with thick hoarfrost.

"We are here on the boarder of Yellowstone Park," said Tim. "But we can't drive in."

"Why not?"

"It's against the law. Noisy, heavy snowmobiles would bother one kind of animals – you guess which."

"Elk." "Coyotes." "Bears." "Buffalo." "Eagles." The answers kept coming.

"Nope. All those critters wouldn't mind us much. It's the mice who would be bothered."

"Mice?" asked Dan. "For heaven's sake, who cares about mice?"

"They live now under the snow," explained Tim, "running in little tunnels, sheltered from the storms. They find enough grain from old grasses."

375

"And?" asked Jeff.

"They are close to the bottom of the food chain, and many of the larger animals depend on them. If owls, eagles, coyotes, foxes and even bears can't find anything bigger or better to eat, they'll all take mice. Without them, many of the big animals would starve to death."

"So we stay away to protect the mice?" I asked.

"Yeah." Tim mounted his sled again. "In the park snowmobiles are allowed on only one road from the town of West Yellowstone to Old Faithful. Nowhere else." With that he turned his engine around. "Let's go home now. We'll take a different trail. Bet you'll like it."

Slow in turning, I wound up as the "caboose" of our group. They barely waited for me, and I just heard the last words of Tim's explanation. "This is a 45 degree slope, not even half a mile long. You have to go down straight. If you try to make turns, you'll flip the sled. It's too steep for that."

Before I could sputter an objection, he was off, and the rest followed him. For gosh's sake, what could I do? Don't turn sideways, he had said. So I went down straight. Believe me, 45 degrees is steep! First I moved as slowly as the machine would go, but when I was still on top of my sled after a hundred feet, I let go, went fast and – I hated to admit it – had a ball.

Tim and the others waited on the bottom.

"Good job," he said. "Let's do it once more. Anyone who doesn't want to come along, can wait. We'll be back." He looked at me.

I pretended not to notice.

Going up and around that slope, I was right behind Tim. Yeah. Down the second time, I whooped it up with the rest of them and even beat Kenny. What a feeling! What a day!

In the evening, Jeff asked, "Mom, in the end you liked it, didn't you?"

"M-hm. Once I wasn't scared, it was great." I gave both my kids a hug.

"See," said Kenny. "Without us, you'd have missed that fun."

A Less Than Perfect Mother
Part II

When I had again time to sit and reflect, more memories came back to me although I didn't really want them – results of my klutzy misjudgement.

... when we went skiing to Big Sky (see the previous chapter), I did not yet use a travel bureau, but called the airline myself. The sales rep told me of a reduced fare which I gladly accepted. "But the direct flight has no cheap seats left," she said. "So you'll have to change planes." All right, for $100 we could do that. But she hadn't told me where and how often. We had to change planes in Chicago and in Minneapolis-St. Paul and had a half hour stop in Billington, Montana.

Because all those sectional flights were just short hops, no real food was served on board. After several hours of those hop scotch flights we were quite hungry, so in Billings I left the plane to buy lunch.

"Mom, are you sure you'll be back in time? What'll we do if you miss the plane?" asked Jeff.

"Don't worry, I'll tell the stewardess to wait for me."

In the little restaurant on the concourse, the people ahead of me had to kill time between flights, and the waitress was tired.

"Could you give me whatever you have ready? My plane leaves in five minutes," I pleaded.

She handed me cheeseburgers and Cokes.

The three of us sat in one of those narrow tourist class seat rows, with me in the middle. The kids put the food trays down, and I set the drinks and sandwiches on them. Oops, only two straws, must have lost one. No problem. I just took the lid off my drink.

Still excited from the unusual experience of finding take-out food in an unfamiliar airport, I talked a lot and with one sweeping gesture knocked over my large Coke. Most of it hit

379

Jeff, soaking him and his seat; a good bit landed on me, running down my leg; even Kenny, on my other side, got splashed. There was of course no way I could reach my purse under the seat for tissues or anything to blot up the mess.

The kids surprised me. Other than some shocked outcries of "Mom!" they were rather restrained. I'd have expected many more complaints from them, being wet because of such a klutzy mother. Only much later did the stewardess bring us some paper napkins. And is that Coke sticky! After the plane and a drafty airport, we still had a two hour damp and clammy bus ride.

... and Kenny! In my mind I leafed through my diary. We had adopted him when he was four and a half, and during the first year he was always afraid we would leave him somewhere (Sunday School, babysitter's) and then "forget" to pick him up. Therefore he was very clingy and loved to ride piggy-back. My husband often carried him for hours on his shoulders. On me, Kenny had his legs at my waist and somehow grabbed my clothes. Usually I held on to one of his hands or a foot, but I became so used to this sweet and not-so-little burden that at times I wasn't quite aware of him. If you carry a knapsack, you don't *always* think of it either.

Maybe he had dozed off or was interested in something else while I unlocked the door with one hand and balanced a grocery bag in the other. I didn't even feel him slide off. There was just the ugly sound of bone hitting concrete. His head had struck the threshold. What a mother was I anyway? Couldn't I be trusted to take care of my child? Was that bag of groceries more important than Kenny? Of course he cried and hollered, and when I cuddled him that day, I watched anxiously for a concussion which, fortunately, did not develop. Lucky again.

... Kenny's fall reminded me of an event many years earlier. My mother's kid-brother and his young wife had a summer house near a lake. During the vacation when I was 16, I spent a whole month there, swimming, bicycling, enjoying the outdoors. All I had to do was help my aunt a little around the house and watch their one-year-old daughter, Christa. The little one was then crawling swiftly all over the place. While my uncle was at work and aunt out for an errand, I played with the toddler. Then the mail came. I glanced through the newspaper, and an article caught my attention.

"Bang, bang, bang!" Christa had fallen the three high steps from the kitchen onto the patio, banging her head three times. She screamed for 20 minutes and also got a goose egg on her head, but that kid had so much hair, it covered the swelling. I didn't know what to do. Rush her to an E.R.? Confess when my aunt came home? Christa gradually calmed down, and when her mother returned, she was her smiling, lively self.

My aunt didn't ask anything like, "How did it go? Everything O.K.?"

So I kept quiet.

For many years I worried whether Christa would develop normally. Would she, perhaps, be retarded because of the head injury? When she was 30, her father wrote about her professional success, about all the responsibilities she had as the manager of a large department and the innovations she had introduced. What a relief! Now I let them know how glad I was that she hadn't suffered any long lasting damage from that injury years ago.

To judge from my uncle's prompt answer, the family was highly amused by my late confession.

Well, all this happened when I was young and inexperienced. What about now, what about Grandson Chuck? No, I didn't let him fall on his head. No, we had no major mishaps while skiing, waterskiing, rafting etc. But ... oh, yeah!

We went once a year to Seaworld where he enjoyed the huge playground "Capt'n Kids" more than any of the shows. He particularly liked the challenge of the many diverse and artful rope ladders.

One summer, the previous set-ups had been removed and a whole building had been erected: L-shaped, each wing at least 30 yards long and three stories high. All this space was criss-crossed by rope tunnels. What a challenge for six-year old Chuck.

"You know," I said, "I can't come with you. No adults allowed."

"Why?"

"I'd probably get stuck, and lots of grown-ups would be too heavy and tear down the ropes."

"O.K., Grandma. I'll climb to that red rope. See it? Then I come back."

He was off, and several kids followed him while I watched. It's a bit confusing to look through that maze. He seemed already past the red rope, but couldn't turn back with all the people behind him. Where I had thought the path branched off to the left, it apparently didn't. Suddenly I was extremely hot. I thought I could still see him with his white T-shirt and dark shorts. Or was that another kid? Now I was shivering.

I really wondered whether this was the right time for me to get hysterical and cry and scream, but I waited a bit. When I knew that I had lost Chuck, I went to the ground level and stood in the center of that "L". It wasn't crowded, so he had to be able to see me from any place, if he was looking.

A few more anxious minutes passed, and then I saw Chuck walking on the hand of one of the park's employees. She didn't have to ask whether this was the right kid for the right grandma. He took one deep sob, and then we held on to each other in a very long hug. I knew it wasn't his fault, and he knew it wasn't mine. But of course I was responsible.

During our visits in the following years, he didn't even want to come close to "Capt'n Kids," much less go in there and play.

Parasailing – Floating Like A Cloud

We sat at the shore of the lake, resting after a morning of hard water skiing. Jeff, my 18-year-old son, remarked how quiet it was, all the morning activity on the lake had ebbed away. There was only the lapping of the wavelets on the shore, a bird's cry, and far away the hum of an outboard motor. The last wisps of fog dissolved in the warming sun.

As a boat came around the bend, there was a huge, red and white parachute serenely floating over the lake; a startling sight, like something from outer space.

"Oh, Mom," gasped Jeff in disbelief. "What's that?"

"Seems to be a parasail. See, the guy is strapped in a harness to the chute? The speed of the boat lifts the parachute, and the person is taken aloft."

Jeff stood up. He wanted to be a few feet closer to that floating miracle. "Where do you think they come from?"

"They take off just two houses down the road from here at that green dock. Want to try it sometimes?"

Instead of an answer he started walking towards the green dock. Suddenly he stopped. "Say, Mom, how come you know all that?"

"I heard about it last fall and thought it might be fun."

We had reached the place. The boat had just come in, the parasailer was in the water and the chute collapsed behind him. A small crowd of excited young people was on the dock.

The driver of the boat came towards us, a 'what-can-I-do-for-you' look on his face. "I'm Mike."

"We'd like to make a reservation."

"How's eleven o'clock?"

"Just fine." Jeff looked at his watch; only an hour to go.

"How many?" asked Mike.

"Two."

"We'll see you at eleven," he said and walked back to his boat.

Jeff hesitated. "Say, Mom, who is 'two?' "

"One is you, of course."

"And the other?"

I answered with a big grin.

"You, Mom? They won't believe it! What will Dad say?"

"Oh, Dad's far away. When he finds out, I'll be back down."

The truth is, I had been thinking about parasailing all winter long, wanting to try it but at the same time being afraid; would I have the guts to do it once I had a chance?

I had figured out what the dangers could be and had thought of all possible mishaps and their consequences. If the boat would stall, what then? I would slowly float down to the water. The same would happen if the 300 foot rope connecting me to the boat would break. That didn't bother me. I'm a good swimmer an certainly not afraid of water; besides, I'd have a life jacket on. Where would the chute be? Probably behind me. What if it were to come down on top of me? 'Well,' I thought, 'there'd be air pockets between chute and water, and if not, I can always dive around it.' All this reasoning didn't prevent my stomach from twisting in knots.

Back at our cabin, our friends had just finished breakfast. They were ranging in age from 14 to 26; most of them were class mates of my kids.

"Guess what Mom's gonna do!" Jeff shouted in excitement.

My "crazy" ideas often influenced the plans of the whole group.

"She's going up with that thing; it's called parasailing," Jeff explained.

"No, Mom," said Kenny, my 14-year-old. "You can't; you are too old."

'Oh, yeah,' I thought. 'I'll show ya.'

I felt dizzy, but the events progressed too quickly to worry about that: get on the dock, harness on, last minute instructions; the boat gave a roar, and I was in the air.

This was absolutely beautiful. It's strangely quiet as if the sounds from earth could not reach upwards. Slight puffs of wind set me in a gently swaying motion. The dock all but disappeared. We now approached the village church. I was higher than the steeple; over on the other side, I could see the next lake. The breeze seemed to caress me, and when I tipped my head back, I could see the chute, a billowing sail.

Then I looked down. Oh, how tiny all those water skiers were! I could barely make them out. There was the big paddle wheeler, the excursion boat of the lake. It made two runs a day; how nice that it sailed just now, so I could watch it from above. I was sure the passengers were looking at me, so I waved at them.

When my boat turned back, I could see the shadow of the chute on the water. I stuck out my leg far enough so that its shadow could be seen. Now the chute had a leg. Marvelous.

I was so engrossed in watching that, I didn't notice three sea gulls circling me. What did they want? Probably were just curious what kind of bird I was.

"Have you guys never seen a parasail?" I said to them in a loud voice.

Instead of an answer, one of them perched on the rope, about 20 feet from me. "Hey, you think the boat can pull us both?"

The sea gull turned away as if annoyed.

"Sorry, just joking," I said.

He looked again at me, then turned in the direction of the boat, then back at me, like someone watching a tennis match. I don't know how long that bird was sitting on my rope; he sure was nice company. When he had flown away, I looked once more at the clouds and lost myself in the sensation of floating, of weightlessness.

After 20 minutes, which seemed both very long and very short, the boat slowed down; I could see it by the change of its wake. Very gradually I approached the water level and was let down gently. First only my toes splashed in the lake, and finally I was all in the water, just in front of the dock, and two strong young men lifted me out.

Now it was Jeff's turn. We all watched him. I radiated enthusiasm for the rest of the day, and someone said, "Look, she can't stop grinning."

After lunch, the rest of our crowd parasailed too.

"If my mom does it, " said Kenny, "I also have to do it." Pride is strong motivation.

One after the other they took off, hands tightly gripping the harness, doubt in their eyes; they all came down, laughing, grinning, "Wow, what a trip!" "Stupendous!" "Wait till I tell my folks!" "I didn't know I could fly!"

At supper Kenny asked, "Mom, what'll you do when you are seventy and can't walk?"

"We'll strap her wheelchair to the parasail." Jeff laughed. "We'll get her up somehow."

The Majestic And the Comical

Sometimes, funny little events can happen even in an awe inspiring environment. Take the Grand Canyon. Everyone has either seen pictures of it or been there.

A few years ago, my two sons (teenagers then) and I watched with amazement and reverence this place of breathtaking grandeur with its ever varying vistas.

We had signed up for the mule trip into the chasm. All the riders were a bit apprehensive. After checking in, we were directed towards a corral. About 20 mules, seemingly asleep, were tied to the fence.

First, the chief wrangler, Jim, gave instructions. In the excitement, I forgot them instantly.

He assigned each of us to a specific mule. While carefully adjusting my stirrups, he said, "This is *Eldorado,* he is very gentle. Pet him."

I did. "Eldorado," I said. "A ride as smooth as in a Cadillac?"

Jim answered with a hesitant smile.

These animals were as big as horses, only with much larger ears. They were wider around the cinch so that the barrel-shaped belly protruded far beyond the narrowly set feet.

A very pleasant lady-wrangler, Shirley, led our string. Jim ordered me right behind her. I thought he considered me (by far the oldest in the group of sixteen) a poor risk needing close supervision.

Now, the first part of the descent goes over an endless number of switchbacks in a wall of rock that seems vertical. Well, maybe it's only 85 degrees. The trail during most of the stretch is just wide enough for one mule.

Once under way, I looked into the distance. The mountain tops that had been below the canyon's rim when viewed from above, now formed the horizon – a dazzling view.

A sudden jerking movement of the mule lifted me out of the saddle. I could barely hold on. Flustered, I tried to get my feet back into the stirrups, when I heard my kids laughing above me, just around the hair pin.

"That beast must have slipped with all four hoofs at the same time," I said expecting sympathy.

"Naw," said Kenny with ill concealed amusement, "just with three. Your mount held the fourth leg in the air for balance."

Now I remembered Jim's warning: "On slick ground, a mule can slip with all four hoofs as well as a horse. But the mules are not skittish and after the slide will keep on walking as if nothing had happened."

The center strip of the trail consists of exposed, smooth rock. The mules avoid stepping on it. On the outside rim, the trail has gravel – less slippery. So they walk on the free edge. Their downhill flank protrudes already far above the abyss, more so the rider's leg. There was nothing under part of me for 2000 feet! Better not get dizzy.

Halfway down, Shirley asked, "How is Eldorado doing?"

"Oh, fine, I think."

"Good," she said with a hearty smile. "We didn't know how he'd behave. This is his first trip down here."

"What??"

"Oh, he's been on trails before," Shirley tried to re-assure me. "Only not on this one."

So it was the *mule* that needed close supervision, not I. Should I have been scared or proud? I didn't have time to worry.

By noon we arrived at the mid-plateau, dismounted, had lunch and peeked into the inner canyon, where the river was another 2500 feet further down. We were so taken in by all those geographic wonders, we nearly forgot about the mules.

On the two hour return trip, we were tired and hot. The mules, however, walked uphill faster than downhill (footholds are better going up).

"Their heart and lungs are so excellent," said Shirley, "the uphill trek doesn't bother them at all." Amazing creatures.

I nearly dozed off having nothing under part of me for half a mile.

"Watch it, Hertha," I heard Shirley. Too late. First Eldorado had slowed down to gain space of about 100 feet in front of him and now heartily galloped to catch up with Shirley. What a rude awakening! Again I remembered Jim's warning: "Don't let them hang back. They'll run if they have the space." I should have listened.

When we arrived at the corral, Jim received us with a sigh of relief. Maybe not every trip is as uneventful as ours. Maybe Eldorado could have thrown me.

Walking to our hotel, bow-legged and aching, we looked once more into the chasm. "That's where we stopped; over there we had lunch; by that single tree, Eldorado slipped. But I stayed on!"

Weren't those mules funny? Isn't this canyon *grand?"*